CLARENDON LAW SERIES

Edited by

H. L. A. HART

CLARENDON LAW SERIES

Introduction to the Law of Property
By F. H. LAWSON. 1958

Introduction to the Law of Contract
By P. S. ATIYAH. 1961

The Concept of Law
By H. L. A. HART. 1961

Precedent in English Law
By A. R. N. CROSS. 1961

Administrative Law
By H. W. R. WADE. 1961

Roman Law
By J. K. B. NICHOLAS. 1962

CRIMINAL LAW
AND
PUNISHMENT

BY

P. J. FITZGERALD

PROFESSOR OF LAW IN THE
UNIVERSITY OF LEEDS

OXFORD
AT THE CLARENDON PRESS
1962

Oxford University Press, Amen House, London E.C.4

GLASGOW NEW YORK TORONTO MELBOURNE WELLINGTON
BOMBAY CALCUTTA MADRAS KARACHI LAHORE DACCA
CAPE TOWN SALISBURY NAIROBI IBADAN ACCRA
KUALA LUMPUR HONG KONG

PRINTED IN GREAT BRITAIN

TO BRIGID

PREFACE

THE criminal law has as its general aim the prevention of certain kinds of human activity. Since any such prevention of activity by prohibition and punishment involves a restriction on individual freedom, the criminal law is not unnaturally found to represent a compromise between the conflicting interests of protecting the state and the citizen against different kinds of harm and safeguarding as far as possible personal liberty. The purpose of this book is to examine English criminal law against this background and to evaluate the compromise which it has achieved.

Unlike the procedure adopted by textbooks on this subject, which invariably begin with an account of the general principles of criminal liability, the method adopted here has been to start by considering under seven broad headings the different types of conduct prohibited by the criminal law. It is only after a discussion of the various kinds of specific crimes that the reader is then presented with the general principles of liability and the general defences of mistake, necessity, and so on. It is thought that this plan provides a better introduction both for the layman and for the student who comes to the subject for the first time.

The features of the criminal law which serve most to safeguard the liberty of the subject are to be found chiefly in the law of procedure and evidence. These are examined in the chapter which deals with the criminal law at work. Here, though the treatment could inevitably only be cursory, an attempt has been made to discuss the part played by the layman in the machinery of the criminal law, the restrictions on the scope of the criminal law, the rules which protect the liberty of the individual and those which ensure that the defendant obtains a fair trial.

The final chapter is devoted to the problem of punishment. Within the limited space available it considers first the general questions relating to the nature, purpose, and justification of punishment, and then the merits, demerits, and particular problems of the different specific penalties available under the present penal system.

My thanks are due to many who have in various ways assisted me in the writing of this book. At the outset Professor F. H. Lawson and Dr. M. Grünhut made many helpful suggestions. Chief Inspector R. N. Dickson of the Leeds City Police afforded me some useful information about the actual practice regarding the charging of defendants and about the conduct of prosecutions by police prosecutors. Professor H. L. A. Hart's criticisms revealed several serious errors and indicated fruitful approaches to various problems. My special gratitude is due to Dr. A. R. N. Cross, who was kind enough to read through the typescript and who has saved me from innumerable pitfalls. For those into which I have fallen the responsibility is mine alone. Finally I should like to record my thanks to Miss C. Divine, who with unfailing patience deciphered my handwriting and produced the typescript.   P. J. F.

University of Leeds
November 1961

CONTENTS

I

THE CONCEPT OF CRIME

THE criminal law is part of public law. Public law consists of those fields of law which are concerned with the state and its relationship with the individual, as opposed to private law, which deals with relationships between individuals. The criminal law falls under the heading of public law, because it is concerned with those wrongs of which the state takes cognizance. The general aim of the criminal law is to discourage and prevent certain types of conduct, and this aim is pursued by the prohibition of the conduct in question, together with the assignment of a punishment for disregard of the prohibition.

Attempts to provide an adequate definition of the notion of a crime have been complicated by the fact that there are really two different questions involved here. The first problem is to explain what is entailed by the stigmatization by law of any conduct as criminal. The second is to ascertain the distinguishing feature common to all the different types of conduct which are by law classified as criminal.

If an act constitutes a crime in English law, this means that the law prohibits it and provides that its performance shall give rise to certain consequences. These consequences are roughly twofold.

First, crimes are the concern of the state, whereas civil wrongs such as breach of contract and tort are the concern merely of the individual wronged. This means that the initiative with regard to crimes rests with the state, whereas in the case of civil wrongs it is up to the victim to decide whether to go to law against the wrongdoer. If, for instance, Jones refuses to pay a debt to Smith, it is purely a matter for Smith whether or not to take legal action against Jones. If, on the other hand, Jones were to break and enter and steal something from Smith's house, this would become a matter for the state, and whether or not Jones was prosecuted would be no concern of Smith.

This simple distinction between crimes and civil wrongs has been blurred by two factors peculiar to English law. The first, which is of little importance today, is that at one time Parliament sought to prevent certain conduct by providing that if anyone committed the prohibited conduct, any individual could take criminal proceedings against him and recover a monetary penalty. These penal actions whereby the plaintiff sued for a penalty as a common informer are now largely abolished. The second factor is that in England prosecutions are nearly all in theory private prosecutions. Not only may any private person in general prosecute another, but in most cases the prosecutor, who is normally a police officer, prosecutes by virtue of his right to prosecute as a private citizen. This fact is obscured by the fact that on indictment the name of a criminal case always starts with *Rex* or the *Queen*. The name of the case of Roger Casement, for instance, who was convicted of treason, is *Rex* v. *Casement*. In cases tried in Magistrates' Courts, however, the name of the individual prosecutor appears in the title of the case, e.g. *Lester* v. *Pearson*. This peculiarity of English law should not, however, mislead us into overlooking the very real control over criminal prosecutions vested in the Crown. The extent of this control is reserved for a later chapter.

The second consequence of criminality is that whereas a man who is proved to have committed a civil wrong will be made to compensate the victim, one who is convicted of a criminal offence is liable to be punished. If A by negligent driving were to injure B, B could bring an action against him whereby A would be made to compensate B. If, however, A were violently to assault B, then A would be prosecuted and on conviction would be liable to punishment. This distinction between the consequences of a criminal act and an act which is only a civil wrong is to some extent blurred by the fact that in certain cases the Criminal Courts may decline to punish an offender; for example, the judge may think it preferable to take a more lenient course such as discharging the accused absolutely. Secondly, in certain cases the Civil Courts may punish a defendant by ordering him to pay exemplary damages to the plaintiff, as frequently happens in libel actions. Nevertheless, it remains true that the essential object of criminal procedure is to punish the accused and so prevent further offences, whereas the essence of civil proceedings is to compel the defendant to compensate the plaintiff for the injury done to him.

The detailed differences between civil and criminal procedure will be considered later.

To define crime merely as conduct prohibited by law under pain of certain special consequences has seemed to some writers insufficiently informative. There must be something, it has been felt, common to all the different criminal offences known to the law other than the mere possession of the legal label of criminality. Accordingly, some intrinsic common quality has been sought by which to distinguish criminal from non-criminal conduct.

One candidate for this has been the quality of harmfulness. Crimes, it has been suggested, consist only of those acts which are particularly harmful to the community. Support for this view is to be found in certain statements made by the courts. In the eighteenth-century case of *R. v. Wheatley*,[1] where the defendant was accused of defrauding one Richard Webb by delivering to him sixteen gallons of amber and charging him for eighteen, the court refused to regard this as a criminal offence, saying, 'What is it to the public whether Richard Webb has, or has not, his eighteen gallons?' Again, during the period when the judges were developing the criminal law, this element of injury to the public seems to have been the basis of the creation of new offences. 'All such acts and attempts as tend to the prejudice of the community', it was said in the case of *R. v. Higgins*[2] in 1801, 'are indictable.' As late as 1937, the House of Lords in the *Andrews v. D.P.P.*,[3] a case concerning manslaughter by driving, drew a distinction between the case where a man acts with such disregard for the life and safety of others as to merit punishment, and cases where his negligence can safely be left to redress by civil action and does not need repression by criminal sanctions in the interests of the safety of the community. It is also true that this quality of harmfulness to the community is to be found in many of the more serious crimes, such as treason and other attacks on the institution of the state, murder and other offences of violence which threaten the peace and order of society, and offences against property, which is one of the basic institutions of our community. But this quality will not suffice to indicate with certainty whether an act is a crime or not. There are some

---

[1] *R. v. Wheatley* (1761), 1 W. Bl. 273.   [2] *R. v. Higgins* (1801), 2 East 5.
[3] *Andrews v. D.P.P.*, [1937] A.C. 576.

criminal offences where little in the way of harm or danger to the public at large could be found. Certain offences of gross indecency, acts of homosexuality between consenting adults, violations of the Sunday Observance Act would, by many people, be thought to fall into the category of conduct constituting no particular threat to society in general. On the other hand, there are certain types of conduct which do not amount to criminal offences, but which may be harmful to the community. Breaches of contract, negligence leading to the destruction of property, and adultery resulting in the break-up of a marriage, while all outside the purview of the criminal law, can cause widespread injury to society. The attempt to elucidate the test of criminality in terms of harmfulness to the public is not, therefore, wholly successful.

Another suggestion is that crimes consist of acts which are wrongful or immoral. This too is not without some basis, in that people do in general think of crimes as wrongful acts, quite apart from the law. Many people would be surprised to learn that acts not intrinsically wrong such as speeding are criminal offences. Certainly the term 'criminal' is generally reserved for those who commit crimes of violence and dishonesty. Those with several convictions for careless, dangerous, and even drunken driving would not usually be referred to as criminals. But the law makes no distinction here between crimes consisting of acts considered wrong in themselves, and acts not wrong in themselves, but merely prohibited by the law. Both are alike criminal offences.

Crime and sin are, in fact, intersecting circles. There are many types of conduct, generally looked on as immoral, which are quite outside the view of the criminal law; adultery,[1] lesbianism, and certain kinds of deceit not involving deprivation of property afford examples of behaviour frowned on by morality, but not by law. Equally, there are many criminal offences such as betting in a public house, shooting game on Sunday, which few people would consider wrongful, apart from their illegality. Many of these offences are the creation of statute and other legislation passed to regulate the welfare of society with regard to trades and industries, and are the results of increasing socialization and the emergence of the welfare state.

[1] Adultery is, however, a crime in some countries, e.g. many of the United States. See American Law Institute's Model Penal Code Tentative Draft 4, pp. 204, 279.

The distinction between crimes which are morally wrong and crimes which are merely legally wrong is certainly one which is popularly made. Most people, for instance, would not talk of betting in a public house as a crime. Much of the problem of road traffic offences arises from the fact that the public, including juries, refuse to regard such offences as morally wrong and, therefore, as real crimes like murder and stealing. In this context it is interesting to notice that while the Articles of Association which regulate limited companies commonly provide that a company director convicted on indictment of a criminal offence automatically ceases to be a member of the board, there is generally a saving clause to the effect that this rule will not apply to convictions for road traffic offences. This distinction of crimes into those intrinsically wrong, *mala in se*, and those merely legally wrong, *mala prohibita*, has also been made by judges and certain authors. Many criminal offences such as offences against the Food and Drugs Act would not find their way into general textbooks of criminal law.

On the other hand, the distinction has incurred considerable disfavour at the hands of certain academic writers. Their attack has been launched on two different flanks. Men's views of what is right and wrong, it is argued, vary from place to place and from time to time; some communities think it wicked to smoke, drink, and gamble, while others seem to devote all their energy to such activities. Euthanasia, though practised in ancient Sparta and by certain Eskimo peoples in recent years, is not countenanced in this country.\From this, the conclusion is drawn that no offence can be said to be intrinsically wrong. This attack is misconceived. Important as it is to realize that no code of morality commands universal acceptance, it is a mistake to think that this realization commits us to abandon what is suggested by the distinction between *mala in se* and *mala prohibita*. The distinction claims that there are certain offences which can only be condemned on legal grounds, types of behaviour which, had they not been legally prohibited, would incur no blame, and that there are other offences such as murder which can be condemned not only on legal but also on moral grounds, types of behaviour which would incur blame quite apart from their illegality. The only reason for our duty to abstain from the former is our general duty to obey the law, while there are extra reasons for abstaining from acts of the second class. Admittedly different societies at different times take different views about what conduct is right and wrong; and whether a crime is thought wrong in itself or only legally wrong will depend on the moral code current in a society. But acknowledgement of this relativity should not blind us to the fact that moral codes are current in societies.

The second attack is a more subtle one. Offences such as murder and theft are often advanced as examples of offences wrongful in themselves. It is argued, however, that what constitutes theft or murder in England depends on the complicated intricacies of English law. Suppose a nurse is under the duty of taking care of an invalid and omits one day to give the patient a necessary injection, intending to cause the patient's death. If the patient dies as a result of this omission, this would generally amount to murder, but if the death occurred more than a year and a day after the omission, the nurse in English law would not be guilty of murder. This requirement as to the interval of time is a peculiarity of English law; no reflection on morality informs us that murder is confined to cases where the death occurs within a certain time. Likewise with regard to stealing. Suppose A owes B £5, but wrongfully thinking that he owes B £10, gives £10 to B. If B, realizing A's mistake, pockets the extra money, he is not in English law guilty of stealing, or indeed of any offence. Here again, reflection on morality and honesty would not have led us to expect that the crime of theft would not extend to cover dishonest conduct of this kind. But the fact that the offences of murder and theft in English law do not cover every case which might be considered morally as murder or theft does not alter the fact that the basic notions of murder and theft are those of immoral acts.

Those who have wanted to define crime in terms of wrongfulness or tendency to injure the community were right in feeling that Parliament and the courts have not acted arbitrarily in creating crimes and that the reason why many acts have become crimes is because of their tendency to injure the community. This principle can be seen at work underlying the judicial creation of such criminal offences as incitements, attempts, and public mischief. It is interesting to note that negligent conduct has for the most part remained outside the criminal law, with the exception of those cases where negligence may be particularly harmful, e.g. on the roads. Moreover, there have been written into the criminal law certain general principles limiting criminal liability, such as those principles relating to lack of choice, lack of intention, mistake, duress, and so forth. A full understanding of the notion of crime must take into account these general principles, which are, of course, common to all criminal offences.

Nevertheless it is a mistake to overlook the fact that whether or not any conduct constitutes a crime in English law depends solely on whether or not such conduct has been proscribed as criminal by the law. The hallmark of criminality is that it is a breach of the criminal law. As was said in a leading case 'the criminal quality of an act cannot be discerned by intuition; nor can it be discovered by reference to any standard but one: is the act prohibited with penal consequences?'

To discover, therefore, whether certain behaviour constitutes a crime it is necessary to look to those portions of the law containing the rules relating to criminal offences. In some countries, for instance India, France, or Germany, the criminal law is for the most part contained in a code. English law has not yet arrived, however, at the state of codification. In the nineteenth century various attempts were made to introduce a Criminal Code, but always without success. The provisions of our criminal law, therefore, are to be found in other sources. Many of the older and more serious offences were created and defined by the judges; for example, murder, stealing, and conspiracy. Of these, some, like stealing, have now been statutorily defined; others, like murder, have been modified, but not wholly defined by statute, while others yet again, like conspiracy, are still entirely the creature of judge-made or common law. The criminal law then is to be found in statutes such as the Larceny Act, 1916; in regulations made by Ministers and others to whom Parliament has delegated the power to make subordinate legislation, e.g. the regulations made by the Minister of Transport; and in the reports of judicial decisions. Besides these sources there is also the authority of certain writers of legal textbooks; the works of Coke and Blackstone, for instance, are accepted in the courts as authoritative and some of the definitions of the older crimes are to be found in such writings.

Formerly the judges played a prominent part in developing the criminal law, extending it by analogy to cover conduct not hitherto specifically prohibited, and at the same time in using analogical reasoning to develop and expand the general part of the criminal law, which is concerned with defences and excuses. But as more and more of the criminal law began to be enacted by Parliament, the judiciary played a correspondingly smaller part in the creation of new crimes. That their creative powers, though dormant, were not extinct became apparent in the case of *Manley*[1] in 1931. In that case the accused falsely informed the police that she had been robbed, thereby causing them loss of valuable time and rendering other people liable to suspicion. There being no statutory crime prohibiting such behaviour, she was convicted of the common law crime of effecting a public mischief, the court asserting that all acts tending to the prejudice of the community were criminal. The obvious breadth of this rule, whereby the courts could in fact penalize as criminal any act of which they disapproved, encountered severe criticism, and in 1954 the judiciary retreated from this position and stated that in present conditions, when Parliament meets more frequently than formerly, the creation of new crimes was the province of the legislature rather than the judiciary.[2] The year 1961, however, saw the pendulum swing back and the House of Lords in the *Ladies' Directory Case*[3] reaffirm the view that the hand of the common law is still powerful to penalize conduct which Parliament has not proscribed. The accused published a booklet mainly containing advertisements by prostitutes and was convicted amongst other things of conspiracy to corrupt the public morals, in that he had conspired with others to induce members of the male public to visit the advertisers' addresses for fornication and in some instances for participation in perversive practices. In English law the crime of conspiracy is wide enough to cover not only agreements to commit crimes but also agreements to commit 'unlawful' acts, such acts having been held to include certain kinds of civil wrong, certain immoral acts, and certain acts tending to the public mischief. The defence contended that though in earlier times the courts had assumed the role of guardian of the public morals, in present times such matters were the

---

[1] [1933] 1 K.B. 529.   [2] *R.* v. *Newlands*, [1954] 1 Q.B. 158.
[3] *Shaw* v. *D.P.P.*, [1961] 2 All E.R. 446.

concern of Parliament, and consequently there was no occasion for the courts to create new crimes. According to the defence only agreements to commit acts already stigmatized as 'unlawful' should amount to conspiracies. The category of 'unlawful' acts was closed and did not extend to the conduct of the accused. Rejecting this argument and holding that a conspiracy to corrupt public morals was punishable as a conspiracy to effect a public mischief, the House of Lords reiterated the claim of the courts to act as *custos morum* and affirmed the existence of a residual power inherent in the courts to punish conduct prejudicial to the public welfare where Parliament has not intervened to supersede the common law.

Few cases in recent years have been quite so disturbing as this. The resuscitation of the judicial power to create crimes runs counter to two cardinal principles of free and democratic government. In the first place, the idea of the rule of law, on which English lawyers have lavished so many panegyrics, is based on the demand that the citizen should be ruled by laws and not by the whims of men. In the sphere of criminal law this idea has become crystallized as the principle of legality, a principle according to which only breaches of existing criminal law should be punishable. The justification of this principle, which has been adopted as an actual rule in some legal systems, though not in the English legal system, is that the citizen should be able to know beforehand what conduct is permitted and what forbidden; for only in this way can he order his affairs with certainty and avoid coming into conflict with the law. It is this demand for certainty with regard to the provisions of the criminal law that militates against retrospective criminal legislation. When Parliament creates a new crime, it almost invariably legislates for the future only. This, however, is just what the courts cannot do. Our legal system is such that a court can only decide a point of law which arises in some actual case before the court, and consequently the court's decision always relates back to the facts of this case, facts which of course precede the decision. If, therefore, a court manufactures a new crime, it thereby determines after the event that the defendant's conduct, which at the time of commission was not prohibited by law, is a criminal offence. To countenance this type of retrospective criminal legislation means that certainty and consequently freedom are at an end. Bentham long ago pointed out that when the judges make law like this, they are treating the citizen as a man treats his dog, hitting him every time he does something to which the master takes exception. Animals and young children can only be trained in this way. Sane and adult members of a free society, however, are entitled to demand first to be told what conduct is forbidden so that they may choose whether or not to keep within the law.

There is a further objection to the creation of new offences by the courts. Even suppose that a court could decide that the kind of act which the defendant had done would in future, though not in the instant case, constitute a crime, there is still the objection that this type of proceeding is not consonant with democratic government. If Parliament creates a new crime, the citizens whose liberty is thereby restricted have the consolation that this was done by their elected representatives whom they chose to perform this sort of activity, and whom in due course they may re-elect or reject. The judges, on the other hand, are appointed by the Crown, virtually irremovable and in practice accountable to no one. That such a body should have the power to decree that certain acts shall constitute crimes is totally incompatible with the notion of democracy.

II

TYPES OF CRIMINAL CONDUCT

CRIMINAL offences may be classified in several different ways.
One important distinction is the practical one between serious
offences which are tried on indictment and minor offences which
are dealt with in the Magistrates' Courts. This distinction will
be considered later in the section concerned with the procedure
of the criminal law. In textbooks of criminal law, which are devoted mainly to indictable offences, crimes are normally divided
into public offences, i.e. crimes against the state, and private
offences, i.e. crimes against individuals; and the second category
is subdivided into offences against the person, and offences
against property. Another subdivision of indictable offences
which should be noticed, though it is of less significance today
than formerly, is the distinction between felonies and misdemeanours. Felonies are those offences which at one time involved
on conviction automatic forfeiture of the felon's property to the
Crown, and all the more serious offences such as murder, burglary, and theft fall into this category. Misdemeanours did not
involve this forfeiture. Though this particular consequence was
abolished by statute in 1870,[1] the distinction between felonies
and misdemeanours still entails certain practical consequences
to be noticed later.

Here, it is proposed to attempt a rough classification of
offences looked at rather from the point of view of the wrongdoer, and since the aim of criminal law is to discourage certain
sorts of activity, it is proposed to consider in outline what are
the kinds of activity which the criminal law seeks to discourage.

Since the use of the criminal law to prohibit any kind of activity entails a corresponding restriction on liberty, it would not
be feasible for every kind of conduct to be forbidden. A balance
has to be struck between the need to protect the citizen against
injury and the need to allow freedom of activity. Such conduct
as is outside the ambit of the criminal law is so either because it
is devoid of harmful tendencies or because the harm which it

[1] Forfeiture Act, 1870.

occasions is of a merely trivial nature. For the most part the law is concerned only with behaviour which is seriously injurious either to the individual or to society and its institutions.

The kind of harm to which the individual is most obviously susceptible and against which he most clearly needs protection is physical injury. The frailty of the human body necessitates the prohibition of attacks deliberately directed against his life and safety. Accordingly, the first category of offences which must be considered are crimes of violence, e.g. murder, wounding, and assault.

A second type of harm against which the individual must be safeguarded is the deliberate infliction of economic loss. Even a society where all property was owned and enjoyed in common would need some legal protection of property. On the one hand diminution of the economic wealth of the community by damage or destruction of its property could not be tolerated; on the other hand no one person could be permitted to take and keep for himself alone property which belonged to the whole community. Furthermore, even such a society as this would be forced to afford some protection to possession. Food could not be eaten, clothing worn, or implements used if the consumer, the wearer, and the user were constantly exposed to the possibility of loss of possession. Without some measure of guarantee of quiet enjoyment of such things life could not go on. Even, for example, in a religious order whose members were forbidden to own property individually, some respect would have to be accorded to possession; if Brother Lawrence, say, were free to snatch the bread out of Brother John's mouth, the habit off his back, and the spade out of his hand, the whole life of the community would be disrupted. Moreover, because of the vital importance of possession and quiet enjoyment, any interference with these tends to result in violence and disorder. In our own society, where private acquisition and ownership of property is recognized and accepted as a basic institution, it is all the more necessary that rules of law should have been developed to protect people against deprivation, damage, or destruction of their property. Accordingly, the next two categories of criminal conduct to be examined consist of crimes of dishonesty, e.g. stealing and receiving, and crimes of malicious damage to property.

Now so far as the victim is concerned, it makes little difference whether the damage done to him is caused deliberately or negligently; the amount of suffering is in both cases the same. A Criminal Code interested only in the welfare of the injured party might well penalize careless conduct on the same footing as violence and malicious damage. In English law, however, negligence does not for the most part constitute a crime, the reason being partly perhaps that carelessness is less morally culpable than deliberate wrongdoing and partly that the careless person is less of a menace to the community than the person who deliberately injures his fellow men. While in general, therefore, the criminal law has been content to leave such matters to the civil law, which compels the wrongdoer to compensate his victim, there are nevertheless certain important crimes of negligence, which accordingly comprise the next category to be examined. It is under this head that are to be found the various offences against the rules laid down for the social welfare and safety of the community, i.e. the legal rules relating to the conditions in factories, the sale of food, and so forth.

The next type of conduct to be considered may be conveniently described as 'nuisance'. Any communal or social life involves some degree of give and take, and the corollary of allowing the individual some freedom of action is that his neighbour must put up with a certain measure of trivial discomfort and annoyance. A limit is reached, however, where the discomfort and annoyance become more than trivial and the law steps in to penalize such conduct. Under this head fall to be discussed behaviour causing annoyance to individuals, e.g. threatening behaviour, abuse, and trespass, and conduct resulting in annoyance to the community in general, e.g. the various types of public nuisance, obscenity, and affronts to public decency.

The different kinds of conduct so far enumerated consist of acts calculated to cause physical injury, loss of or damage to property, and interference with comfort. There exists also in English law a class of offences which may be conveniently grouped together as crimes against morality. These consist of contraventions of the accepted, or officially accepted, canons of moral conduct and are concerned in the main with sexual behaviour. Some of these, such as rape, could logically be classified with crimes of violence in that they involve physical attacks on unwilling victims; others, notably homosexual offences, involve no such attack, but consist of conduct that is unnatural in that it deviates from the usual pattern of sexual behaviour; yet a third subclass comprises conduct which is neither violent nor unnatural but which is contrary to the officially accepted moral code, e.g. bigamy, blasphemy, and conspiracies to corrupt public morals.

Finally, we come to what might loosely be termed political or public offences, i.e. crimes against the state and its institutions. Under this head we shall examine treason and kindred offences, crimes against the administration of justice, and offences against public order.

I. VIOLENCE

Convictions for violence fortunately form a relatively small proportion of the total number of convictions today. In 1960, for instance, of a total of 1,035,212 convictions only 1 per cent. consisted of convictions for violence, together with 1·2 per cent. for non-indictable assaults.[1] Yet clearly offences of violence form one of the most important categories of crimes, since any society is bound to make provision for the protection of its members against physical attack upon their person. In any legal system we should expect to find rules prohibiting violent behaviour. To provide merely that the victims should recover compensation from the wrongdoer would obviously not suffice, since in some cases the wrongdoer might not have the means to afford such compensation, while in others, where fatal injuries are caused, compensation is no longer possible. In any event, nothing is so likely to lead to disorder and disruption of the peace as an attack of violence by one person against another. It is not surprising, therefore, to find that in English law, quite apart from the fact that the victim may sue the wrongdoer for damages in the Civil Courts, the criminal law seeks to prevent such conduct by prohibition and threat of punishment.

The law related to violence is complicated. Most of the relevant provisions are to be found in the seventy-nine sections of the Offences against the Person Act, 1861. With regard to certain offences, however, such as assault, battery, and murder, we

[1] These and all other figures regarding the incidence of crime are taken from the Criminal Statistics issued by the Home Office. The figures refer to 1960 unless the contrary is stated.

must look for the definitions in the reports of decided cases
and in the writings of such authors as Coke, Blackstone, and
Stephen.

(a) Lawful Use of Force

In seeking to repress violence the aim of the law is not to prevent all use of force, but only the unlawful use of force. For the
use of force is not necessarily undesirable in all cases, and is
accordingly not necessarily unlawful. There is here a latent conflict since ideally the use of force should never be tolerated, but
since reality falls short of the ideal, the law has to take account
of the fact that on occasions force must be met with force and
the members of the community must be allowed to defend themselves against wrongdoers. We may distinguish roughly four
different grounds, on which the use of force may be justified.

First, force used in the execution of a public duty in the public
interest is in certain cases of necessity permissible. Were this not
so, a soldier could not lawfully attack the enemy, a policeman
could never lawfully arrest a resisting offender, and the hangman would commit murder each time he carried out an execution. Police and private citizens are entitled (indeed it may be
their duty) to use force to prevent the commission of dangerous
felonies. Secondly and akin to the lawful use of force in the public
interest is the use of force by parents and teachers to punish
children. Though the law will not permit excessively severe
chastisement, it accepts the view that in some cases corporal
punishment of children is necessary and desirable.

Thirdly, the private citizen is allowed by law to use force to
protect himself. When one man assaults another, the latter
cannot be expected to submit peacefully and rely solely on the
machinery of the law to bring the attacker to justice. Instant
threats demand instant measures. Here the law is in accord with
common sense, in permitting the citizen to use force to defend
himself against attack. His right of self-defence extends also to
defend those near and dear to him against attack and further to
defend his property against attack. But because it is allowable
to use force in self-defence, it does not necessarily follow that
force may lawfully be used in self-help. Self-defence applies to
the case where a man protects himself or his property against
an actual or imminent attack. Self-help is concerned with a

different situation, namely the case where he wishes to assert some legal right which is being denied him. If A tries to drive B out of B's house or if he tries to take B's wallet from him, B would be entitled in both cases to use force in defence of his property, but if A succeeded in getting possession of the house or the wallet, then B's claim to be allowed to recover his property forcibly would have to rest not on a right of self-defence (for the attack is now over), but on the right of self-help. At this stage, however, B is not in immediate danger and clearly the policy of any legal system would be to discourage forcible self-help, which is liable to cause disturbance of the peace, and to substitute some legal process whereby B could recover his property. Here English law differentiates between the recovery of land and the recaption of movable property. Since land and houses do not disappear, there is no immediate necessity for the owner to recover them forcibly from the trespasser and since 1381 the Statute of Forcible Entries has prohibited rightful owners from forcibly entering on their land and evicting their dispossessors. The owner's proper course is to bring a civil action to be restored to possession. Articles of movable property, however, such as wallets may be impossible to recover unless immediate action is taken by the loser to prevent the thief making off with them. Here English law allows the lawful owner to use a reasonable amount of force to recover his goods.[1]

Fourthly, the consent of the victim is in many cases a complete justification for the force used upon him. If this were not so, no surgeon could ever lawfully operate upon a patient, no doctor could examine him, no one could tackle an opposing player on the rugby field, and no boxer could punch his opponent. The slightest application of force in the course of everyday life, e.g. each handshake, each kiss, would constitute a battery. In such cases it is rare to find consent to the use of force expressly given. For the most part it is implied by law; the footballer, the boxer, or the patient are taken in the circumstances to have given their consent. It is important, however, to remember that the law will not imply consent to an unlimited amount of force. A boxer will only be taken to have consented to such attacks as are normal within the rules of boxing, so that if his opponent kicked him in the stomach or punched him deliberately below the belt, here

[1] *Blades* v. *Higgs* (1865), 11 H.L.C. 621.

there would be no consent. Secondly, the victim's consent must be freely given. Consent obtained by threats or fraud would not qualify as true consent. So if a doctor were to persuade a young boy to submit to an injection by falsely pretending that the boy's father had said that the boy was to have the injection, here there would be no true consent and the doctor would be guilty of assault. A third limitation on the operation of the victim's consent is that the law will not allow a person to consent to all degrees of force. There comes a stage when the amount of force becomes too great for even the victim's consent to afford a defence. As English law stands, no one may consent to be killed and a person who deliberately kills even a willing victim is guilty of murder. Similarly, one cannot by law consent to the infliction of very serious deliberate harm, so that if two men fight a duel or indulge in prize fighting, the consent of the injured party will not absolve the other from criminal responsibility for causing grievous bodily harm. In medical operations, surgeons do sometimes inflict very serious injuries, but the law here accepts the patient's consent since the operations are performed in the interests of the patient's health. But there are illegal operations, to which consent affords no defence. For instance, abortion outside the limits at present set by law is such an operation, where the consent of the woman operated on affords no defence to the abortionist.

In all these cases where the use of force by one person against another is lawful either in the public interest, in the protection of private interests, or by reason of the victim's consent, the limiting factor is that of reasonability. The rule is that no more force may be used than is reasonably necessary. For instance, a policeman is entitled to use force if necessary to effect an arrest, but this does not mean that at the least show of resistance he would be entitled to kill the prisoner. Similarly, while a parent may punish his child, he must not overstep the bounds of reasonability. A spanking is within the law; flogging with a cat-o'-nine-tails is not. In self-defence, too, no more force may be used than is reasonably necessary to repel the attack. If A attacks B with his bare fists, B will not normally be justified in shooting A dead. Indeed, it has been suggested that when attacked a man may not lawfully kill his assailant until he has first retreated as far as he possibly can with safety and that only when he is at bay may he take his assailant's life.[1] By contrast, if A tries to force his way into B's house it has been said that here B is under no obligation to retreat first before killing A, since to retreat would be to give up the very thing which the law allows him to defend.

(b) The Grading of Offences of Violence

Crimes of violence in English law range from assault, where in fact no force at all is inflicted on the victim, to murder, where the result is the victim's death. The gravity of the offence depends partly on the harm done to the victim and partly on the amount of harm intended.

At the bottom of the scale come simple assaults and batteries where comparatively little harm is caused. The crime of assault consists not so much in violence as in the threat of violence, for assault strictly speaking consists of some physical display of force against another which leads that other to believe that force is going to be used against him, and the essence of the offence is the victim's apprehension. One cannot, therefore, strictly assault someone who is asleep, someone who does not know that the assailant is there or someone who is for some reason ignorant of the threat. Secondly, the threat must be a real one. If one man threatens another with his fists, but both are standing on opposite sides of a wide river, this would not amount to a real threat of an immediate force. The rule, if it exists[2], that mere words alone do not constitute assault without some physical display of force would seem to be based on the view that verbal threats unaccompanied by gestures do not constitute sufficient real menace of immediate force.

But the term 'assault' is often applied to offences which are strictly speaking batteries. A battery is the unlawful application of force to another person. In contrast to assault proper, where the victim must be aware of the threat, there is no need in the case of battery for the victim ever to know that force has been applied to him. So it is legally possible to commit battery on

---

[1] *R.* v. *Smith* (1837), 8 C. & P. 160.

[2] The only authority for this proposition seems to be *Mead and Belt*'s case (1832), 1 Lew. 184. In *Fairclough* v. *Whipp*, [1951] 2 All E.R. 834, Lord Goddard C.J., in stating that 'an assault can be constituted . . . by a threatening gesture or a threat to use violence against a person', would appear to suggest that mere words might amount to an assault.

someone who is asleep and who is not woken by the application
of force. The penalties for assault and battery on summary conviction are a maximum of two months' imprisonment.

More serious are assaults aggravated either by the fact that
more harm is caused, or by the accused's intention to cause
more harm. In the former class are assaults causing 'actual
bodily harm', i.e. some more than trivial interference with
health and comfort, or 'grievous bodily harm', i.e. really serious
bodily harm. The second class comprises such offences as assault
with intent to steal. For these aggravated assaults the maximum
penalty is five years' imprisonment.

Yet more serious are offences where the offender causes actual
or grievous bodily harm with intent to wound, disable, or cause
grievous bodily harm. Here we have the assault aggravated
both by actual harm caused and by the offender's intention to
cause harm. The maximum penalty for these crimes is life imprisonment. Of equal gravity is the crime of manslaughter.
Manslaughter as will be seen later is a composite crime, but in
what is called 'involuntary manslaughter', i.e. manslaughter
proper, as opposed to murder reduced to manslaughter, the
gravity of the offence results not from the accused's intent, but
from the harm caused to the victim. Where A assaults B and the
blow is not calculated to produce serious injury, but B owing to
some constitutional weakness dies as a result of the blow, A is
dealt with as severely as if he had intentionally caused serious
injury less than death. The maximum penalty for manslaughter
is the same as for inflicting grievous bodily harm with intent,
i.e. life imprisonment.

At the top of the scale stands murder. In the typical case the
accused kills the deceased intending to cause death or grievous
bodily harm. Actual intent, however, is not essential. Recklessness, i.e. foresight of death or grievous bodily harm as the probable consequence of his conduct together with indifference to
the consequence, is enough. Furthermore, actual foresight is not
necessary; provided that the accused aims a voluntary unlawful
act at the deceased, it is enough if a reasonable man in the circumstances would have foreseen that death or grievous bodily
harm was the probable consequence. Here the penalty is fixed
by law, being in certain cases death and in others life imprisonment.

Most of these crimes involve harm occasioned by the direct application of force, but this is not essential in all cases. It is possible, for example, to commit the offence of inflicting grievous bodily harm indirectly. A man who maliciously turned out the lights in a theatre was found guilty of inflicting grievous bodily harm on those members of the audience who were injured in the resulting panic.[1] In murder and manslaughter it is never necessary for the accused to cause death by the direct use of force, and, as we have seen, assault proper is committed without force or harm of any kind being actually inflicted on the victim.

(c) The Accused's State of Mind

Little need be said about the intention required by law on the part of the accused in most of these crimes, though special attention must be devoted to the state of mind of the accused with regard to murder. So far as the other crimes are concerned, two facts should be noted. First, it is not necessary that the accused should in all cases actually intend to injure the victim. Sometimes recklessness is as good as intent. So if A throws a stone into a seething crowd and seriously injures B, he is just as guilty of causing grievous bodily harm as if he had intended B's injury. Just as the law forbids people to hurt others, so it refuses to allow them to gamble with the safety of others.

The second factor concerns the doctrine of 'transferred malice'. According to this doctrine if the accused attempts to produce harm of a certain kind, but in fact produces different harm of the same kind, this makes no difference to his culpability. On the other hand, if instead he brings about harm of a totally different kind, he incurs no guilt for producing this harm. In this context the law distinguishes between two different kinds of harm, namely injury to the person and damage to property. If, for example, X throws a stone at Y, misses and hits Z, X produces different harm from that intended, but still harm of the same kind. X's malice with regard to Y is said to be transferred to Z and he is held as guilty as if he had actually injured Y. If on the other hand, the stone which missed Y had not hit Z, but had broken a window, here the harm caused would have been in the eyes of the law of a totally different kind, and X's malice with regard to Y would not be transferred to the window and he

[1] R. v. Martin (1881), 8 Q.B.D. 54.

VIOLENCE

would not be guilty of damaging property. He might be guilty of malicious damage to the window if he had acted recklessly so far as the property was concerned (i.e. if Y had been standing in front of the window, it might be argued that X's recklessness with regard to the window was as good as intent to damage the window). Just as malice can be transferred from persons to persons, but not from persons to things (including animals), so conversely it can be transferred from things to things, but not from things to persons. If A throws a large stone at B's dog and breaks B's window, malice could be transferred and A would be guilty of malicious damage to property. But if the stone had in fact hit and injured B, A would not be guilty of malicious injury to the person unless it could be shown he had acted recklessly with regard to B's safety.

This rule, which operates to transfer malice only within the same category of object, is a curious one. We might expect that a logical legal system would take one of two different views: either the accused should be guilty of harm caused and intended and not guilty of harm caused but not intended; or he should be guilty of harm caused even if not intended, provided he intended to produce some unlawful harm and in both cases the question of the type of object injured should be irrelevant. Today perhaps the more popular view would be the former; a man should only be punished for harm which he intends to cause and does cause. If he fails to achieve his purpose, but in the attempt produces some different harm, then all he should be guilty of is the attempt to produce unlawful harm. If X aims a blow at Y, but hits Z he should be guilty only of attempting to injure Y. He never intended harm to Z and the fact that the harm resulted from an act which was unlawful should not operate to render X guilty of injuring Z, any more than it would do if it resulted from an act which was lawful. The older view would be that where a man intends to cause unlawful harm and causes some harm other than that intended he should be just as guilty as if he had intended to cause the harm actually caused. In the above example X should be just as guilty as if he had intended to injure Z. The justification for this rule would be that where a man engages in some unlawful activity, he faces not only the possibility of punishment if he succeeds, but also the extra hazard that if he fails to bring about the precise harm intended he may still be as guilty as if he had succeeded. A doctrine of transferred malice would provide just such an extra hazard. English law, however, gives us a compromise between these views. The second approach operates if the harm caused is of the same legal category as the harm intended. Where the categories are different, the first approach is adopted. The restriction of the operation of the transference of malice can be supported on the following grounds. Injury to the person, in general, is much more serious and more heavily punishable than damage to property. Consequently, if the accused intended to damage property, but injured a person instead, it would be unfair (unless he had been reckless) to expose him to the extra hazard of being found guilty of a much more serious crime than the one intended. Malice should not, therefore, be transferred from property to persons. The converse restriction whereby malice cannot be transferred in the opposite direction from persons to property would seem to stem from a desire for symmetry within the law.

(d) Homicide

Special notice should be made of crimes of homicide, crimes consisting of unlawful killings. Here we shall consider briefly, murder, manslaughter, and some related crimes.

(i) Protection of life

In this context the aim of the law is obvious, the protection of life. Now the law only forbids the taking of life; it does not go further and demand the prevention of death. In general, it would be true to say that the law adopts the view that, 'thou shalt not kill, but needest not strive officiously to keep alive'. To push a man into a river so that he drowns would be a crime; to watch him drowning and to make no efforts to save him would (whatever the view of the coroner) constitute no offence in English law. The moral rule that we must love our neighbour, translated into legal terms, becomes an injunction to avoid acts likely to injure our neighbour. There are, however, certain occasions where the law of homicide goes further than this and imposes a positive duty to take active steps to prevent death. The law imposes such a duty where there is a specific relation between the two persons, such that in law the one has a duty to look after the other. The prime example of this is the relation between a parent and his child of tender years. If a father abstained from saving his child from drowning, he would incur criminal responsibility. The duty of looking after another person may also be undertaken voluntarily, as is the case with a doctor and his patient, a nurse and her charge. But once assumed, the duty cannot be relinquished at will. Having undertaken the duty the doctor or nurse is bound to perform it. Failure to treat or care for the patient would, if death resulted, be treated as a criminal offence.

Another aspect of the fact that what the law forbids is merely the taking of life is the corollary that there is no prohibition of the prevention of life coming into existence. While killing is a crime, family planning is not.[1] The criminal law is only interested in the protection of already-existing life. This raises a difficult question, namely at what point should the law consider that life begins to exist. One obvious point would be the moment of birth, another the moment of conception, and yet another the moment when the foetus is capable of being born alive. The first of these, birth, is the point selected by the common law, the moment of birth being the moment at which the body of the child has wholly quitted that of the mother, there being in law no need for the umbilical cord to be severed. Only living persons (in Coke's words, 'reasonable creatures in being') can be killed in law. To kill an unborn child is neither murder nor manslaughter. This does not mean, however, that injuries inflicted on an unborn child which cause him to die after being born are outside the law of homicide. Once the child is born the law protects his life even against pre-natal injuries. If A intentionally causes injury to B, an unborn child, who having been born dies as a result of that injury, A is guilty of murder.

Now if the law is prepared to protect the life of the living child even against pre-natal injuries, why should it not equally protect the life of the unborn child against such injuries? Why should the beginning of life not be pushed back a stage to the point where the foetus becomes viable? What this would mean is that if A in the above example had caused the unborn child

[1] There is a considerable amount of law on this subject in the United States, where the sale and distribution of contraceptives is in many jurisdictions criminal. In Connecticut the mere use of contraceptives is an offence. On this topic see St. John-Stevas, *Life, Death and the Law*, pp. 55 ff.

to die before birth, he would still be guilty of an offence. This step has in fact been taken by the law. The crime of *child destruction*, created by the Infant Life Preservation Act, 1929, prohibits the intentional causing of a child to die before it has an existence independent of the mother, provided that the child is capable of being born alive. To prove this capability the prosecution will normally produce medical evidence, but if the pregnancy has lasted twenty-eight weeks this is prima-facie evidence. The law has not, however, taken the step of putting this crime on the same footing as murder. In the first place, there is no fixed penalty for child destruction, but merely a maximum penalty of life imprisonment. Secondly, the prosecution must prove that the accused was not acting in good faith to preserve the life of the mother. So, although the law has assumed protection of the unborn life, it is not so fully protected as the separately existing life and it may have to take second place to the already existing life of the mother.[1] There is a third aspect in which legal protection of this unborn life falls short of the protection accorded to existing life. We have seen that in certain cases the existence of a duty may render the omission to prevent death criminal. This does not apply, however, to child destruction. No one, not even the mother, has a duty to see positively that the unborn child is born alive, and failure to do so does not amount to child destruction.

At this point one might wonder why the law should not go even further and protect even the life of the foetus which is not yet viable. One might expect the law to extend its protection of life to the moment of conception. The objection to this is that in general a person should be allowed by law to do what he likes with his own body and many feel that accordingly a woman should have the right to terminate her own pregnancy. The counter-argument is that there is more than just the woman's own body involved and that the foetus, even before it is viable, is not so radically different from a human being as to be denied all legal protection. The law has adopted the second view and the offence of *abortion* under the Offences against the Person Act, 1861, is committed if an instrument is unlawfully used on a woman, or a drug unlawfully administered to her, with intent

---

[1] For a valuable discussion on this topic see Glanville Williams, *The Sanctity of Human Life and the Criminal Law*, pp. 139 ff.

to procure her miscarriage. Because it is not always easy to prove that there has been conception, the law provides that this offence can be committed even when the woman is not pregnant. It cannot be committed by the woman herself, however, unless she is actually pregnant. Like child destruction abortion carries a maximum penalty of life imprisonment. Here, too, the law has attempted a compromise: the life of the unviable foetus is protected, but not to the same extent as that of the unborn child.

To few crimes has there been such opposition as to that of abortion. Apart from the view prevalent that the termination of a pregnancy should be the mother's own responsibility, there is also the practical difficulty that the outlawing of abortion drives pregnant woman to unskilled abortionists who operate in back streets without skill and without due safeguards, with the result that more harm is caused than if abortion was openly allowed. English law does allow pregnancy to be lawfully terminated if done in good faith to preserve the life of the mother. In the celebrated case *R. v. Bourne*[1] the judge directed the jury not to construe this requirement narrowly. A young girl had been raped and a doctor procured her abortion in order to prevent her from becoming a mental or physical wreck. On his trial for abortion the jury were instructed that this would count as preserving the life of the mother and the doctor was acquitted. Those who wish to abolish the crime of abortion want the law to go further than this and allow all pregnancies to be terminated. This would be to exalt the mother's interest at the expense of that of the foetus. The law forbids a mother to kill her child; it is not wholly unreasonable that it should forbid her to destroy her foetus.

(ii) *The lives protected*

Not every life is protected. Clearly this is necessary, because otherwise the soldier who killed the enemy, the policeman who killed an escaping prisoner, and the public executioner carrying out his duties could never lawfully perform their functions. The principles relating to the lawful use of force apply in general to the law of homicide. It is not unlawful to kill another person in the course of executing certain public duties. An obvious example is that of the public hangman. The latter must, of course,

[1] *R. v. Bourne*, [1939] 1 K.B. 687.

carry out the execution in the manner prescribed by law. Were he instead to poison the prisoner, he would be guilty of murder. So far as the private use of force is concerned, killing in self-defence will not be unlawful if it is absolutely necessary, i.e. if no other step would have sufficed to protect the person attacked.

The one rule which applies in general to the use of force but does not apply to homicide is the rule concerning consent. The consent of a victim to be killed will not absolve the killer from guilt. This means that mercy killing and euthanasia are not allowed by law. Here again, there is considerable opposition in some quarters to the law as it stands.[1] It should be possible, so it is argued, to put sufferers out of their misery if the sufferers themselves so desire. One objection to this is the religious view that man has no right to dispose of his own life, the giving and taking of life being a matter entirely for his Creator. This objection is insufficient to support the continued criminality of mercy killing, since the immorality of an action does not entail that it should be legally prohibited. If the matter of disposition of life is a matter for man's Creator alone, the contravention of this principle can be said to be equally a matter for the Creator alone. There are, however, practical grounds for supporting present law. To allow mercy killing might open the door to fraud. It would be only too easy to fake evidence that the deceased desired to die. Secondly, it would be an easy step from killing those who requested to die, to killing others, such as imbeciles, on the ground that it would be better for all concerned if they were out of the way. There is one further objection akin to the religious objection and this is the feeling that human beings should not be treated as animals and put out of their misery.

The ineffectiveness in law of the victim's consent meant that suicide was unlawful. Although successful suicide was beyond the reaches of the law, attempted suicide was a crime. Moreover, anyone assisting another to commit suicide was guilty of a murder. The Roman soldier who held the sword for Brutus to die upon would, in English law, have been guilty of murder. The doctrine of transferred malice, too, operated harshly in this context, for if a suicide failed to take his own life and killed

---

[1] See Glanville Williams, op. cit., pp. 277 ff.; St. John-Stevas, op. cit., pp. 262 ff.

another, he was guilty of murder. If X aimed a gun at his own head, but the gun kicked and he missed and killed Y, this was murder.

The law here is in a transitional stage. Various reasons have been advanced to support the illegality of suicide, for example, the immorality of disposing of one's own life and the harm done to society by depriving it of the services of one of its members. Yet to fix a penalty for suicide is futile. For one thing it will if anything spur the offender to success rather than act as a deterrent; for another it is generally agreed that what the person with suicidal tendencies needs is not punishment, but sympathetic treatment.

The Suicide Act, 1961, modifies the law to abolish the unlawfulness of suicide so far as the principal agent is concerned, so putting an end to prosecution for attempted suicide and obviating the harsh result of the rule of transferred malice. With regard to accessories the moral position is less clear. In the agony of the moment a man may against his better judgement express a desire to kill himself and it would be only reasonable for the law to prevent others (particularly those who might benefit from his death) from actively assisting him to carry out his intention, before he emerged from his suicidal frame of mind. In one respect the harshness of the law in this context had already been mitigated by the Homicide Act, 1957, which provided that where two people form a suicide pact, but only one dies and the other survives, the survivor is no longer guilty of murder, but only of manslaughter. Although the maximum penalty for the latter offence is life imprisonment, the judge in his discretion may award any sentence less than this and treat the survivor with leniency. The Suicide Act, 1961, has gone further and provides that any person who aids, abets, counsels, or procures the suicide of another or attempts by another to commit suicide will be liable on conviction to imprisonment for a term not exceeding fourteen years.

(iii) *Killing*

Killing, as we have seen, must, apart from the cases where there is a special relationship, be caused by positive acts; causing death by omission will not normally amount to homicide. The general requirement is that the accused must actively cause the death of the deceased. Here the difficult questions of causation arise. Because of the difficulty of establishing that the death resulted from the injury inflicted, the judges restricted homicide to cases where the death resulted within a year and a day of the injury and this is still the law today.

More difficult problems arise where the death results partly from the accused's act and partly from other circumstances. Here the law has adopted a general rule that the accused is not guilty of homicide if some abnormal circumstances or some deliberate voluntary act by a person other than the accused intervenes. If A knocks B down and a tree then falls on B and kills him, this intervening abnormality absolves A of responsibility for B's death. The intervening event must, however, be abnormal. If A knocks B down and leaves him lying on a road carrying heavy traffic, A can hardly escape responsibility here if B is run over and killed by a vehicle. Likewise, if the accused knows of and intends to make use of the intervening abnormality, the intervention will not absolve him from guilt. If A in the first example knew that the tree was about to fall and left B lying under it, he would be responsible for B's death. Secondly, the abnormality must intervene; an already present abnormality will not exempt the accused. This has specific relevance to the physical state of the deceased. If the latter, unknown to the accused, suffers from some constitutional weakness, such as an eggshell skull, then if the accused unintentionally causes his death by some intentionally inflicted injury, he will still be guilty of homicide. This principle is enshrined in the maxim that a wrongdoer must take the plaintiff (in criminal law, the victim) as he finds him.

So far as intervening voluntary human acts are concerned, it should be noted that nothing less than a full voluntary act by the deceased or some third party will suffice to exonerate the accused. If the deceased brings about his own death in attempting to escape from the accused, the deceased's act, if it is a reasonable one to take in the circumstances, will not count as fully voluntary, because he has no free choice. So if Y, to escape severe injury at the hands of X, jumps out of a window to his death, X may be held responsible for Y's death, provided the latter acted reasonably in the circumstances.[1] If he jumps out of

---

[1] *R. v. Pitts* (1842), Car & M. 284.

a first-floor window, a jury might consider this reasonable; to precipitate himself from the top of the Empire State Building, however, would not be reasonable and would intervene to exempt X from responsibility.

Similar problems arise where the deceased helps to bring about his own death but acts as he does as a result of the injury inflicted on him by the accused. In the eighteenth century Governor Wall[1] punished a soldier by an excessive flogging, after which the soldier drank some spirit. Twenty years later, when tried for the murder of the soldier, Wall argued that it was the deceased's own rash act which caused his death. It was held, however, that Wall, by his illegal conduct had put the soldier into such a dangerous situation that his act was a natural one in the agony of the moment and not fully voluntary; and Wall was accordingly convicted (and executed) for murder. In another case where the accused deliberately inflicted a finger wound on another and the latter's refusal to have it amputated resulted in his dying from gangrene, his failure to submit to the operation did not suffice to exonerate the accused.[2] Today, increased medical knowledge would probably render such a refusal unreasonable and the deceased would probably be held to have occasioned his own death. There might, however, be cases where the victim is faced with an exceedingly difficult choice. Suppose, for example, the result of an injury inflicted on a man is that his only hope of surviving is to submit to the amputation of all his limbs. If the victim refuses to take such a step, either hoping to survive without such a drastic remedy, or preferring to live out what time remains rather than preserve life in such a terrible condition, it might be held that his refusal to submit to the operation is not the cause of his death. The alternative is so dreadful that his choice might well be considered less than completely free.[3]

---

[1] *R. v. Wall* (1802), 28 St. Tr. 51.

[2] *R. v. Holland* (1841), 2 Mood & R. 351.

[3] A difficult case concerning problems of causation arose in the case of *R. v. Smith*, [1959] 2 All E.R. 193, in which the accused was convicted of murdering a fellow soldier by stabbing. Unknown to anyone, the wound had pierced the deceased's lung and the medical treatment he received was, as it subsequently transpired, disastrous; had he received other treatment, he might not have died. The Courts-Martial Appeal Court refused to set aside the conviction, distinguishing the case from that of *R. v. Jordan* (1956), 40 Cr. App. Rep. 152, where it was held that death resulting from any normal treatment employed to deal with a felonious

(iv) *The state of mind of the accused*

Whether unlawful homicide amounts to murder or manslaughter depends on the state of mind of the accused when he did the act resulting in the victim's death. Murder is unlawfully killing with malice aforethought, manslaughter is unlawful killing without malice aforethought.

Murder. Malice aforethought today means an intention to kill, or cause grievous bodily harm. It is not necessary that the accused intended to kill the person actually killed. If the accused fires at Smith, but kills Jones instead, the doctrine of transferred malice will render him guilty of the murder of Jones. Nor is it necessary for the accused to intend actually to kill the victim; it is enough if he merely intends to cause him grievous bodily harm. We have seen that grievous bodily harm means really serious bodily harm. Where the grievous bodily harm intended is so serious as to bring the victim to the brink of death, it is reasonable enough to hold the accused guilty of murder if the victim actually dies. One may object, however, to the rule whereby the accused is guilty of murder by reason of an intent to cause harm amounting in law to grievous bodily harm, but not calculated to bring the victim anywhere near death. Morally we differentiate between an intent to kill and an intent to injure and we regard the latter as less culpable than the former. Even if the actual result is in both cases the same, i.e. the death of the victim, the moral gravity of the accused's behaviour differs in the two cases. The criminal law's failure to reflect this important moral distinction, it is suggested, is unsatisfactory.

We have seen that in criminal law recklessness is generally as good as intent, and this holds good for the law of murder. If the accused does an act which he knows is likely to kill or cause grievous bodily harm to his victim and the victim dies, the accused is guilty of murder. Parallel to the two kinds of intent, therefore, we have two kinds of recklessness. If, for instance, X plants in an aircraft a bomb timed to go off during flight, in order to destroy the plane, he knows that it is extremely likely

---

injury may be regarded as caused by the felonious injury, but that the same principle does not apply where the treatment employed is abnormal. In that case the deceased, after being stabbed, was injected with Terramycin, to which he had already shown an intolerance.

that the crew and passengers will be killed or seriously injured.
If they are killed X will be just as guilty of murder as if he had
planted the bomb in order to kill them. The justification of
treating recklessness on the same footing as actual intent is that
a man must not gamble with the lives of others.

There is a third type of situation where a man may be guilty
of murder without intending or foreseeing death or grievous
bodily harm. In 1960 the House of Lords decided in the case of
D.P.P. v. *Smith*,[1] that it would be enough to render a person
guilty of murder if he aimed at the deceased a voluntary, unlawful act which a reasonable man in the circumstances would
realize to be likely to cause death or grievous bodily harm. Prior
to this, some lawyers had taken the view that the real question
was whether the accused himself realized the possible consequences of his action and that evidence as to what a reasonable
man in the circumstances would have realized would only operate to help the jury to decide what the accused himself actually
realized. The House of Lords, however, disapproved of this
view, stating that the only question is whether a reasonable man
in the circumstances would have known that the act was likely
to cause grievous bodily harm.[2] The facts of *Smith*'s case were,
that a policeman jumped on the running-board of the accused's
car intending to investigate whether there was stolen property
concealed in the car. Smith, to escape from the policeman,
drove off and shook the policeman off the car into the path of
oncoming traffic, as a result of which the policeman was killed.
There was some evidence to the effect that Smith neither intended to cause the deceased any serious injury nor even knew
that serious injury was the probable result of his action. This
according to the House of Lords was irrelevant, since all that
mattered was whether a reasonable man in Smith's place would
have known this. Taking the view that any reasonable man
would have known that serious injury was the probable result
of Smith's action, the House of Lords (reversing the decision of

[1] *D.P.P.* v. *Smith*, [1961] A.C. 290.
[2] Lord Denning in his Lionel Cohen lecture 'Responsibility before the Law',
January 1961, at the University of Jerusalem, contends that the decision of the
House of Lords was to the effect that the objective test was to be used as evidence
in establishing whether the defendant subjectively foresaw the consequences. This
contention, however, seems difficult to reconcile with the Lord Chancellor's speech
in that case.

the Court of Criminal Appeal) ordered that Smith's conviction for murder be restored.

Now what is not always realized is that this decision applies to two very different kinds of case. The first is the obvious case where the accused acts in the heat of the moment and does something which (had he stopped to think) he would have known would cause serious injury or death. Here we can say, in a way, that the accused did really know the probable consequenecs of his action. The result of Smith's case is that it is no defence for the accused to say, 'I did not realize, in the heat of the moment, what the result of my act would be.' Those who applaud the decision do so largely on the ground that most crimes of violence are committed in the heat of the moment and it would stultify the law of murder to acquit an accused who did not stop to think. They are satisfied that the law should demand that people in Smith's position must stop to think. To this the same sort of objection can be made as is made against counting an intent to cause grievous bodily harm as equal to an intent to kill. To do something which results in another person's death, knowing that your act is likely to have this result, is morally worse than to bring about the same result through failing to realize the probable consequences. Failure to stop to think in such a case does not excuse morally, but it does render the act less morally culpable than intentional killing. Those who object to the decision in Smith's case do so on the ground that this important moral distinction should be reflected in our law.

There is, however, another type of case to which the decision applies and which is less obvious than the one just discussed, where the rule could work serious injustice. Suppose A does an unlawful act aimed at B which kills B and suppose that a reasonable man in A's position would know that A's act would probably have this result, but suppose A lacks this knowledge (not through failing to stop to think, but just because he does not know that this type of act is likely to cause serious harm). An example would be that of a person putting some poisonous substance in another person's drink, perhaps in order to make him sleepy, not knowing that this substance is likely to cause serious harm. This is not a case of the accused mistaking some poisonous matter for something not poisonous, e.g. mistaking arsenic for sugar; it is rather the case of not knowing that arsenic can

R v Cunningham.

kill. Here we have a voluntary act aimed at the deceased; the act is unlawful, for one man may not administer drugs to another without his consent; and a reasonable man would, of course, know the danger involved. But few would wish to treat A in this case as guilty of the same crime as a person who administers poison knowing it to be dangerous and wishing to kill or seriously injure. Yet the decision in *Smith*'s case would go as far as this and hold that, though genuine mistakes as to particular facts and circumstances operate to exonerate in the criminal law, mistakes about the way things behave, i.e. mistakes about the laws of nature, will only exonerate if they are reasonable. In other words, a man is ignorant of the workings of nature at his peril. In some cases his ignorance may make him guilty of murder. This is perhaps the most serious defect in our present substantive criminal law.[1]

Prior to 1957 there were two other heads of malice: cases of constructive malice where the accused could be guilty of murder without any intent to cause death or grievous bodily harm. The first concerned death caused by an act committed in the course or furtherance of a felony. Originally if the death resulted from any unlawful act on the part of the accused, the latter was guilty of murder. This rule was later qualified by the requirement that the unlawful act must be felonious. When death ceased to be the automatic punishment for all felonies, the harshness of this rule became apparent, and the rule was further qualified by the rule that the felony must be one of violence. Before the Homicide Act, 1957, therefore, the position was that if the accused killed a person in the course or furtherance of a felony of violence, e.g. robbery or rape, he would be guilty of murder even though he did not intend to cause any harm to the deceased. A good example is provided by the case of *Jarmain*,[2] who shot a cashier during the course of a robbery. His plea that the gun went off

---

[1] This 'objective recklessness', as it might be termed, does not apply to all branches of the criminal law. In *R. v. Cunningham*, [1957] 2 Q.B. 396, the accused broke open a gas meter and stole the contents, thereby unknowingly fracturing the gas main, as a result of which gas seeped into the next-door house and the occupant inhaled some of the gas, her life being thereby endangered. Cunningham's conviction for unlawfully and maliciously causing her to inhale a noxious thing so as to endanger her life, contrary to section 23 of the Offences against the Person Act, 1861, was quashed on the ground that he could not be guilty unless he intended or foresaw that the removal of the meter might cause injury to someone.

[2] *R. v. Jarmain*, [1946] K.B. 74.

by accident, even if genuine, afforded no defence, because the death resulted from an act done in furtherance of a dangerous felony, the act in question being that of pointing the gun at the deceased. The other type of constructive malice concerned death caused by acts done with intent to resist lawful arrest by policemen. Dissatisfaction, however, with constructive malice led to the abolition of these two heads of malice by the Homicide Act, 1957.

Murder and treason stand alone in having a fixed penalty. Before 1957 the punishment for murder was death, but dissatisfaction with capital punishment led to a compromise in the law of murder by the Homicide Act, 1957. The Act created a distinction between capital murders for which death by hanging is retained and non-capital murders for which the punishment is life imprisonment. The death penalty is retained for murders done in the course or furtherance of a theft; for murder by shooting or by causing an explosion; for murder done to resist arrest or to escape from legal custody; for murder of a police officer acting in the execution of his duty or of a person assisting a police officer so acting; and for a murder of a prison officer by a prisoner. Capital punishment must also be inflicted for repeated murders, provided that both murders were committed in Great Britain.

This compromise has been much criticized. The Act seems to suggest that it is worse to shoot than to poison and the moral seems to be, 'if you must commit murder do it quietly'. But the distinction is not entirely without reason. The first two types of capital murder are meant to hit at the professional criminal against whom protection is particularly desirable. The retention of the death penalty for murder by shooting does not suggest that Parliament considers shooting worse than poisoning. The rationale is rather that whereas poisoning is deliberate and the poisoner is unlikely to be deterred by any penalty, shooting may happen in the heat of the moment and here the death penalty may serve to deter people from carrying guns. The retention of capital punishment for the next three classes of case is for the protection of the police and prison officers. The reason for keeping the death penalty for repeated murders would seem to be that since imprisonment has proved an insufficient deterrent some greater punishment is required.

One important restriction was made, however, on the infliction of the death penalty. The Act provides that where there is
more than one party to a capital murder, only those who caused
the death or inflicted harm on the deceased shall be liable to
capital punishment. This means that if A and B embark on a
smash-and-grab raid and A sits waiting in the car while B carries
out the robbery, A will not be hanged if B murders the night-
watchman as part of the plan.

Manslaughter. Manslaughter is a residual crime consisting of
unlawful homicides which do not amount to murder. It is traditionally divided into voluntary and involuntary manslaughter.
Voluntary manslaughter covers cases which would normally
amount to murder, because the accused does have malice aforethought, but which are by law reduced to manslaughter on
account of special circumstances. As a general rule, the substantive law of crime pays no attention to mitigating factors, because
after conviction it is open to the court to take account of these
factors in passing sentence. But in view of the fixed penalty for
murder the only way to allow mitigating circumstances to have
any effect is to provide that they shall reduce the offence to
one with a variable penalty. There are at present three cases of
voluntary manslaughter. If the accused was suffering from diminished responsibility—a defence provided by the 1957 Act; if the
accused was acting in the course of a suicide pact with the deceased; if the accused was acting under provocation—murder is
in each case reduced to manslaughter. Diminished responsibility
is more aptly treated together with the problem of insanity and
will be dealt with later. Suicide pacts have been already considered and it is not proposed to deal with them further. Provocation will be considered under the chapter reserved for
defences.

Involuntary manslaughter consists of unlawful killing without any of the different heads of malice aforethought which we
have previously examined. This type of manslaughter may be
committed in two different ways. In the first place, if the accused
does an act likely to cause some harm to the deceased, but not
likely to kill or cause grievous bodily harm, then, should death
result, the accused is guilty of manslaughter. If the accused, for
a joke, pulls another person's chair from under him and the
other dies from the resulting fall, here, since the death results

from an unlawful act likely to cause some harm (though certainly not very likely to cause serious harm), the accused is guilty of manslaughter. This has important application to illegal operations. If a woman dies as a result of an unlawful abortion, the abortionist is guilty of manslaughter. If a woman dies as a result of a lawful operation (including a lawful abortion), the surgeon is not, in the absence of negligence, guilty of manslaughter, for though his act is likely to cause some injury, it is not an unlawful act.

The other type of involuntary manslaughter consists of causing death by negligence. This is one of the exceptions to the rule that the criminal law takes no account of negligence. The negligence in question must be gross: what would amount to mere civil negligence will not suffice. This type of manslaughter is not strictly a crime of violence, since violence involves the intent to inflict some harm and it will be more conveniently discussed in the section dealing with negligence.

Manslaughter unlike murder does not carry a fixed penalty. It has no minimum penalty, but a maximum of life imprisonment. Before 1957 it was greatly to the accused's advantage to reduce a murder charge to manslaughter to avoid the death penalty. It is still to his advantage if he is being prosecuted for capital murder; and even on a charge of non-capital murder, it will still benefit him, for the penalty for non-capital murder is still a fixed penalty of life imprisonment, whereas in manslaughter life imprisonment is only a maximum penalty.

2. DISHONESTY

Of all crimes those which loom largest in the popular imagination are crimes of dishonesty. Less serious than crimes of violence, which they outnumber by about four to one, and less frequent than road traffic offences, which usually account for over 50 per cent. of convictions, they none the less enjoy a certain pre-eminence in the public conception of crime. The reason for this is not merely that such offences constitute an attack on one of the fundamental institutions of our society, based as it is on the acquisition and ownership of property; it is that crimes of dishonesty are the work of the professional. In this country at least we are not familiar with the professional murderer, and even those drivers most prone to accidents would

L 30-45

only rank as amateur criminals. The professional criminal today is the thief, the burglar, the fence—in other words the man who makes a living out of dishonesty.

In ordinary language dishonesty connotes an element of deceit. Perjurers and pickpockets would be reckoned dishonest, a highwayman not. For however reprehensible the highwayman's conduct may be, it has one redeeming feature—it is open and above board. Dishonesty, on the other hand, consists of underhand behaviour, such as cheating at cards or shoplifting. In law, however, dishonesty connotes not so much deceit as fraudulent misappropriation of property. Armed robbery would rank as a crime of dishonesty, while perjury and kindred offences would not.

Crimes of dishonesty whereby one man misappropriates another's property are mostly to be found defined in the Larceny Act, 1916, the nearest thing in English law to a code of dishonest offences. Within its fifty sections are contained the definitions of stealing, embezzlement, fraudulent conversion, robbery, burglary and housebreaking, blackmail, obtaining by false pretences, and receiving. A notable absentee is forgery, which has an Act of its own, the Forgery Act, 1913. It would be outside the scope of a work of this nature to embark on a detailed discussion of each of these offences. It is proposed rather to concentrate on the three basic crimes of dishonesty: stealing, swindling, and receiving.

(a) Stealing

The basic offence of dishonesty is theft. Theft, or larceny as it is termed, is to property what assault is to the person. It may be roughly defined as fraudulently taking a man's property from him with the intention of depriving him of it permanently. The serious light in which the law regards this crime may be seen from the fact that the maximum penalty for certain sorts of larceny, e.g. larceny by a servant, is fourteen years' imprisonment, more than double the maximum penalty for the offence of unlawful wounding, or inflicting grievous bodily harm.[1]

[1] The maximum penalty for unlawful wounding is five years. For wounding with intent to murder, however, and for wounding with intent to maim, disfigure, or disable or do some other grievous bodily harm, the maximum penalty is imprisonment for life.

(Offences against property will often be found more heavily punishable in English law than offences against the person, the reason possibly being that in the days when the criminal law was developed and punishments were first assigned, our lawmakers were much less liable themselves to attacks on their persons than to attacks on their property.) The maximum penalty for simple larceny is five years' imprisonment. More severe penalties are provided for aggravated larcenies, e.g. fourteen years for larceny from the person, fourteen years for larceny from ships, and life imprisonment for larceny of postal packets. A special type of aggravated larceny is the offence of *robbery*, which consists in stealing a person's property from his person or in his presence against his will by force or threats. Simple robbery carries a maximum penalty of fourteen years, while armed robbery and robbery with violence are punishable with life imprisonment.

(i) *Restrictions on the scope of larceny*

You can steal a horse, but you cannot steal a ride, it has been said, so highlighting at least two of the restrictions on the scope of the offence of larceny, namely: (i) that only material objects can be stolen, and (ii) that borrowing is not stealing. In view of the important role played by larceny in the defence of property against attacks of dishonesty, some of the earlier limitations on the offence are to our present ways of thinking surprising. The category of objects capable of being stolen was narrow. Larceny could only be committed by wrongfully taking objects in the loser's possession out of his possession. If the wrongdoer had already obtained possession legitimately he could not commit larceny. It was essential that the thief should take the goods without the owner's consent. Finally, the thief had to have, at the time he took the goods, an intention to deprive the owner permanently of them. The history of the law of larceny is the account of the narrowing of these restrictions, the widening of the bounds of the offence, and the closing of the various gaps through which dishonest rogues escaped. There still remain even today several gaps which it is hoped may eventually be closed.

Stealable property. By no means all the property which a person may own is legally capable of being stolen. A man's wealth may consist, not only of land, goods, and money, but also shares in

companies, patent rights, and other intangibles, but the law of
larceny is restricted to tangible objects. It is not possible at common law to steal an idea for a book, an invention, a ride on a
horse, or a peep at a football match. Ideas and inventions are
protected by the law of copyright and patents. Railway companies and similar undertakings have protected themselves by
private Acts of Parliament prohibiting people from stealing
rides without paying. The Road Traffic Act, 1930, has prohibited 'joy-riding' by creating the offence of driving a motor-
car without the consent of the owner. But the general law of
larceny is confined to tangible things. One notable exception
to this is the case of electricity, the fraudulent abstraction of
which amounts to an offence carrying the same penalty as simple
larceny.

Within the category of tangible things, larceny was yet further restricted to movable objects. Money and goods could be
stolen, but land and anything attached to it could not. A man
might be dispossessed of his land and his house, but they remained where they were so that in this case his civil remedies of
recovering possession and damages for trespass were considered
sufficient. Movable property, on the other hand, could be easily
disposed of and would in many cases be of too little value to
make it worth the loser's while to sue, even if he could catch the
thief. For these reasons, it was obviously desirable to afford
movables the extra protection of the criminal law. The criminal
law gave no protection, however, to things attached to land, such
as crops, plants, trees, and metal ores. The Larceny Act, however, has created specific offences concerning the theft of such
things so that today the only tangible objects outside the scope
of theft are land itself and buildings attached to it.

To be capable of being stolen, however, it has always been
the law that an object must have value. At one time dogs (now
specifically included in the Larceny Act) were not larcenable,
on the ground that they were of no value. But since even such
things as void cheques have been decided to be of value in this
context, this requirement constitutes little restriction today on
the offence of larceny.

Larceny as an offence against possession. The essence of stealing is
taking a man's property out of his possession, for larceny is an
offence against possession, not against ownership. This meant at

one time that if A already possessed goods belonging to B he could not legally steal them. On the other hand, if B the owner fraudulently takes the goods from A the possessor, he is guilty of stealing. A man who left his clock with a shopkeeper, as security for the price of an article which he had bought, and who then secretly took it from the shop, was held guilty of larceny in the case of *Rose* v. *Matt.*[1]

One important consequence of the requirement that the thief must take the goods from the possession of another, is that goods not in anyone's possession cannot be stolen. Wild animals not in captivity fall into this category, for they are not by law considered to be in the possession of anyone. The game on a landowner's estate is not in his possession, so that the poacher is not guilty of stealing the pheasants or partridges which he shoots. Human corpses, except those used in laboratories for anatomical purposes, are likewise in no one's possession. There are, however, special laws relating to unauthorized exhumations and tampering with graves. Living persons are not, in English law, the subject of larceny since they are not capable of being owned and possessed. The Offences against the Person Act, 1861, however, makes it an offence unlawfully to take a child under fourteen years out of the possession of its parent or guardian; to take a girl under sixteen out of the possession of her parent or guardian without his consent; and to abduct a girl under eighteen with intention to have carnal knowledge of her.

Likewise incapable of being stolen are things which have been abandoned, since they are not in anyone's possession. English law, however, tends to abhor a vacuum with regard to possession and does not readily conclude that possession has been abandoned. A householder who put refuse in a dustbin was held not to have abandoned possession, so that dustmen who appropriated it to their own use, instead of handing it over to the corporation, were guilty of stealing.[2] Nor is a lost article necessarily abandoned so far as possession is concerned. If A finds a wallet and keeps it, knowing that it belongs to B, or knowing that he could easily find out who the owner is, he is guilty of larceny by finding. Even if the loser is taken to have abandoned possession the taker may find that the goods have fallen into possession of

[1] [1951] 1 K.B. 810.
[2] *Williams* v. *Phillips* (1957), 41 Cr. App. Rep. 5.

the person on whose land they were lost. Golf balls lost and abandoned on the links have been held to fall into the possession of the golf club, with a result that a trespasser who took them was guilty of stealing them from the members of the club.[1]

But the most important corollary of the possessory nature of larceny was that if the wrongdoer had already got possession before he misappropriated the goods he committed no crime. If X lent his horse to Y, who subsequently absconded with it, Y, since he already had possession, was not guilty of theft. This was one of the greatest defects in the law of theft and allowed dishonesty to flourish unpunished.

To remedy the position the courts and the legislature extended the criminal law to catch within its provisions persons who would have otherwise escaped on the plea that having already acquired possession they could not be guilty of larceny. The first extension related to people such as *servants* and *guests* in physical possession of the goods of their masters or hosts. In the eyes of the law this physical possession was not counted as legal possession, but only as custody; the legal possession remained with the master or host. Consequently, if the butler made off with the silver which he had been cleaning, he committed larceny. The next gap to be closed concerned the *bailee*. A bailee is a person who is temporarily entrusted with possession of an article, e.g. a borrower, a carrier, a warehouseman. A fifteenth-century decision, known as the *Carrier*'s case,[2] held that a carrier who was employed to carry bales of wool, but who broke open the bales and misappropriated the contents, was guilty of larceny. Though he had been entrusted with the bales, he had not been entrusted with the contents, it was said, and so he committed larceny by 'breaking bulk'. This convenient fiction, however, would not work for things like horses, where the distinction between the article and its contents could not be made. It remained for Parliament to intervene and provide by statute that a bailee who fraudulently converts the goods bailed to him is guilty of stealing.

But even this extension of the crime of larceny leaves out of account two important situations affording possibilities of dishonesty. Suppose X gives Y goods or money for Y's master Z,

[1] *Hibbert* v. *McKiernan*, [1948] 2 K.B. 142.
[2] (1473), Y.B. 13 Ed. IV, fo. 9, pasch. pl. 5.

but Y misappropriates them. Here Y does not steal from X, because X parts with possession of his own consent, nor does he steal from Z because the goods were never in Z's possession. To meet this difficulty was created the offence of *embezzlement* which prohibits clerks and servants from misappropriating property received by them for their employers. But this only serves to deal with servants; there still remains the case where someone other than a servant is entrusted with property for another person and the case where one man entrusts property to another, on the understanding that the latter does not have to hand over the identical property, but only property of equal value. A person who lends money does not normally expect the return of the specific coins lent, but only of money to the same value. So, if the borrower or the person entrusted misappropriated the money, he would not be guilty of larceny, since he was under no duty to hand back the specific goods entrusted. Indeed he was given not only the possession, but also the ownership of the property. To penalize such breaches of trust there was created the offence of *fraudulent conversion*, a composite offence covering various types of misappropriation of property (including land) by persons to whom it has been entrusted.

The consent of the owner. Proof of the consent of the owner would be fatal to a prosecution for larceny. Just as in the case of crimes of violence a person by consenting to a battery may render lawful the use of force which might otherwise be unlawful, so in the case of crimes of dishonesty a man may consent to be deprived of his goods and so render innocent an appropriation which might otherwise amount to larceny. With regard to violence, however, we saw that there is a limit to what a person may consent to. No such limit applies to offences against property. The other restriction on the operation of consent noted in the case of violence, namely that consent to be effective must be true consent, is equally applicable in the law of larceny. Consent obtained by force, threats, or fraud does not count as true consent. If A makes B part with his property by force or threat of force he is guilty of robbery. If A merely demands by threats or force that B hand over his property, but does not succeed in obtaining it, A is guilty of blackmail.

If, on the other hand, the owner's consent is obtained by fraud the position is not so simple. This is because the law distinguishes between the case where the owner consents to part only with the possession of the property and the case where he consents to part with the ownership as well as the possession. If X tricks Y into lending him his watch on some pretext and then makes off with it, this is a case of larceny by a trick. But if X tricks Y into giving him his watch, e.g. in return for counterfeit money, here Y consents to part with his entire interest in the watch and X is not guilty of larceny. He is, in fact, guilty of the crime of obtaining by false pretences. The distinction is less important today than formerly so far as the criminal law is concerned, for the Larceny Act contains procedural provisions whereby in such cases a person may be convicted, even though it turns out that the offence committed is not the offence charged. In the civil law, however, the distinction entails highly important consequences.

The owner's consent to part with possession may also be nullified by a spontaneous mistake of his own, not induced by any fraud on the recipient's part. The law here, which is one of the most difficult aspects of the whole of the law of larceny, seems to make a distinction analogous to the one made with regard to consent obtained by a trick.

If the owner's mistake leads him to part with possession only and the recipient takes fraudulent advantage of the mistake, he commits larceny. So, if X, intending to pay £10 to Y, hands the money by mistake to Z, larceny is committed if Z fraudulently takes advantage of the mistake to pocket the money; for here X never intended to pass the property in the money to anyone but Y, and his consent to pass possession is nullified by his own mistake and Z's dishonesty. Likewise if A, intending to pay B £10, miscounts the money and hands over £11, larceny is committed by B if he takes fraudulent advantage of A's mistake; for A never intends to give B the ownership of the extra pound and his consent to part with possession is negatived as before. But suppose the owner makes some mistake which leads him to intend to part not only with possession, but also with the property, then there is no larceny. If in the last example, A, through wrongly calculating the debt owed by him to B, thinks that he must pay B not £10, but £11, here A means to give B the property as well as the possession in the whole of the money. As we saw earlier, when property passes as well as possession, consent is not negatived by fraud, nor it seems is it negatived by mistake. But whereas in the case of fraud the recipient is guilty of obtaining by false pretences, in the case of mistake he is not guilty of any offence. He is not guilty of larceny because the property passes to him and there is no offence of 'obtaining by spontaneous mistake of the owner'. Accordingly, B in the last example would be guilty of no offence; A would be left to his remedy of suing in the Civil Courts for 'money had and received'.

(ii) *The accused's state of mind*

An essential feature in the crime of stealing is, of course, the dishonesty of the thief. Larceny consists not in taking another's property, nor even in wrongful taking, but in dishonest taking. Consequently, if the taker mistakenly thinks that the property is his, e.g. he takes the wrong umbrella, his taking is wrongful and therefore in civil law a trespass, but not dishonest, so no larceny is committed. In such cases prosecutions for larceny would fail, because the accused could show that he was acting 'with a claim of right made in good faith'. This defence is open to anyone who honestly thinks he has a right to take the property, e.g. because he thinks it belongs to him, because he thinks the property is abandoned or belongs to nobody, or because he thinks the owner would consent to his taking it. In all these cases he would, of course, be liable in civil law to the true owner. Usually such mistakes are simple errors of fact, as in the case where A mistakes B's umbrella for his own. Sometimes, however, the mistake is one of law. Suppose X sells his radiogram to a swindler, Y, who pays for it with a dud cheque thereby committing the crime of false pretences. Y then sells it to an honest third party, Z. According to English law, Z's right to the radiogram is preferred to X's and Z becomes the true owner. It is just in this type of case where civil disputes arise between two innocent parties, that it becomes vital to establish whether the wrongdoer committed larceny by a trick, or false pretences; because if the crime was larceny, the former owner can recover the property; but if the crime was false pretences, the new owner's title prevails. Now, suppose in this example X, being ignorant of this branch of the law, sees the radiogram in Z's shop and takes it from him. X, though acting wrongfully in law and rendering himself liable to Z, does not behave dishonestly and so is not guilty of stealing.

This affords a notable exception to the general rule that ignorance of the law is no excuse.

A second essential requirement of the crime of larceny is that the taker must intend to deprive the owner permanently of the property. In one respect the legal notion of stealing is wider here than the popular notion. Usually a thief takes another man's property in order to gain some advantage for himself, but in law there is no need for this. It is sufficient if he merely intends to deprive the owner permanently of it. So if A took B's hat and threw it on to a bonfire in order to destroy it, A would commit the crime of larceny. In another respect, however, the offence of larceny may be thought to be unduly narrow because of this requirement, for it means that it is no crime merely to 'borrow' another's property. In general this is reasonable because the owner eventually gets his property back, but it is not hard to imagine cases where hardship might be caused by dishonest borrowing and where prohibition by the criminal law might be advantageous. Suppose X makes a living by hiring out television sets and Y fraudulently borrows one of X's sets for six months without paying for it, here X, in fact, loses six months' rental on the set. Or suppose Y borrows it and treats it so carelessly that X does not recover it in its original condition. Or again, suppose A takes and keeps for a long time some article of B's such as a car battery, which only has a short working life. In all these cases it is arguable that the criminal law should be extended to discourage and prevent this sort of conduct. At present, the only kind of dishonest borrowing which attracts the sanction of the criminal law is the offence of taking and driving away a motor-car without consent of the owner, an offence prohibited by the Road Traffic Act, 1960.[1]

One of the most difficult aspects of the law of larceny relates to the requirement that the taker's dishonest intent must be simultaneous with the taking. The basic principle is that an innocent taking followed by a fraudulent intent does not amount to larceny. So if A finds money belonging to B and takes it in order to return it to B, but then later decides to keep it, he commits no crime. A partial justification for punishing only a taking accompanied with fraudulent intent and leaving unpunished

[1] Local by-laws may to some extent fill the gap. For example an Oxford City by-law of 15 Sept. 1958 prohibits dishonest 'borrowing' of bicycles.

a taking followed by fraudulent intent is that the former conduct
is a direct attack on property and therefore more harmful than
the latter, which involves no original attack. It is also arguable
that the former conduct is more reprehensible than the latter,
since in the latter case the temptation is stronger. Perhaps the
distinction is connected with the general principle already noted
to the effect that the criminal law leans against punishing omissions. The criminal law forbids us to take other people's property with intent to deprive them permanently of it, but does
not go so far as to require us to hand back property which we
have taken innocently.

However, the requirement of simultaneity does not provide
as many loopholes as might be expected. Usually an innocent
possessor will either be a bailee or a trespasser. A bailee, as we
have seen, commits larceny if he misappropriates property entrusted to him. A trespasser too will be guilty of stealing if he
converts the property to his own use on learning of his mistake.
If X takes Y's umbrella by mistake he commits a trespass and if
on realizing his mistake he decides to keep it, he commits larceny. This result was achieved by a judicial fiction developed
in the celebrated case of *R. v. Riley.*[1] In that case twenty-nine
black-faced lambs belonging to Riley and ten white-faced lambs
belonging to the prosecutor were in a field belonging to a third
party. When Riley drove his lambs out to take them to market,
the morning mist prevented him from noticing that one of the
prosecutor's lambs had attached itself to his flock. He only became aware of this when, arriving at a near-by farm, he offered
to sell the twenty-nine lambs to the farmer, who counted the
flock and pointed out that there were in fact thirty. Riley then
sold all thirty lambs to the farmer. His conviction for larceny
was upheld on the ground that where innocent taking amounts
to a trespass, there is a continuous taking throughout the whole
of the time the taker has the property, so that if the taker decides
to misappropriate it, his intent is fictitiously simultaneous with
his taking. In cases where the owner makes a mistake as to the
property he hands over, we saw that if the owner merely intended to part with possession, a fraudulent recipient taking advantage of that mistake would be guilty of stealing. Sometimes,
however, the recipient himself does not learn of the mistake till

[1] (1853), Dears C.C. 149.

later. Suppose O, meaning to give R a shilling, hands him a
sovereign; R too thinks that it is a shilling, but on finding later
that it is a sovereign decides to keep it. In this type of case,
though the law cannot be said to be settled, judges have sometimes decided that the recipient does not take until he knows
what he has got, so that in the above example the fraudulent
intent would be, again by virtue of fiction, simultaneous with
the taking.[1] The requirement of simultaneity does, however,
still leave some loopholes through which dishonesty can escape.
An example of such a loophole was provided by the case of
Moynes v. *Cooper*.[2] The accused had obtained an advance from
his employers of £6. 19s. 6½d. against his weekly wages. The
wages clerk, unaware of the advance, subsequently paid him
his full wage of £7. 3s. 4d. As the money was handed to the
accused in an envelope, he did not discover the mistake till
later, but on discovering it he decided to keep the excess. He
was held not guilty of stealing the £6. 19s. 6½d., since at the
moment he took possession of the money he had no intent to
steal. This case differs from the example above concerning the
sovereign, in that in that example O did not intend R to have a
sovereign; in this case the wages clerk did intend the accused to
have all the money in the envelope, so that possession was obtained at the time the envelope was handed over. Other possible
loopholes are the case of a person who finds property and at
first intends to hand it to the owner, but later changes his mind;
the case of a person who receives property due to a mistake on
the part of the owner, intends at first to put the matter right, and
later decides to profit from the mistake. The abandonment of
this requirement would greatly simplify the law, obviate the
need for fictitious reasoning and prevent dishonest conduct
escaping punishment.

(b) Swindling

Various factors seem to have militated against the recognition
by the law of swindling as a criminal offence. A fool and his
money are soon parted, runs the saying, and the courts at first
took the view that the victim of the fraud had only himself to
blame for his folly. 'Shall we indict one man for making a fool

[1] *R.* v. *Ashwell* (1885), 16 Q.B.D. 190.
[2] [1956] 1 Q.B. 439.

of another?', asked Chief Justice Holt at the beginning of the eighteenth century, when an attempt was made to secure conviction for obtaining money by fraud.[1] In commercial dealings this was an era when the maxim *caveat emptor* flourished and it was up to the buyer to see that he was not cheated by the seller. If the seller sold short weight or short measure then it was the buyer's fault for not keeping sufficiently close watch. But the buyer could not be expected to take more precautions than common prudence dictated and if the seller resorted to the use of false weights or false measures—something which even common prudence could not guard against—the criminal law intervened and held him guilty of the offence of common-law cheating.

A second factor has been the reluctance of the criminal law to punish what it considers to be mere civil breaches of contract. Where X defaults in the performance of contractual obligations owed to Y, this is regarded as a matter concerning X and Y alone, not as an event deserving the sanction of the criminal law. Breaches of contract and non-payment of debts are often the result not of dishonesty, but of supervening financial difficulties; and criminal measures which might unduly restrict speculation and business ventures would not be advantageous to the economic health of a society based on a capitalist system. Non-payment of debts is not regarded today as so morally reprehensible as certain other behaviour and we are now committed to the policy of reserving imprisonment for fraudulent debtors only, i.e. debtors who are ordered by court to pay, who have the means to pay, but who refuse to do so.

Thirdly, even the dishonest swindler may be considered less dangerous and less morally guilty than the outright thief. Wrong as it may be to trick a man into parting with the ownership of his property, this is not so bad as taking it from him by force or stealth. The latter is a direct attack upon his interests, whereas the former involves at least some co-operation on the victim's part. It would be feasible to withhold punishment for fraud, leaving it to each individual to take care not to be defrauded, but a property-owning society could not continue if its members had to run the risk that their goods might be taken with impunity from them by force or when their backs were turned.

---

[1] *R. v. Jones* (1703), 2 Ld. Raym. 1013.

Although, in due course, specific offences had to be devised to protect society against the swindler, a distinction has always been maintained between stealing and swindling and while the former constituted a felony, the latter only amounted to a misdemeanour.

(i) *False pretences*

This offence consists in fraudulently persuading a person by some false pretence to part with his property. In many ways the offence is analogous to that of stealing. There must be for this offence, as for larceny, some dishonest or fraudulent intent on the part of the accused. If X deceived Y into handing over some goods to him, but X honestly thought that he was entitled to the goods, he would commit no crime. Secondly, like larceny the offence of false pretences is restricted to certain kinds of property. It is confined, in fact, to such things as were larcenable at common law, i.e. movable objects of value.

Things not originally larcenable but now larcenable by statute may nevertheless not be obtained by false pretences. It has been held, for example, that it is not possible to obtain a dog by false pretences since a dog is not capable at common law of being stolen. Thirdly, we saw that with larceny it is not essential for the offender to act with a view to personal gain; it is sufficient for him to intend to deprive the owner of the property. Similarly, in false pretence there is no need for the accused to derive any benefit himself from the fraud. Normally, of course, the accused obtains the goods himself by the false pretence, but the offence may equally well be committed by persuading the owner to hand over the goods to a third party.

The basic difference between theft and swindling is that the thief takes the owner's property without his consent, while the swindler persuades the owner to part with his property. We have seen, however, that in larceny consent to pass possession is negatived if it is obtained by fraud and that certain kinds of fraud amount to the crime of larceny by trick.

Consequently, the difference in law between larceny and false pretences is not so much the basic difference between obtaining with, and obtaining without, consent; the difference in law is that in larceny the accused only obtains possession of the property, whereas in false pretences he obtains both possession and ownership. This distinction has already been examined. It might perhaps be more rational to group together all the cases where the offender persuades the owner by fraud to hand over his goods, instead of classifying some of these under the heading of larceny and others under the heading of false pretences.

The false pretence may be made by conduct as well as by words. To wear an army officer's uniform, for example, would be to represent impliedly that the wearer held a commission in the Army. But whether express or implied, the false pretence must consist in some representation of past or present fact. It must first of all be a statement or assertion; a promise, however unprepared the maker may be to keep it, does not amount to a false pretence. Counsel have argued that when a person makes a promise, he impliedly represents that he now has a certain intention, i.e. to keep it, or that if, in fact, he does not mean to keep his promise he is falsely pretending to have this intention. Criminal Courts have not favoured this argument and remain unprepared to treat a promise, or even a statement of intention, as an assertion of fact sufficient to amount to a false pretence. So far do the Criminal Courts resile from the danger of penalizing breaches of contract. Occasionally, a promise may imply the existence of certain facts, for example the promisor's ability to fulfil his promise. If X, a married man, dishonestly obtains money from Miss Y, by promising to marry her, he implies by this promise (unless he has expressly informed her of his inability to marry her) that he is legally free to marry her; and since this implied assertion is untrue, he is guilty of obtaining money by a false pretence.

Secondly, the false pretence must be an assertion of fact not a mere expression of opinion. The underlying notion here is that while misrepresentation of facts can mislead, matters of opinion and valuation are common ground and it is up to the loser to form his own opinion rather than rely on those of other people. Moreover, sellers have always been allowed a certain latitude in advertising their wares. Mere puffing does not amount to a false pretence, but here too care must be taken to avoid express or implied representation of fact. To say of a certain washing machine that it is the best that money can buy would be a mere expression of opinion. To go further and claim that it completes the operation in half the time taken by any other machine would be a statement of fact. Thirdly, it is only representation of present or past fact which counts as false pretence. Representation as to the future will not suffice.

Like larceny, false pretences carries a maximum penalty of five years' imprisonment. The less serious view which the law takes of false pretences, however, is shown by the fact that unlike larceny, it is not a felony, but a misdemeanour.

(ii) *Obtaining credit by fraud*

This is a less serious crime than the one just considered. Like false pretences it is a misdemeanour, but the maximum penalty for the offence is one year's imprisonment.

The crime consists in incurring a liability, and obtaining credit by fraud. An example of this would be to borrow money never intending to pay it back. If A dishonestly borrows money from B with no intention of ever repaying the loan, A is guilty of obtaining credit by fraud, since all three elements of the offence are present. A has incurred a liability, namely to repay B; he has obtained credit; and he has obtained it by fraud, because B would not have lent money had not A concealed his dishonest intention not to honour the debt. In one respect the offence is wider than obtaining by false pretence. The fraud by which credit is obtained includes not only false pretences, but also other sorts of fraud which do not qualify as false pretences. The example just described provides us with an instance of this, since there the fraud consisted in a dishonest intention which would not amount to a false pretence.

(c) *Receiving*

Perhaps the most serious menace to a property-owning community is the 'fence'. Were it not for the existence of someone ready and willing to pay for stolen property, the professional thief would be hard put to dispose of his loot and to make a living out of his chosen career. The elimination of the market for stolen property would go far towards putting other professional criminals out of business.

The substantive law of crime draws no distinction between the professional and amateur receiver. The man who on one occasion receives stolen property is as guilty of the offence of receiving as the man who does so in the course of carrying on the business of a receiver. If either is caught he is guilty of the same offence. However, a distinction which is not drawn in the substantive criminal law can be reflected in the sentencing policy of the courts. If the judge is satisfied that the accused has committed only an isolated offence, he may well be inclined to treat him more leniently than if he were sure that the offence was part of a general course of conduct.

Receiving consists in dishonestly receiving property which has been dishonestly acquired. The property must be stolen, obtained by false pretence, or acquired by some other conduct amounting to a felony or misdemeanour. The receiver must know at the time of receiving the property that the property has been dishonestly acquired. If A buys goods from B and later learns that B had stolen the goods, this knowledge does not render A a receiver. Nor will refusal on A's part to hand back the goods to the true owner make him guilty of receiving. In practice, it is not easy for the prosecution to show that the accused realized at the time he received the goods that they had been dishonestly acquired. To simplify the prosecution's task and prevent receivers escaping conviction the laws of evidence have been specially relaxed with regard to this offence. Normally, the prosecution may only advance evidence to show that the accused committed the offence charged; they cannot bring evidence of bad character or evidence that the accused has committed other offences, in order to show that he is the sort of person likely to commit the actual offence charged. In a prosecution for receiving, however, this sort of evidence may be given, in order to show what kind of person the accused is and to show that it is probable that he received the goods knowing that they were 'hot'. Evidence may be given that other property stolen within the previous year was found in the accused's possession and that the accused has within the last five years been convicted of an offence of dishonesty. Moreover, if recently stolen goods are found in the accused's possession, failure by the accused to give a reasonable explanation will entitle the jury to infer that he received the goods knowing them to be stolen.

Knowingly receiving stolen goods does not amount to a crime, unless the accused receives them with a dishonest intention; an honest motive takes the receiving out of the criminal category. Were this not so, the police would be guilty of receiving every time they took stolen property away from a thief. Further, an honest receiving followed by a change of heart will not amount to a crime. If A receives goods from B, knowing them to be stolen from C and intending to hand them over to C, and if A subsequently changes his mind and decides to keep the goods, he does not become guilty of receiving. Like larceny, receiving requires simultaneity of act and intent. The obvious danger, however, of such a defence is that the jury may be reluctant to believe that the accused receives the goods honestly in the first place.

3. MALICIOUS DAMAGE

The chief hazard to which property is exposed is misappropriation. Second only in importance to this is the other great danger, namely wanton damage or destruction. In 1960 malicious damage accounted for 1·7 per cent. of the total number of convictions in the Criminal Courts.

This field of our criminal law provides yet another example of the excessive complexity of English law. A simple yet totally adequate rule of law could prohibit malicious damage to any kind of property, prescribe a penalty for the offence, and set out a list of factors which would aggravate the crime. One such aggravating factor might be the danger to other persons resulting from the offence, another might be the amount of damage caused. The English criminal law relating to malicious damage is far less simple than this and needs 78 sections of the Malicious Damage Act, 1861, to contain its provisions.

The main reasons for this undue complexity is that the Act, which consolidated all the previous provisions relating to malicious damage, retains two distinctions which are absolutely unnecessary. The first distinguishes between the different methods by which damage is caused. Apart from the general offence of causing damage by some unspecified method, the law singles out damage caused by burning, by explosion, and by rioters. Secondly a distinction is made between the different kinds of property which are damaged. Instead of a general section providing that it will be an offence to cause damage to any property, the Act has a number of special *ad hoc* sections concerning damage to buildings, machinery, trees, fences, mines, ponds, railway carriages, animals, ships, and various other objects, and finally a section relating to damage to any sort of property. Damage to each of all these different kinds of property constitutes a different, specific offence.

(a) The Property Protected

The law with regard to dishonesty, as we saw, is concerned primarily with the protection of movable property; land and buildings are virtually outside its scope. For it is precisely movable property, money, and goods, which are easily disposed of, while immovable property, such as land and buildings, cannot be so easily disposed of dishonestly.

When we turn to malicious damage we find that the converse is the case. Because goods are liable to misappropriation, for this very reason they are less prone to being damaged and destroyed; whereas just because land and buildings are not so liable to misappropriation they are all the more likely to be exposed to damage and destruction. Those who commit crimes of dishonesty, crimes of gain, are interested in property which is easily disposed of; those who commit crimes of malicious damage are interested in property that is valuable rather than disposable. As we should expect, therefore, offences of malicious damage may be committed not only with regard to goods, but with regard to buildings and other immovable property. Indeed, the oldest crime of malicious damage, arson, is concerned almost solely with buildings and immovable property.

Originally *arson* consisted in burning another person's dwelling-house. It was subsequently extended to cover setting fire to any buildings, ships, crops, haystacks, and even ordinary goods. But for the offence to amount to arson the goods must be in, against or under a building and must be set fire to in such circumstances that if the building caught fire, the accused would be guilty of arson of the building. In other words, the accused must intend to set fire to the building or must act recklessly with regard to it. In *Faulkner's*[1] case, a sailor who whilst stealing rum from a ship set fire to the rum, which in its turn set fire to the ship, was held not guilty of arson, because he neither intended nor foresaw that the ship would be burnt. So even where goods are involved, the law of arson is in reality protecting not the goods burnt, but the building in which they are burnt; and

[1] (1876), I.R. 11 C.L. 8.

apart from this type of case it is not arson to set fire to goods and chattels. This would, however, constitute the offence of malicious damage, which can be committed in respect of any type of property.

Normally people do not set fire to or damage their own property. If a man does, however, choose to damage his own house or goods, then the law takes the view that he may do what he likes with his own, so long as no one else is injured or exposed to danger. The law of arson and malicious damage is only concerned with *unlawfully* setting fire to and *unlawfully* causing damage to property. If a man sets fire to, or damages, property owned or possessed by himself, this is, generally speaking, not a crime. English law has no place for the view that the destruction of one's own property should be prevented on the ground that it will result in the diminution of the property of one's successors, or in the lessening of the general wealth of the community. On the other hand, where ownership and possession reside in different persons, either would be guilty of a crime if he damaged the property. If X hires Y's car, X cannot lawfully damage the car, just because it is in his possession. Conversely, Y would not have the right to damage the car while the hiring continued, just because it was his own property.

There are, however, some important exceptions to this rule that a person can damage his own property with impunity. Three such exceptions are provided by the law of arson which lays down that it is an offence for a person to set fire to his own dwelling-house in such circumstances that those of his neighbours are injured. Here we have a case of reasonable protection being afforded by law to the property of others. It is also an offence to set fire to a dwelling-house, even one's own dwelling-house, when there is a person inside it; and, in fact, the offence is complete even when the only person inside is the offender himself. Here the law is aiming at the protection of human life and safety of third parties. It is, moreover, an offence to set fire to certain types of buildings with intent to injure or defraud. If a man sets fire to his house, in order to bring a fraudulent claim against his insurance company, this amounts to arson. What the law is really prohibiting in this case is a type of inchoate obtaining by false pretences. These special exceptions provided by the law of arson have no parallel in the general law of malicious damage. So far as the latter is concerned, a man's right to destroy or damage his own property is not limited by reason of the damage to others, or by reason of his fraudulent motive. If an owner damages his car in order to bring a claim against his insurance company, he is not guilty of malicious damage; his crime, if any, would be an attempt to obtain money by false pretences.

Apart from the exceptions in the above paragraph, there is one other important restriction on a person's right to do what he likes with his own property (in so far as others are not injured). The view that animals, although they bear no rights in law, should not be exposed to unnecessary suffering has obtained statutory recognition in the Protection of Animals Act, 1911, which prohibits intentional or negligent causing of unnecessary suffering to any animal. There are, moreover, restrictions on the experiments which may legally be performed on live animals. There has even been one case, *R. v. Parry*,[1] where a person has been found guilty of causing malicious damage to an animal, even though it belonged to him.

(b) *The State of the Defendant's Mind*

To be guilty of malicious damage or arson a person must act unlawfully and maliciously. If he has a right to cause damage, e.g. in most cases if the property is his own, he acts lawfully. Where he has no right to cause the damage, e.g. if the property belongs to someone else, or if his conduct comes under one of the exceptions discussed, then his act is unlawful.

What is not finally settled is whether he acts lawfully or not in the case where he mistakenly thinks that he has a right to cause damage. If his mistaken belief arises from a mistake of fact, no offence is committed. So if A throws B's hat on a bonfire in mistake for his own, he commits no offence. Where the mistaken belief arises from a mistake of law, the position is less clear. Generally speaking ignorance of law is no excuse. The law relating to malicious damage can either follow this general rule and exclude defences of mistake arising through ignorance of law, or it can follow a rule analogous to the 'claim of right' rule in the law of larceny. This rule, as we saw, provides that a mistaken belief that he has a right to take the property will

[1] (1900), 35 L. Jo. 456.

exonerate the taker, even though the belief arises from a mistake of law. Now at different times the law of malicious damage has followed both these rules. In one case, a woman who through a mistake as to the general law thought that she had a right to burn furze on a common was held not guilty of arson.[1] In another case, however, a man who wrongfully thought he was entitled to shoot a dog chasing a hare on land over which he had sporting rights, was held guilty of malicious damage.[2] Hares and similar animals are not in law in the ownership of anyone until they have been taken possession of, so that in this case the accused, though he thought he was protecting a proprietary interest, had no such interest to protect. Since this branch of the law serves to protect people from malicious and spiteful damage to their property, it would seem preferable for the courts to accept ignorance of law as a defence, so as to avoid punishing acts committed without ill will, just as the law of theft refrains from punishing taking committed without dishonesty. The owner of the property would, of course, have the right to receive compensation in the Civil Courts for the wrong done.

The requirement that the accused must act maliciously means that he must either intend the harm caused or must act recklessly. The rules concerning recklessness and transferred malice which have been discussed with regard to offences of violence apply equally in this context. A man who threw a stone at some persons with whom he had been fighting was held not guilty of malicious damage when the stone broke a window in a neighbouring house.[3] He had not intended harm of the same legal type as that which he caused; consequently his malice could not be transferred. There is this further similarity between offences of violence and offences of malicious damage, that both are concerned with intentional or reckless conduct. Malicious damage cannot be committed by negligence.

(c) Methods of Causing the Damage

Two important methods are singled out for special treatment by the law; namely, damage by fire and damage by explosives. It is natural that deliberate burning should have early on

[1] *R.* v. *Twose* (1879), 14 Cox C.C. 327.
[2] *Gott* v. *Measures,* [1948] 1 K.B. 234.
[3] *R.* v. *Pembliton* (1874), L.R. 2 C.C. 119.

attracted the attention of the criminal law, since this is one of the simplest and at the same time most dangerous methods of causing damage. What is quite unnecessary is that arson should be retained today as a separate crime.

One interesting feature of the crime of arson is that it does not consist of damaging property by burning, so much as in setting fire to property. If any part, however trifling, of a building is burnt, arson is committed. A person who succeeded only in charring and scorching one floorboard was held guilty of arson of the building. While the harm sought to be prevented is the damaging or destroying of the property, the law does not wait until the object is achieved, but steps in to punish what is, in fact, an attempt to achieve the object. The success of the object is immaterial to the offender's guilt. Likewise the law of stealing aims to protect property owners against permanent deprivation of their property, but instead of waiting for this object to be attained, steps in to penalize the attempt to achieve it.

Explosions, like fire, are so fraught with danger that it is not surprising to find special provisions to deal with them. Apart from the fact that higher penalties can be imposed for damaging property by explosion than by ordinary malicious damage (fourteen years' imprisonment as opposed to two years), the most interesting feature of the attitude of the law here is the penalizing of certain inchoate offences. The Malicious Damage Act, for instance, lays down that it is an offence merely to place explosive substances near any property with intent to damage it and that it is an offence even to have such substances in one's possession in order to commit such a crime. The Explosive Substances Act, 1883, forbids the causing of an explosion likely to injure life or property and the keeping of such substance with intent to cause such an explosion. It goes further, however, than the Malicious Damage Act, in that it even renders it an offence to make or have in one's possession explosive substances without being able to show that this is done for a lawful purpose. Here we have an exception to the general rule that people are punished for what they have done, rather than for what they are or have in their possession.

The penalty for the various offences of this type varies. For most kinds of arson the maximum penalty is life imprisonment. Arson of one of Her Majesty's ships or a naval dockyard is punishable with death. Causing damage by explosion is punishable with fourteen years' imprisonment. Of the residual kinds of malicious damage prohibited by the residual section of the Act, the penalty varies according to the amount of damage done. Damage exceeding £20 attracts a maximum penalty of two years; damage in excess of £5 but less than £20 is punishable summarily with three months' imprisonment or a £20 fine. For damage less than £5 the offender may only be dealt with summarily and is liable on conviction to imprisonment for two months or a fine of £5.

4. NEGLIGENCE

The gravity of a crime, we have seen, is largely a function of two factors; the accused's intention to produce harm and the actual harmfulness of his conduct. Offences of violence provide excellent examples of this. Assault is more heavily punished if actual or grievous bodily harm is inflicted on the victim. Assault occasioning grievous bodily harm is further aggravated if the accused intended to kill or seriously injure the victim. Again, murder is a more serious crime than manslaughter by reason of the accused's intent to kill or cause grievous bodily harm; it is more serious than the crime of causing grievous bodily harm with intent, by reason of the extra harm caused, i.e. the victim's death.

Reversing the telescope, as it were, we can see this principle operating in reverse. To take intention first, we find that the smaller the harm intended, the smaller the offence. So, for example, an ordinary assault is a less serious crime than an assault with intent to kill or to cause grievous bodily harm, or an assault with intent to rob. Eventually we reach the vanishing-point, where no harm whatsoever is intended and the conduct is no longer within the province of the criminal law. For example, to injure a person without any intention to do so (and without recklessness, which counts as intent) is no crime. The careless infliction of injury is no offence. So again, to damage property without intending so to do (and without recklessness) is no offence. Carelessness again is not enough.

Likewise with regard to the other factor, the harmfulness of the conduct, we find that the less harmful the conduct, the less serious the crime. For instance, wounding with intent to kill is less grave than murder. Here again we eventually reach the vanishing-point, where the conduct is so harmless as to fall outside the scope of the criminal law. One reservation, however, must be made here. If the lack of harmfulness is due to the accused's failure to succeed in his venture, this will not serve to exempt him from the sanction of the criminal law, which contains special provisions relating to attempts to commit crimes. Nevertheless, the attempt to commit a crime is less heavily punished than its actual commission. The vanishing-point occurs where the conduct consists in acts (other than attempts to commit crimes) which cause physical harm neither to persons nor property. Conduct which merely annoys, such as insult, borrowing, and trespass, is for the most part outside the criminal law.

It may seem strange that negligence, which plays such an important role in the Civil Courts, should but rarely make an entrance on the criminal stage. The courts developed only one crime of negligence, viz. manslaughter. As for non-fatal injuries, the injured party is left to his civil remedy. If, through gross carelessness, I knock out your eye with my umbrella, I commit no crime. In the eyes of the law this is entirely a matter for you and me alone. One notable exception to this principle arises from Parliament's intervention to protect children against neglect. The Children and Young Persons Act, 1933, prohibits the wilful neglect of a child under sixteen. Even here the neglect must be wilful; neglect through inadvertence does not contravene the Act. Nevertheless, to this extent the Act does penalize negligence in that there is no need to show that the accused positively intended to injure the child. It is sufficient to prove that he acted intentionally and that he realized that the child was likely to suffer as a result of his conduct.

Of negligent damage to property the Criminal Courts knew nothing. Today the position is much the same. If I wilfully cause a few shillings' worth of damage to your house, I am guilty of malicious damage; if through carelessness I bring about its total destruction, I commit no offence. There are isolated instances where Parliament has stepped in to punish negligent damage to property. These instances chiefly concern people in special positions with special duties. A seaman, for example, contravenes the Merchant Shipping Act, 1894, if through drunkenness he

commits acts tending to the destruction of his ship. To cause
the destruction of a submarine cable by culpable negligence is
an offence contrary to the Submarine Telegraph Act, 1885.
Here, however, Parliament was bringing English law into line
with the law of other states.

It would be wrong, however, to imagine that negligence is
overlooked by the criminal law entirely. Apart from the important common-law crime of manslaughter, there are two other
branches of the criminal law which concern negligent behaviour.
These are the law relating to road traffic and the law relating to
social welfare.

But before considering these different types of negligent behaviour which are contrary to the criminal law, let us first
inquire why it should be that in general the courts and the
legislature have been so reluctant to punish negligence. Negligence consists in failing to take due care. Whether this failure
results from taking an unjustified risk, from a miscalculation,
from inadvertence, or from mere clumsiness, the essence of
negligence is the agent's failure to attain the standard of care
demanded in the circumstances. Outside the law, the standard
required is that dictated by common prudence and varies
naturally from situation to situation. We expect a man to be
more careful with a loaded gun than with a hose-pipe. The law
is, for the most part, content to adopt the standard of common
prudence and to require that people should take reasonable
care, i.e. as much care as would be taken by a reasonable man,
but the essence of negligence is the agent's failure. In other
words, negligence is a type of omission rather than a positive act.
As we have already seen, the criminal law leans against punishing omissions. Underlying this reluctance to punish omission,
there would seem to be the idea that to enjoin positive action on
penalty of punishment would be too great an interference with
individual liberty.

Secondly, it may be suggested that carelessness cannot and
need not be deterred by punishment. Since most acts of negligence arise from inadvertence, the actor would not in any case
have the thought of the penalty before his mind at the relevant
time. This is not wholly convincing. Children are frequently
punished at home or at school for carelessness, and this means
that they (and others) act more carefully in the future. The

suggestion that carelessness need not be deterred (or need not be deterred as much as deliberate wrongdoing) is based on the idea that carelessness is less of a danger than deliberate wrongdoing. Certainly intentional wrongdoing causes greater alarm and a violent or dishonest man would be regarded as a greater menace to society than a man who is merely negligent. Until fifty years ago such a view would probably have been justified. In recent years, however, the harm that can result from mere carelessness has been increased a thousandfold by the invention of the motor-car. In terms of human suffering at any rate it can hardly be doubted that a really negligent driver is a greater menace to the community than a murderer. The potential danger of negligence in this context has, of course, been recognized by the criminal law, as we shall see.

Another possible reason for not punishing carelessness is that failure to take due care is not generally considered a moral failing. Admittedly, it is morally wrong to take an unjustifiable risk, but we tend not to blame people for negligence arising from error, miscalculation, inadvertence, or clumsiness. Everyone makes mistakes and slips from time to time and we tend to think of this as a misfortune, rather than a vice. If we believe the offender when he says, 'I didn't mean to do it', we tend to withhold blame, and all the more so, because we feel that such an error or miscalculation might have happened to ourselves. It is probably this feeling more than anything else (i.e. the feeling, 'anyone might have made such a slip, I could have done the same myself'), which originally made courts and Parliament and later made juries reluctant to see people punished for negligence. Although not all crimes are sins, the most important ones are, and these are the things that the public regard as crimes and the things for which the public feels that punishment should be inflicted. In the popular view a man convicted of one offence of dishonesty becomes a criminal, but a man convicted of dangerous driving time out of number never acquires this title. For we think of criminals as people who deliberately flout the laws and institutions of our society and refuse to come to terms with them; and carelessness is very different from this.

So far as the motor-car is concerned this popular attitude is a serious hindrance to the prevention of road accidents. It is no good, however, lamenting with some of the judges, that juries never convict of manslaughter or dangerous driving. Either we must try to persuade the public to look on negligent behaviour in the field of road traffic as immoral, so that they will be less hesitant to accept the idea of punishment for careless and dangerous driving; or we may have to abandon the attempt to treat such conduct as criminal and try to find a different approach to the problem of accident prevention. A useful analogy might be found in the approach to flying accidents. In the Royal Air Force, pilot error (other than error arising from deliberate disobedience to orders, e.g. unauthorized low flying) is not treated as a crime, but the accident-prone pilot may be temporarily grounded or relieved of flying duties altogether. Such an approach might well be fruitful in relation to road accidents. It might be much better not to punish an accident-prone motorist with fines and imprisonment, but to disqualify him temporarily or permanently from driving. Disqualification not as a punishment but merely as a preventive measure would seem to be the obvious remedy for negligent drivers. Whether the Criminal Courts or Magistrates' Courts, however, constitute the most suitable instrument for dealing with this problem is open to doubt. It might be better if the problem were entirely removed from the Criminal Courts and divorced from the criminal law and placed in the hands of a panel of motoring experts, possibly under the supervision of the motoring organizations. If it is thought that such tribunals might be unduly lenient to the careless driver, it is worth reflecting that the Royal Air Force tribunals which investigate flying accidents are mostly composed of air-crew officers, and yet they can hardly be said to be too tender-hearted. Just as the Royal Air Force aims to maintain a high standard of flying and just as professional bodies like the Law Society endeavour to maintain a high standard of professional conduct, so the motor organizations, if given power to deal with careless driving, could try to maintain high standard on the roads.

Let us now consider some of the exceptions to the general rule that negligent conduct is no crime. Such exceptions arise, either where the harm caused is exceptionally great, e.g. death; where there is great potential harm, e.g. in the field of road traffic; or where the interest to be protected is highly valued, e.g. the care of children.

(a) *Manslaughter*

The major crime of negligence is manslaughter. We have already seen that manslaughter is a composite crime and we have considered voluntary manslaughter, i.e. those cases where special features operate to reduce murder to manslaughter. We have also described one type of involuntary manslaughter, namely manslaughter consisting of death resulting from an unlawful act likely to cause harm less than death or grievous bodily harm. The remaining type of involuntary manslaughter concerns death caused by gross negligence. The typical example of this crime is that of killing someone by very negligent driving.

To render the accused guilty of manslaughter, however, his negligence must be gross. Ordinary negligence such as would make him liable in a civil action or even such negligence as would amount to dangerous driving is not enough. What amounts to gross negligence is not fully defined, but the courts have held that there are degrees of negligence and that the jury must ask themselves whether the accused's conduct was such that it goes beyond a mere matter of compensation between the parties. The assertion that there are degrees of negligence has puzzled those who have thought of negligence as consisting of inadvertence or an absence of care. Since inadvertence or absence of care are essentially negative things, how, it is sometimes asked, can there be degrees of nothing? If we remember, however, that negligence consists in falling below the standard required, it is easy to see how one person can fall further below this standard than another, so that there is nothing difficult in the notion of different degrees of negligence.

It might be thought that where death results from dangerous or careless driving, the driver should be automatically guilty of manslaughter, on the ground that death results from an unlawful act, likely to cause physical harm. In *Andrews* v. *D.P.P.*,[1] however, the House of Lords decided that in such cases the right approach is to direct the jury to consider whether the accused was acting with criminal negligence and that it would be a misdirection to direct the jury that all they need consider is whether the death results from dangerous driving. The justification of this is that dangerous and careless driving differ from unlawful

[1] See p. 3 n. 3.

acts like assault and abortion which feature prominently in cases of constructive manslaughter. The unlawfulness of dangerous driving arises from the driver's failure to take care; it is itself a crime of negligence. The driver is performing an act, i.e. driving, which is not in itself unlawful, but he is performing it so negligently that his conduct becomes criminal. Consequently, when considering whether the accused is guilty of manslaughter it is only reasonable to determine his guilt according to the degree of negligence.

(b) Road Traffic Law

Contrary to the popular conception of the criminal as a thief or a thug, the typical criminal today is the motorist. In recent years over half the convictions recorded concerned road traffic offences. For example, in 1960 motorists accounted for 60·1 per cent. of the total number of convictions. The invention of the motor-car led to such an increase in the potential danger resulting from negligence that special measures were necessary to protect the public and since the common law took no account of negligence, the legislature had to intervene. There had been, since 1861, one provision on the statute book prohibiting wanton or furious driving of carriages resulting in bodily harm. Apart from this solitary provision, the rules relating to road traffic are contained in the road traffic legislation enacted since 1930 and the regulations made thereunder; most of the law relating to road traffic offences is now to be found in the Road Traffic Act, 1960.

This legislation had three aims. It tried to ensure that only competent drivers and suitable vehicles should be allowed on the road. It attempted to regulate road traffic by providing for the installation of traffic signs, speed limits, &c. Finally, it endeavoured to prevent negligence on the roads by creating special offences of negligent driving.

To secure the first objective, rules were made concerning the licensing of drivers. No one is allowed to drive without a licence. Before obtaining a licence, a person must have reached the age of seventeen, must have passed a driving test, and he must be physically fit to drive. Moreover, for certain offences a driver may be disqualified by a court order from driving. If such a person should drive while disqualified, he would be flouting the order of the court; and for such contumacy Parliament has ordained that he must be sent to prison, unless there exist special reasons for not imposing a prison sentence. Such special reasons must be circumstances concerning the offence committed and not the offender himself. For instance, the need to fetch medical aid in an emergency would amount to a special reason. The defendant's previous good record and similar matters are not special reasons for this purpose. One very important provision relates to compulsory third-party insurance. If a driver injures another person through negligence, the injured party has, of course, the civil right to sue for damages, but this right will be of little value unless the defendant is in a position to satisfy the judgment. To insure that third parties may not be prejudiced by motorists' lack of money, Parliament has decreed that every driver must be insured against injuries to third parties. To drive a vehicle without such insurance or to let another person drive a vehicle without insurance is an offence punishable with up to three months' imprisonment. People like bus drivers, however, and others who are employed to drive vehicles, can hardly be expected themselves to be responsible for the insuring of their vehicles; and the law provides that such persons are not guilty of any offence under this head, provided that they neither know nor ought to know that no insurance policy is in force.

The control of traffic is contained in regulations concerning pedestrian crossings, traffic signs, speed limits, the procedure to be adopted in case of accidents, and many other matters. The interesting feature in these rules is that the legislature (or in some cases the Ministry of Transport, in others the local authorities) has not been content with a general prohibition of negligence; it has gone further and laid down the standard of care which the driver must attain. For instance, the regulations have not merely prohibited unreasonably fast driving; they have allowed for the fixing in certain areas of a standard speed, excess of which constitutes an offence. Likewise, the rules not only require the motorist to take care when entering a major road from a minor road; they provide for the setting up of traffic signs ordering the motorist to stop or slow down. The Ministry of Transport has also drawn up for the guidance of motorists a set of rules known as the Highway Code. This code does not have the force of law and breach of its rules does not itself amount to an offence. On the other hand, in a prosecution for some actual offence such as careless driving, the offender's failure to observe the rules of the Highway Code may well constitute evidence that he has committed the offence charged. Even the best-known rule, the rule of the road, has no legal force. It is not an offence in itself to drive on the right-hand side, but failure to observe this rule would be one way of committing such an offence as careless or dangerous driving.

Of the various special offences created by road traffic law, the most important are careless driving, dangerous driving, drunken driving, and causing death by driving. *Careless driving* consists in driving a vehicle on a road without due care and attention or without reasonable consideration for other road users. It is a summary offence, for which disqualification may be ordered and on a second conviction a motorist may be sent to prison. This offence is aimed partly at drivers who fall below the standard of care by error or miscalculation and partly at competent but selfish motorists who disregard the safety of others. The courts apply an objective test of carelessness, by asking what the reasonably prudent motorist would have done in the circumstances. If the defendant has made an error which a reasonable driver would not have made, he is guilty of careless driving and the cause of his error is irrelevant. Mere inexperience is no defence; for instance, the law expects as high a standard of care from the learner as from the expert. *Dangerous driving* consists in driving recklessly or at speed or in a manner which is dangerous to the public having regard to all the circumstances. Conviction for this offence renders the driver liable to be sent to prison for four months, or, if tried on indictment, for two years. On a second conviction the motorist must be disqualified, unless there are special reasons for not disqualifying him. The objective test applied to careless driving also obtains in the case of dangerous driving.

The greatest danger on the roads perhaps arises from alcohol. To drive drunken motorists off the roads Parliament created a pair of offences relating to drunkenness and the motor-car. *Drunken driving* is the offence of driving or attempting to drive while under the influence of drink or drug, to such an extent as to be incapable of having proper control. The penalties are much the same as those for dangerous driving, except that in the absence of special reasons, disqualification is compulsory even for a first conviction. The lesser offence of *being in charge* of a vehicle when under the influence of drink or drug, &c., entails compulsory disqualification only for a second conviction. It is a defence to such a charge, if the defendant can show that he did not drive after becoming unfit to drive and that there was no likelihood of his driving the vehicle while under the influence of the drink or drug.

The reluctance of juries to convict motorists for manslaughter led to the creation in 1956 of the new offence of *causing death by reckless or dangerous driving*, for which the maximum penalty is five years' imprisonment.

(c) Social Welfare

Just as laws have been enacted with regard to road traffic, so rules have been made to regulate trades, industries, and other activities. The Factory Act, Food and Drugs Act, and many other statutes, together with the regulations made thereunder, have created a host of specific offences. Like road traffic legislation these rules not only demand that employers, shopkeepers, and people engaged in various activities should attain a certain standard of care, but go further and prescribe what that standard is. For example, rule 23 of the Building Regulations, 1948, made by the Minister of Labour in the interests and safety of those working in the building trade, provides that every board or plank forming part of a working platform shall be not less than 8 inches wide, or, in the case of boards exceeding 2 inches in thickness, not less than 6 inches wide. These provisions are not usually found in textbooks on criminal law. They are contained rather in the special works concerning trades and industries and in the manuals used by magistrates. For these are for the most part summary offences. Many of them are also offences of strict liability, i.e. the defendant may be guilty without intention or even negligence on his part.

5. NUISANCE AND TRESPASS

With conduct which involves no physical harm or danger of physical harm the criminal law has little concern. Annoying or molesting people, borrowing their property without their consent, and trespassing on their land are outside its scope. For one thing, there has to be a certain amount of give and take in any community and people have to put up with some degree of inconvenience. For another, the law does not concern itself with trifles. Were every act of annoyance, however trifling, to be made a crime, more would be lost in the encroachment on individual liberty than would be gained in the protection of private interests. In such matters the victim's remedy, if any, is to apply to the Civil Courts for an injunction to restrain the wrongdoer.

In certain cases, however, the criminal law does intervene to prevent conduct aimed at the person or property of others, even though no harm is actually caused. We have seen that the law takes account of threatening behaviour. The crime of assault consists essentially of the threat of force. Demanding with menaces is an offence, popularly known as blackmail. Certain forms of intimidation constitute offences against the Conspiracy and Protection of Property Act, 1875. The Public Order Act, 1936, provides that it is an offence to use insulting words in a public place with intent to provoke a breach of the peace.

Interference with the liberty of others, even without the use of actual force, is prohibited by the offence of False Imprisonment. Verbal abuse too may in certain circumstances amount to criminal conduct. Written matter which is likely to bring another person into hatred, ridicule, or contempt, will, if calculated to provoke a breach of the peace, constitute the offence of criminal libel.

In this context trespass to property deserves special notice. Malicious damage and misappropriation are not the only possible infringement of a person's property rights; mere interference and intermeddling constitute an invasion of those rights. If I borrow your umbrella, or walk across your field, I commit a civil wrong against you for which I may be made to pay damages. On the other hand, such interference is on the whole outside the scope of the criminal law, which leaves the injured party to his civil remedies. Wrongful borrowing with one statutory exception is no offence.[1] Trespass to land is in general no crime. Accordingly, the warning 'trespassers will be prosecuted' is often referred to as the 'wooden lie', since trespassers cannot be

[1] The exception is taking and driving away a motor-car without the consent of the owner, an offence prohibited by the Road Traffic Act, 1960, s. 217.

prosecuted, they can only be sued. The threat, therefore, is an empty one.

So far as concerns trespass to land, the civil remedy is by no means adequate. It is little comfort to the occupier that he can bring an action at his own expense for damages which may amount to little and which the trespasser may be unable to pay. What he really needs is a way of preventing the trespass. He can, of course, eject the trespasser, using no more force than is reasonably necessary, and if the trespasser refuses to go, he may be guilty of an offence under the Public Order Act, 1936. Moreover, if the police assist the occupier in ejecting a trespasser and the latter refuses to leave the premises, he can be arrested, on the ground that he was creating a disturbance of the peace. But this does not serve to protect the occupier against the trespasser whom he cannot catch, but who persists in entering on his land against his will. It would be open to him to apply to a Civil Court for an injunction against the trespasser, whose disobedience of the injunction would then render him liable to be put in prison for contempt of court, but such proceedings take time and money and are of little use against casual trespassers. The best protection for the occupier would be the prohibition of trespassing by the criminal law.[1]

Now, although trespassers cannot in general be prosecuted, the criminal law does take cognizance of trespass in certain cases. If the trespass is done with a view to the commission of certain crimes, usually of dishonesty, it becomes a criminal offence. Secondly, landowners and certain special undertakings have succeeded in acquiring a certain measure of protection from the criminal law against trespassers.

Where the trespasser intends to steal or commit some criminal offence, his conduct may amount to *burglary, housebreaking,* or some kindred offence. Burglary and housebreaking are usually classified as crimes of dishonesty. This is not in fact quite accurate. An essential element of these offences is the commission of, or the intention to commit, a felony in the building in question. The felony, though it almost invariably is an offence of

---

[1] In certain countries trespass has been made an offence. Trespassing on enclosed land is a crime in South African law. See Gardiner and Lansdown, *South African Criminal Law and Procedure* (6th ed.), pp. 1414, 1784. In Scotland trespass is prohibited by the Trespass Act, 1865.

dishonesty, need not be; it could equally well be a crime of violence such as murder.

Burglary, for which the maximum penalty is life imprisonment, consists in breaking and entering the dwelling-house of another, by night, with intent to commit a felony. It may also be committed if the accused enters the house with intent to commit a felony and then breaks out; or if, having entered without felonious intent, he then commits a felony and breaks out. 'Breaking' here signifies some interference with the security of the building, such as opening a closed door or window. Merely entering via an open door or window would not amount to breaking. To enter via the chimney, however, is to break in, since this is a hole which is not expected ever to be closed. 'Night' in this context means the time from 9 p.m. to 6 a.m., Greenwich Mean Time or Summer Time, according to whichever is in force.

If certain of the requirements for burglary are missing, the accused may be guilty of one of the lesser offences of housebreaking. For instance, if he breaks into a house during the day; or if the building is not a dwelling-house; or if he enters a dwelling-house by night with felonious intent, but without breaking—in all these cases he commits housebreaking, for which he is liable to be imprisoned in some cases for fourteen years and in others for seven years. Akin to this are certain offences contained in section 28 of the Larceny Act, 1916, which provides among other things that it is an offence punishable by five years' imprisonment to be found by night in any building, with an intent to commit a felony therein. The Vagrancy Act, 1824, lays down that it is an offence punishable by three months' imprisonment or £25 fine to be found in a building or inside an enclosed yard, garden, or area for a criminal purpose.

These provisions, however, would not serve to protect landowners against poachers, since poaching is not by common law a felony; nor would they protect undertakings such as railways against trespassers who have no intention of committing a felony. Landowners secured protection by the Night Poaching Act, 1828, and the Game Act, 1831. A trespasser by day in search of game, for instance, is punishable with a £2 fine and if the trespasser refuses to give his name, refuses to leave the land, or persists in returning, he may be arrested. Higher penalties are prescribed for entering land by night to poach if the trespasser is armed.

Certain bodies carrying on public work have had statutes passed to protect them against trespassers. For example, it is an offence against the Civil Aviation Act, 1949, to trespass on a licensed aerodrome providing that warning notices are displayed. The Military Manœuvre Act, 1937, makes it an offence to trespass on military camps during manœuvres. Wilful trespass on railway tracks is forbidden by Regulation of Railways Act, 1840, 1868, and the British Transport Commission Act, 1949. The Merchant Shipping Act, 1934, lays down a maximum penalty of six months' imprisonment or £20 fine for any unauthorized person who goes on to a ship and remains there after being warned to leave. Lastly, trespass on enclosed or ornamental gardens in a town is an offence contrary to the Town Gardens Protection Act, 1863, and is punishable with a fine of forty shillings or fourteen days' imprisonment. These examples suffice to show that the warning that trespassers will be prosecuted is not always the empty threat which it is sometimes considered to be.

Akin to trespass are certain forms of behaviour such as eavesdropping and prying. Though these fall short of breaches of the peace, they constitute blemishes of the peace, and the Justices of the Peace Act, 1361, empowers magistrates to deal with such eavesdroppers and peeping Toms by binding them over to be of good behaviour.[1]

So far we have considered conduct which molests or interferes with others. Conduct which is merely a nuisance only attracts the sanction of the criminal law if it causes substantial annoyance to the community in general.

At common law it is the offence of public nuisance to do an act whose effect is to endanger the life, health, property, morals, or comfort of the public, or to obstruct the public in the exercise or enjoyment of rights common to all subjects of the realm. This is clearly a wide and compendious offence and has been held to include such diverse activities as obstructing the highway, behaving as a common scold, and refusal by an innkeeper to admit travellers to an inn when he has accommodation. Under the rubric of acts interfering with the comfort, enjoyment, and health of the public have been held to fall such matters as

---

[1] See C. K. Allen, *The Queen's Peace.*

erecting a privy near a highway, selling food unfit for consumption, and keeping animals whose smell or noise annoys the public. Nuisances which involve danger to the public have been held to include the keeping of a ferocious dog unmuzzled and the throwing of fireworks in the street. A third head of public nuisance comprises acts endangering the public morals, decency, or order, and extends to indecent exposure, obscene libels, indecent exhibitions, keeping brothels, gaming-houses, and betting-houses.[1]

The common law on public nuisance has been to a large extent supplemented and supplanted by statute. Today these matters are for the most part regulated by such enactments as the Food and Drugs Act, 1938; the Public Health Act, 1936, which prohibits the discharge of excessive smoke, fumes, and similar items; the Noise Abatement Act, 1960, which seeks to prevent the increasing nuisance caused by excessive noise. Many of these matters also form the subject of by-laws which local authorities are empowered to enact to regulate affairs within their localities. Detailed consideration of such enactments is outside the scope of textbooks on the criminal law and is to be found either in works specially concerned with these subjects or in the manuals used by the magistrates, since the majority of these offences are summary offences and triable therefore in the Magistrates' Courts.

6. IMMORALITY

Originally conduct contrary to the accepted notions of private morality fell within the province of the Ecclesiastical Courts, which punished forms of behaviour such as drunkenness and adultery. Later, when such matters came to be dealt with by the Criminal Courts, the latter confined their attention to two categories of acts, those involving some element of violence and those affected with some degree of unnaturalness. Into the first category fall such offences as rape and indecent assault, where force is used against an unwilling victim. The second class consists of bestiality and homosexual offences between males. Behaviour which offends neither on the score of violence nor of

[1] The law relating to betting and gaming has been considerably modified by the Betting and Gaming Act, 1960.

unnaturalness, e.g. adultery, has been left outside the scope of the criminal law.[1] There is, however, a third group of miscella-neous offences against public morality.

(a) Rape and Kindred Offences

What the law aims to prohibit here is the taking of unlawful sexual liberties with women or young children of either sex. The major offence is rape, which is punishable with life imprison-ment. Assault on a woman if accompanied by indecency con-stitutes the offence of Indecent Assault, which is punishable with two years' imprisonment. The abduction and defilement of females is forbidden by a group of offences concerning the ab-duction of women under the age of twenty-one and the unlawful removing of females under sixteen from the custody of their parents or guardians. There are also provisions of the criminal law prohibiting the exploitation of women for immoral pur-poses, e.g. living on the immoral earnings of prostitutes. Curiously, if the assault is committed on a male person the maximum penalty is five years.

The essence of rape and similar offences is that the accused takes sexual liberties with a woman against her will. Where the woman consents, this will generally operate to prevent any offence in law being committed. Rape, for example, cannot be committed against a consenting victim. As always, however, consent must be true consent. Consent obtained by force or threats will not count. Fraud too may vitiate consent in certain circumstances, if the victim was led to consent by some fraud either as to the nature of the act or as to the identity of the agent. To obtain intercourse with a woman by persuading her that she is undergoing a surgical operation or by impersonating her husband amounts to the crime of rape.

In this context there is one important further restriction on the operation of consent. We saw how in relation to offences of violence that there were certain things to which a person is not by law entitled to consent; he cannot, for instance, consent to be killed. Likewise with regard to crimes under the present heading the law refuses in certain cases to take account of the victim's consent. Girls of tender years must be protected against

---

[1] It is interesting to compare the position on this matter in the United States. See p. 4, n. 1.

those who would take advantage of their immaturity. The age set by law is sixteen, the age at which one has legal capacity to marry. A girl below this age is, in the eyes of the law, too young to be permitted to consent.

So far as rape is concerned, actual consent is always a defence. Accordingly special offences have been created to punish the unlawful carnal knowledge of girls below the age of sixteen. In these cases the girl's consent is no defence. The interesting feature of these crimes is that even an honest mistake by the accused as to the girl's age will not avail him. This rule can be unduly harsh. Police and probation officers with experience of such cases have stated that many of the girls who appear in school uniforms in the witness-box bear a strikingly different appearance in the outside world, where sophisticated use of clothes and cosmetics enables them to pass easily for nineteen or twenty. Indeed the law recognizes this by relenting from its extreme position in two cases, provided the girl is not under the age of thirteen. An honest mistake as to the girl's age will exonerate the defendant either if he believed himself to be married to the girl, or if he himself is under twenty-four and has not been previously convicted of such an offence.

These exceptions apart, mistake is no excuse. It is no defence to a charge of indecent assault on a girl under sixteen even in the second of the above exceptions. So while a man under twenty-four and not previously convicted will have a good defence to a charge of unlawful carnal knowledge, on the ground of honest mistake, he will have no such defence if charged with indecently assaulting her. Here one must rely on the good sense and fairness of the prosecuting authorities not to bring such a charge, and on the common sense of the courts if such a charge is brought. The justification for ruling out the defence of honest mistake is that the law sets a higher value on the interest of protecting young girls than on the general interest of not penalizing those who break the law through mistake of fact. Such refusal to allow for mistake here is no doubt assisted by the feeling that the accused is in any case acting immorally, and that men who have extra-marital intercourse with young girls do so at their peril, so far as the law is concerned. If the girl is just below the statutory age, an offence is committed. To acquiesce in the punishment of persons who innocently break the law on the ground that their behaviour is in any event immoral is far from satisfactory. In these days most people take the view that the law should concern itself not with immorality but illegality, and that the immorality or otherwise of a man's conduct should be irrelevant.

(b) Unnatural Offences

This category comprises sexual acts committed with animals and homosexual behaviour between men. Lesbianism is unnoticed by the criminal law.

The punishment of some homosexual behaviour can be justified on the same grounds as that of the offences considered in the last section. Obviously the 'rape' of a male victim should be prohibited like rape itself. Likewise the law would be defective if it afforded no protection to young boys against corruption analogous to the protection provided for young girls. What is less obvious is whether the law is justified in penalizing unnatural conduct not committed against an unwilling victim and not calculated to corrupt.

The Wolfenden Committee, set up to consider this problem, recommended in 1957[1] that homosexual behaviour between consenting male adults should not constitute any criminal offence. Such conduct should only be punished, they suggested, where there is some element of corruption or some affront to public decency. Their recommendation was based on the view that it is not the province of the criminal law to enforce morality but rather to prevent acts harmful to the community or to individuals. Other reasons advanced were that the existence of such offences creates opportunities for blackmail and that those who live in the twilight world of homosexuality need, if anything, treatment rather than condemnation. So far these recommendations have not been implemented.

(c) Miscellaneous Offences

Outside these two classes of offence come certain types of conduct which are nevertheless punishable by the criminal law. Organized vice and drug-peddling are prohibited on account of the potential danger to the community. Here the law seeks to protect people, in their own interest, against the insidious

[1] Cmnd. 247.

hold of drug addiction. Conduct which offends against public decency is justifiably prohibited by law; for the members of a community are entitled to claim that within limits they should not have to put up with the spectacle of disgusting and nauseating behaviour. Indecent spectacles, obscenity, and open prostitution are offensive to the majority of people, and are to be prevented for much the same reason as conduct amounting to public nuisance.

Two special offences are worthy of particular consideration. Incest, which is a crime against the Punishment of Incest Act, 1908, and Bigamy, contrary to the Offences Against the Person Act, 1861, are crimes for which the rationale is not entirely clear. In so far as incest serves to protect women against the undue influence over them of male relatives, it is no doubt worth retaining on the statute book. Where, however, both parties commit incest with full consent, this might seem to be one of the cases where the law is trying to enforce morality. If the proper province of the law is only to prevent acts harmful to individuals or to the community in general, it would not seem at first sight easy to justify retention of the crime of incest to deal with such cases. The real justification for the criminality of incest, however, is the need to prevent the undesirable effects on the possible children of the union produced by matching recessive traits, as is particularly likely with in-breeding. It is noteworthy in this context that the Mental Defectives Act, 1913, which prohibited carnal knowledge of mental defectives, provided that consent on the part of the defective should not count as a defence.

Bigamy is in reality an offence against the marriage ceremony. There is much to be said in favour of retaining it to punish those who trick people into 'marrying' them by dishonest suppression of fact. Where, however, both parties are fully aware of the previous marriage, there is little justification in punishing them for going through a second marriage ceremony.

This is particularly so in view of the fact that they commit no crime if they merely live together and put it about that they are married. Why then should the actual celebration of the ceremony attract criminal sanctions? The falsification of the marriage register is in any case an offence and needs no crime of bigamy to prevent it. Here again we have an instance of the law penalizing conduct which offends against religious and moral codes, but which causes no harm to anyone. We should be little the worse for it if the crime of bigamy were abolished.

(d) The Enforcement of Morals

Having briefly considered offences of immorality, let us now turn to the question whether the retention of such offences in the criminal calendar can be justified. The need for such justification arises from the fact that the use of the criminal law, involving as it does the imposition of penalties, entails the infliction of suffering. It is generally accepted that such infliction of suffering should be avoided if possible and should be tolerated only where it results in the obtaining of some good which outweighs the evil caused by the misery inflicted.

Now since the justification of the retention of such offences is itself a moral question, the answer to the problem will depend on the moral views of the person arguing for or against such retention. One of the difficulties in this regard is the lack of uniform agreement as to what should be the function of the criminal law.

With regard to the other classes of crimes which we have considered it is not hard to find agreement as to the justification for their existence in law. Few would deny that a man has the right to defend himself against physical attack and to defend his property likewise against attack. So far as negligence is concerned, most people would agree that where the harm or potential harm is serious, a man is entitled to use some measure of force to protect himself against such harm. Nuisance is perhaps less easy to justify as a crime, but here again most people would accept the proposition that a person is entitled to protect himself to some extent against offensive activities; he has a right to demand that others do not, by producing unpleasant fumes, noise, and so on, render his life intolerably unpleasant. Offences against public decency are in the same case. People have a right to demand that certain behaviour which disgusts or nauseates them should not take place in public. With regard to nuisance and indecency, however, the offence to the person affronted has to be weighed against the hardship involved in preventing the person committing the offence from continuing the activity in question. The justification of the existence of all these types of crimes is based on the right of the individual to protect himself against certain types of harm; his private right is supplemented and to some extent supplanted by state prevention of these activities.

The punishment by law of offences of immorality can sometimes be justified on similar grounds. Some of these offences, like rape, involve physical assaults, and here the justification is the same as for ordinary offences of violence. Others, while free from violence, involve a measure of corruption, where one of the parties is young, inexperienced, or economically dependent on the other. The justification for punishing corruption is that even if it were admitted that everyone should be free to choose his own way of life, nevertheless the young and inexperienced should be protected against their own immaturity until they are old enough to appreciate what is involved in this choice. Sometimes the punishment of these offences can be supported on the ground that they are committed in such circumstances as to offend against public decency. This still leaves the case of those offences whose commission involves neither violence nor corruption nor indecency, viz. homosexual behaviour between consenting adults in private.

It is perhaps curious that the only type of private sexual immorality punishable by law is homosexual conduct between men. Lesbianism, adultery, and fornication remain outside the criminal law. In certain other countries, however, notably certain of the United States, adultery and fornication are criminal offences.

Such offences differ in one very important respect from ordinary crimes, in that it is only those who commit them that are obviously and directly affected. Such conduct is not other-regarding as is violence or dishonesty. No clear and direct attack is made on third parties by such behaviour. In order, therefore, to defend the imposition of penalties on those who behave in this way, it must either be shown that it is somehow good in itself to prevent people from so behaving or that their conduct does in reality affect other people, who consequently have a right to be protected against the harm caused by it.

Not many champions are to be found of the first of these views. Enforced conformity to a moral code merely for the sake of such conformity would not generally be thought in these days to be in itself of any value. To force a person by fear and threat of punishment to act according to certain moral standards is not to make him act morally, though it could of course be argued that a man who was forced by law not to give way to certain sexual passions might end up by resisting them purely for moral reasons. Today, however, the imposition by force of moral standards for their own sake is not generally accepted as defensible. Most people would agree with the Wolfenden Committee that the function of the law in this context is to preserve public order and decency, to protect the citizen against what is offensive or injurious, and to provide safeguards against corruption and exploitation. The committee concluded that private immorality should not be the concern of the law and recommended that homosexual behaviour between consenting adults in private should no longer be an offence.

Many people, however, while accepting the premiss as to the proper function of the criminal law, would refuse to draw the same conclusion as the committee as to this particular problem. Such refusal is based on the view that such conduct, though not directly injurious to the citizen, is indirectly so. It has been argued that those who indulge in such practices with consenting adult partners may later extend their activities to corruption of the young. The Wolfenden Committee concluded here, however, that factual evidence did not support this proposition.

A different attempt to show that such behaviour is not merely self-regarding but is in fact injurious to others has been made by Lord Devlin,[1] who denies the validity of the distinction between public and private morality. His main argument is that the established morality of a society is as necessary to its continued existence as are the institutions of government and that just as a society is justified in defending itself against subversive activities resulting in the overthrow of its government, so it is entitled to protect itself against the disintegration which would follow from the loosening of moral bonds resulting from failure to observe the rules of the established morality.

Now it is true that if the accepted moral standards with regard to violence and dishonesty were weakened, the good order of our present society would be difficult to maintain. On the other hand this analogy between sexual immorality and treason has been challenged, notably by Professor H. L. A.

[1] *The Enforcement of Morals*, Maccabaean Lecture, 1959 (O.U.P.).

Hart,[1] who points out that the argument rests on several un-proved assumptions. In the first place there seems little evidence that failure to enforce sexual morality in the past has led to the disintegration of societies. Secondly, it is by no means estab-lished that the failure by some members of a society to observe certain rules of a moral code will lead to the abandonment of all the rules of the code by all the members of the society. Thirdly, mere failure to conform to a moral rule or standard is a quite different matter from a direct attack on an institution of the state; a closer parallel would be an attack on the moral standards made by a person advocating a change of attitude. This brings us to the next unproved assumption, viz. that a society is justified in resisting change, a view which would seem to entail that it is defensible to use the law to stifle criticism and reform and block the way of all peaceful change of the con-stitution and of all alteration of moral attitudes. Yet moral codes and political constitutions change without effecting the disintegration of society. Finally it is by no means clear that there in fact exists such unanimous moral agreement in our society on this matter as Devlin assumes; the established morality may well on closer inspection be found to be more like the Established Church, accepted in practice only by a minority of the citizen body.

A different attempt at justification of the retention of crimes of homosexuality might be made by arguing that the law should serve to promote the common good of society by providing amongst other things an environment in which the citizen can best pursue the end of living a moral life.[2] The toleration of immoral conduct makes it more difficult to produce such an environment and is accordingly to be deprecated. To implement the recommendations of the Wolfenden Committee, it is argued, might well mislead some people into thinking that homosexual behaviour is not immoral and so in fact lead to a decline in moral standards. In accord with this line of thought would seem the recent decision of the House of Lords in *Shaw* v. *D.P.P.*,[3]

---

[1] H. L. A. Hart, 'Immorality and Treason', *The Listener*, 30 July 1959; 'The Use and Abuse of the Criminal Law', *The Oxford Lawyer*, Hilary 1961.

[2] See St. John-Stevas, op. cit., ch. 1. It is not possible in the limited space avail-able to do full justice to Dr. Stevas's position; the text does not purport to be an accurate summary of his views.

[3] *Shaw* v. *D.P.P.*, [1961] 2 All E.R. 446.

where it was held that the production of a directory in which prostitutes were enabled to advertise their services constituted a criminal conspiracy to corrupt public morals, even though the persons corrupted would comprise adult members of the community. While punishment for corrupting the young is justified by the need to protect them until they reach maturity, the notion that the adult community should be protected by force against those who might corrupt them is less easy to support. The claim of the courts to act as guardian of morals rings strange to modern ears. Children need guardians, and benevolent despots may be regarded in the same light by their subjects, but the ordinary adult members of the English community would hardly consider themselves in need of the tutelage of some twentieth-century Areopagus. The objection to which this approach is open is that in a community where moral attitudes to such matters diverge, one must weigh the good to be attained in the form of preserving the morals of one group from corruption against the misery involved in using the weapons of the criminal law against those who may not share such moral views.

If there are difficulties in justifying the punishment by law of private immorality, there are not wanting reasons for objecting to the enforcement of morals in this private sphere. The police and the courts would be better occupied in dealing with conduct which is unanimously agreed to need prevention, e.g. violence and dishonesty. Secondly, laws against private immorality are difficult to enforce and their enforcement, therefore, tends to be haphazard and to result in inequality. Thirdly, the intrusion of the criminal law and the institutionalized organs of crime prevention into the private life of the citizen is undesirable. For example, while the basic wrongfulness of adultery lies in its attack on the institution of the family, legalized prohibition of adultery would also run counter to the interests of the family by permitting an invasion of that privacy which is accepted as an important feature of family life. Lastly, there must not be forgotten the factor which gives rise to the necessity of justifying the legal enforcement of private morality, viz. the actual suffering involved by such enforcement, which has to be outweighed by the good achieved if such enforcement is to be defended.

7. POLITICAL AND SIMILAR OFFENCES

So far we have considered conduct injurious (or potentially so) to individual members of the community. There remains for discussion conduct constituting a danger to the state itself and to the institutions of the state. The matter may be conveniently dealt with under three headings. First we may take treason and other offences against the safety of the state. Secondly, we shall consider crimes against the administration of justice. Lastly, we shall discuss various types of behaviour prohibited on account of their disorderly nature.

(a) Treason

The fundamental requirement of any society is the ability to protect itself against annihilation or subjection; and the chief duty of any government is to safeguard the state and its institutions against external and internal attack. A government which fails in this duty cannot provide and ensure the freedom and stability necessary for the members of society to work out their own destinies in peace. Without such guarantee of stability the rest of the law, both civil and criminal, is for the most part inefficacious.

To ensure its safety a state relies primarily on its military strength and on its police forces. The function of the criminal law is to act as a deterrent by the prohibition of acts injurious to the well-being of the state and the prescription of penalties for such acts. But whereas the state must defend itself both against external and internal assault, the scope of the criminal law is for the most part confined to attacks on the state by actual members of the state itself. So while a citizen of this country would be guilty of treason if he assisted the Germans in either of the two world wars, a German soldier committed no offence by fighting against England. For treason and other such offences can be committed only by persons who owe allegiance to the Crown.

The reason for this restriction on the scope of the offence of treason is to be found in its history and development. In medieval times each vassal owed a duty of allegiance to his lord, who in his turn owed a similar duty to his overlord, and so on. Conversely, each lord had a duty to protect his underlings and had jurisdiction over them. A breach of a vassal's duty of allegiance constituted treason, petit treason in the ordinary case and high treason if the allegiance broken was that owed to the supreme overlord, the king. Lords and kings of equal status, however, were bound by no such duties towards one another; nor did the vassals of one lord owe allegiance to any but their own lord and his overlords. Accordingly, the king of one country would have no right and jurisdiction over the kings of another country or over the latter's subjects. Today the counterpart of this rule is that no state has jurisdiction over another state or (with certain exceptions) over the citizens of another state.

This restriction may be justified, so far as concerns individuals, on the ground that intolerable difficulties would be created by any extension of jurisdiction. To hold an enemy soldier guilty of an offence for obeying the orders of his superiors and fighting against this country would put him in an impossible position, and the law rightly refuses to expose such people to this sort of conflict of duty. There has been, however, one extremely important development which has made inroads on the soldier's right to obey all superior orders with impunity. The brutality of warfare has been to some extent mitigated by the emergence of international laws of war. Of customary origin, these rules are now mainly contained in international treaties such as The Hague Conventions of 1899 and 1907 and the Geneva Convention of 1949. The rules of war prohibit amongst other matters the maltreatment of prisoners of war, the killing of civilians, the military use of gas, and various other things. Before the Second World War it was recognized that a belligerent was entitled to try and punish enemy combatants for war crimes. After the war the allied courts, consisting partly of military tribunals and partly of special tribunals, tried and convicted vast numbers of enemy soldiers and civilians of offences against the laws of war. These trials established that superior orders do not necessarily afford a defence. As was argued by Sir Hartley Shawcross at Nuremberg, 'Political loyalty and military obedience are excellent things, but they neither require nor do they justify the commission of patently wicked acts. There comes a point where a man must refuse to answer his leader if he is also to answer to his conscience.' There was precedent for this in the German case[1]

[1] *Annual Digest of Public International Law Cases 1923–4*, No. 235.

of the *Llandovery Castle* (1921)where a German court convicted
the accused of killing defenceless persons in lifeboats during the
1914–18 war and rejected a plea of obedience to superior orders
on the ground that the order was universally known to be
against the law. The test according to the Nuremberg Court is
whether moral choice was a possibility for the accused.

So far as concerns foreign states, foreign governments, and
heads of governments, the difficulty has been the traditional
view of the community of states as a primitive society whose
members live in a Hobbesian state of nature with one another.
No rule of international law forbade the waging of war. By the
end of the nineteenth century certain limits had been set to the
amount of force which one state could lawfully use against
another short of actual war. Restrictions were placed on what
could be done by way of reprisal, intervention, or self-defence.
The drawback was, of course, that so long as war remained a
lawful activity, any state exceeding the limits set by international
law to the peaceful use of force could escape all responsibility by
declaring war. After the First World War the covenant of the
League of Nations attempted a limited prohibition of war and
provided that before engaging in war the members of the League
should first submit their dispute to pacific settlement or to the
Council of the League and that they were not to resort to war
until three months after the failure of pacific settlement. This
moratorium, it was hoped, might provide sufficient cooling time
for national feelings and make it impossible for any rulers to
lead their country into war. This was followed in 1928 by the
Pact of Paris, signed by over sixty states and condemning re-
course to war and renouncing it as an instrument of national
policy. The difficulty which now arose was that measures which
obviously amounted to war were claimed only to constitute use
of force short of war. For example, in 1937 50,000 Japanese
forces were engaged over a thirty-mile front near Shanghai
against a Chinese army of 1,500,000. Simultaneously in North
China 100,000 Japanese were advancing against 300,000
Chinese; over 50 battles were fought between 20 August and
16 September, and Japan maintained a naval blockade over
1,000 miles of China's coast. Yet on 2 September 1937 the
Japanese Foreign Minister stated that this was not a state of war
but only a major conflict. Indeed there had been no declaration

of war by either state, nor had diplomatic relations even been severed.[1]

After the Second World War the leaders of the Axis Powers were prosecuted at the Nuremberg and Tokio Tribunals, established by the major allied powers, for various offences including crimes against peace, i.e. beginning a war of aggression. There has not been wanting serious misgiving and criticism concerning these trials. Some have questioned the legal right of the victors to set up tribunals to try the vanquished; others have argued that the crime against peace was a new invention and that the victors were creating retrospective law to convict the accused *ex post facto*. Legal dispute with regard to the trials is now largely of historical interest only, in view of the fact that the principles established thereby were unanimously accepted by a resolution of the United Nations General Assembly on 11 November 1946 and have thus become accepted as part of international law by universal acclaim.[2] In pursuance of the instructions of the Assembly, these principles were subsequently formulated by the International Law Commission in the Draft Code on Offences against the Peace and Security of Mankind.

War crimes and crimes against peace, however, are strictly matters of international law and fall outside the scope of ordinary municipal criminal law, which is concerned rather with acts detrimental to the state committed by people owing allegiance to the Crown. In determining the class of people owing such allegiance, English law could have adopted either a territorial principle to the effect that everyone within the territory of Great Britain owes allegiance, or it could have adopted a principle of personal loyalty, whereby people who had never lived within this territory might owe such a duty by virtue of personal ties of birth and descent. The law has in fact adopted a mixture of both principles. In the first place all those who are citizens of the United Kingdom and Colonies owe a duty of allegiance regardless of their place of birth or residence. This class, however, does not include British subjects other than citizens of the United Kingdom and Colonies. Moreover, such a citizen cannot throw

---

[1] See, for example, *Kawasaki Kisen Kabushiki of Kobe* v. *Bantham S.S. Co. Ltd.* (*No. 2*), [1939] 2 K.B. 544, where an English court had to decide whether a provision in a charter party for termination by war could be invoked in these circumstances.   [2] Resolution of United Nations General Assembly, 11 Nov. 1946.

off his allegiance in time of war by taking out citizenship of the enemy state. Secondly, the duty extends to aliens resident in this country, who therefore enjoy the protection of the Crown. A resolution of the judges in 1707 declared that if such an alien returned home leaving here his family and property under the protection of the Crown, he might be guilty of treason.

The category of persons owing allegiance was extended after the Second World War by *Joyce*'s[1] case. A citizen of the United States, Joyce went to Germany just before the outbreak of war, with a British passport which, while resident in England, he had obtained by fraud. After war broke out he assisted the Germans by broadcasting to this country. His possession of a British passport constituted sufficient ground in the view of the House of Lords for the decision that he owed a duty of allegiance and was guilty of treason by assisting the enemy. This decision raised considerable controversy. It was criticized by some on the basis that possession of a passport gives the holder no right in English or international law to state protection, so that Joyce had no actual right to protection. On the other hand, once war had begun, it could hardly be said that he enjoyed any actual protection from the Crown. The decision was in fact an extension of the law of treason to cover a situation which had not previously arisen; and in so far as the House of Lords was creating new law, this was bound to evoke dissatisfaction, for the judicial extension of the criminal law to penalize conduct not already declared to be criminal (especially in a capital case) is not readily accepted today.

Treason, considered the most heinous of crimes, gained early recognition from the law and was punishable by particularly barbarous methods of execution. As early as 1351 the statute book acquired a Treason Act, which decreed that certain actions would be punishable as treasons. Such actions consisted in fact of breaches of the feudal allegiance owed to the person of the king: and one of the most interesting aspects of this branch of the law is the way that the judges in later centuries by construction and interpretation adapted these archaic provisions to the needs of our modern society where the citizen is bound rather by a political tie under a constitutional monarchy. The act of 'compassing the king's death' (for which the regicides of Charles I

[1] *Joyce* v. *D.P.P.*, [1946] A.C. 347.

were prosecuted) was extended to cover the compassing of his political death, e.g. by promoting a revolt in a colony. The act of 'levying war against the king in his realm' was stretched to include attacks on any general class of the king's subjects, e.g. the incitement of anti-papist riots, and to forcible attempts to change the policy of the Government. The head of treason under which those who assist the enemy in war-time are charged is that of 'adhering to the king's enemies in his realm giving them aid and comfort in the realm or elsewhere'. The trial of *Casement*,[1] who during the First World War incited British prisoners of war in Germany to join the enemy and take part in an expedition to land arms in Ireland, decided that treason could be committed although both the adherence and the giving of aid to the enemy took place outside the realm. Casement, who pleaded that the adherence must take place in the realm, complained that this decision, which involved construing the words 'giving them aid and comfort in the realm' in apposition to the words 'adhering to the king's enemies in his realm', meant that he was to be hanged by a comma.

Increasing stability during later centuries led to the decline of treason trials. Because of the death penalty juries became reluctant to convict. Accordingly in 1848 the Treason Felonies Act provided that these constructive treasons could be prosecuted as treason felonies, for which the penalty should be life imprisonment. Today treason is probably not regarded in this country as such a terrible offence as it once was. In recent years more understanding has been shown to the efforts of subject peoples to throw off foreign domination. Even rendering assistance to the enemy in war-time might not be considered so villainous in these times, when we are accustomed to seeing ideological loyalties preferred to national ties. Nevertheless, assisting the enemy remains a serious danger and both world wars reaped a small harvest of treason trials, for which the death penalty was exacted.

Besides the crime of treason there are certain lesser offences which consist of acts injurious to the state. Sedition is a common-law crime which is committed by writing or uttering seditious intent. A seditious intent includes an intention to excite disaffection against the Government or Parliament, to raise

[1] [1917] 1 K.B.

discontent or disaffection amongst Her Majesty's subjects, and
to promote feelings of ill-will between classes of subjects. The
attempt to seduce members of the forces from their allegiance is
itself an offence against the Incitement to Disaffection Act, 1934.
Incitement to Mutiny is prohibited by the Incitement to Mutiny
Act, 1797. Acts calculated to cause disaffection in the police
forces are contrary to the Police Act, 1919. To protect secret
information against transmission to the wrong quarters there
was passed in 1911 the Official Secrets Act, which provided heavy
penalties for wrongfully disclosing such secret matter. Apart
from these crimes it is worth noting two other offences. Enlisting
in the forces of a state at war with a state with which England is
at peace is an offence against the Foreign Enlistment Act, 1870,
under which the organizers of the Jameson Raid were prosecuted. The Public Order Act, 1936, created a number of offences
to prohibit the organization in this country of any political
association similar to the S.S. in Germany, and provided that it
is an offence to train or organize a political association to usurp
the functions of the police.

(b) Offences against the Administration of Justice

At common law any act done with the intention of perverting
the course of justice is an offence. The fabrication of evidence
and conspiracies to pervert the course of justice are punishable
by law. Other examples of such offences are Maintenance, un-
justifiably procuring a person to carry on civil litigation;
Champerty, agreeing to support a litigant in return for a share
in the proceeds of the action; Common Barratry, unlawfully
stirring up litigious quarrels; and Embracery, the corruption of
jurors.

But the best-known crime against the administration of justice
is Perjury, contrary to the Perjury Act, 1911, and punishable
with seven years' imprisonment. This offence consists in wilfully
making on oath a statement known to be false or not believed to
be true. Those who are by law allowed to affirm instead of taking
an oath may nevertheless be guilty of perjury. One important
requirement is that the statement must be one material to the
proceedings.

So if a person accused of some crime gives false evidence to the
effect that he did not commit the offence, he commits perjury.

If he is convicted of the crime charged, prosecution for perjury rarely follows; such prosecutions are reserved for flagrant cases where it is patent that the accused and his witnesses have concocted false evidence, on which the accused was lucky enough to be acquitted. If an accused prisoner informs his counsel that he did commit the crime, counsel may not call his client to give evidence which counsel knows to be false, since this would amount on the barrister's part to aiding and abetting the prisoner to commit perjury. In such a case he has three possible courses. He may withdraw from the case. He may appear on a plea of guilty and make a speech in mitigation. Or he may defend the prisoner on a plea of not guilty, without calling evidence but attacking the prosecution case either on some technical point of law or on the ground that there is insufficient evidence to convict the accused. This is quite permissible, since in English law the accused has a right to call on the prosecution to prove its case. Accordingly, to plead 'not guilty' in such a case is not perjury on the part of the accused; it amounts merely to a refusal to admit the charge and a demand that the case be proved against him.

Akin to perjury are certain offences concerning the making of false statutory declarations in documents required by statute. False declarations to the Inland Revenue are perhaps the best-known example of this. Such offences are for the most part punishable with up to two years' imprisonment.

(c) Disorderly Conduct

The need to preserve order has led to the creation of various crimes under this head. The most important are Unlawful Assembly, Rout, and Riot. Unlawful assembly is committed when three or more people gather together for the purpose of committing a crime involving violence, or to carry out some purpose in an unlawful way likely to involve violence; and in both cases it is necessary that their behaviour should be such as to provoke in the minds of ordinary reasonable men apprehensions of violence.

Rout consists of an unlawful assembly on the move. As soon as the unlawful gathering takes steps towards the execution of its purpose, the offence of rout is committed.

Riot is committed by an unlawful assembly which is carrying

out its purpose with violence, or with intent to use violence to resist opposition, in such a way as to cause alarm to ordinary citizens. If there are twelve or more rioters, the Riot Act, 1714, lays down that if a Justice of the Peace reads the 'riot act', i.e. the proclamation in the act calling upon them to disperse, and if they do not disperse an hour after the proclamation has been read, they are guilty of statutory riot, an offence punishable with life imprisonment.

Besides these crimes, there are many other offences in this field of the criminal law, such as carrying fire-arms to prevent arrest, obstruction of the police in the execution of their duty, using threatening, abusive, or insulting words or behaviour in a public place with intent to provoke a breach of the peace. There is also the ancient common law offence of Affray, committed by two or more persons fighting in a public place in such a way as to alarm other persons, or by one person going armed in a public place to the alarm of others.

At one time it seemed as if any conduct tending to the prejudice or detriment of the community might amount to an offence. Certainly there was authority to the effect that all such conduct amounts to the crime of Public Mischief. This could be a useful weapon in the hands of the courts to deal with conduct not specifically prohibited because it had not perhaps been envisaged. Making false reports to the police about non-existent crimes and wasting their time, calling out the fire brigade to non-existent fires, and similar behaviour could be conveniently prosecuted under this head. On the other hand the existence of a common-law crime of public mischief prohibiting all acts tending to the prejudice of the community would be too powerful an instrument of oppression if the courts wished to create new crimes. Any conduct could be held to be in some way detrimental to the community. The Court of Criminal Appeal expressed the view that judges should not use the crime of public mischief to convict people for conduct not specifically prohibited by law, and that such conduct should be dealt with under the heading of conspiracy.[1]

Conspiracy, a common-law misdemeanour, is an agreement between two or more people to commit a crime; an agreement to do some unlawful though not criminal act, e.g. to perform

[1] See p. 8, n. 2.

some fraud on another; an agreement to do some immoral act, e.g. to seduce a woman, to run slowly in a race so as to enable a confederate to win bets; or an agreement to do acts tending to the public mischief. As we have seen, the House of Lords in *Shaw*'s case decided that a conspiracy to corrupt public morals was indictable as a conspiracy to effect a public mischief and that the concept of public mischief was not restricted to such behaviour as had previously been expressly determined by law to be a public mischief. Accordingly, though the judges may still lean against the crime of public mischief as an offence committed by a single person, agreements between one or more persons to do anything which in the eyes of the court tends to injure the community may amount to a criminal conspiracy.

III

GENERAL PRINCIPLES:
WHAT COUNTS AS CONDUCT

HAVING considered the different types of conduct prohibited by
the criminal law, we are now in a position to discuss what is
known as the general part of the criminal law. While the special
parts of this law exist for the purpose of prohibiting certain types
of behaviour, the general part serves largely to place limits on
the legal pursuit of this purpose. Accordingly, while the provisions of the special part work against the accused person, those
of the general part operate in his favour. It is in this branch that
there are to be found all the various defences which negative
criminal responsibility.

This part of the criminal law consists of general principles,
some of which are nothing more than broad generalizations
describing the general pattern of the criminal law. Such, for
instance, is the general principle that the criminal law takes no
account of omissions. Others have a higher status than this,
having been elevated into actual rules of law, e.g. the rules concerning infancy, duress, mistake, and other defences.

Such rules are the creation of the judges and form their most
important contribution to the criminal law. As new situations
previously unenvisaged have arisen, the courts have developed
the law by analogical argument. For example, the Infant (Life
Preservation) Act, 1929, laid down that in order to prove a
person guilty of child destruction the prosecution must show
that he did not act in good faith for the sole purpose of preserving the life of the mother. The section of the Offences against
the Person Act, 1861, relating to abortion contains no parallel
provision. Nevertheless, in *Bourne*'s[1] case the judge held that as
that section contains the word 'unlawfully', the prosecution had
to prove on a charge of abortion also that the accused did not
act in good faith for the sole purpose of preserving the life of
the mother. Moreover, he directed the jury not to construe the

[1] See p. 25.

words 'preserving the mother's life' narrowly; he instructed them that to save the mother from becoming a mental or physical wreck would count as preserving her life. The objections to judge-made law on the ground that it is an undemocratic method of legislation and that it involves retroactive law-making does not apply to the development of general principles, which work for, rather than against, the accused.

The general principles of the criminal law might be summed up in two propositions: no one is guilty of a crime without performing an act of some sort; and an act by itself unaccompanied by any criminal intent does not suffice to render a person guilty of an offence.

I. THE NEED FOR AN ACT

The law's refusal to punish anything other than actions involves four different things. In the first place, the law is only concerned with positive conduct as opposed to mere inactivity. Secondly, the law only prohibits acts as opposed to thoughts or intentions. Thirdly, the law only penalizes acts as contrasted with bodily states and forms of involuntary behaviour. Lastly, a man is only punished for his own conduct and not for that of others.

(a) Acts not Omissions

The law's disregard of omission is exemplified in the law relating to violence. The law of homicide forbids killing; it does not command that life be preserved. Another example is provided by the offence of larceny. A finder of an article commits larceny if he keeps it knowing who the true owner is. Mere failure to return the article, however, incurs no responsibility. Like the Ten Commandments, the criminal law consists mostly of prohibitions.

This is partly due perhaps to the difficulty of attributing responsibility to mere inactivity. Where some act is performed which results in injury, it is easy to fasten on this act as the cause of the harm. If A pushes B into a river and B drowns, it is easy to fix on A's act as a cause of B's death. Where the injury results from inactivity, however, the situation is not so simple. Suppose X gets into difficulties while swimming and several people stand back and watch him drown. Here it is not so easy to single out the inactivity of any one of them as the cause of X's death, whereas in the first example there is one obvious person to blame, i.e. the person that pushed B in. In the second example we cannot select any one particular bystander rather than anyone else, for in this example all of them are non-performers.

Where, however, there are present people who can avert injury and such people take no steps to do so, we may hold them morally at fault. This tendency is reflected in our language, which at this point begins to make use of such terms as 'omission' and 'failure'. Lack of a single word to denote 'not doing' leads us to speak sometimes of mere inactivity as an omission. This, however, overlooks the fact that the basic notion of 'omitting' and 'failing' is that of leaving undone something which is usually done and which can be done, and carries with it often the suggestion that the thing left undone should have been done. In the parable of the Good Samaritan, for instance, it was only those who passed by and did not render assistance who could be said to have omitted to help the victim of the robbery. Those never at the scene of the accident could not be said to have omitted to have rendered assistance and could not be blamed on this score. It is worth emphasizing this, since it is often said that the criminal law does not, in general, prohibit omission, when what is meant is that it does not punish inactivity. In those exceptional cases where it does punish inactivity, such inactivity is found to consist in omissions.

It is true, however, that in respect of omissions, as opposed to mere inactivity, law and morals part company. A bystander who refuses to come to the rescue of a swimmer in difficulties may incur moral condemnation, but commits no criminal offence. The same holds true of the law of torts, or civil wrongs. One man is under no duty, at criminal or civil law, to take positive action in the interests of others. The moral rule that we should love our neighbours becomes in law the rule that we must avoid injuring our neighbours.[1] In order to impose upon some other person a legal duty to perform some positive action, generally one must pay him to do it. It is in the realm of contract that such duties are imposed.

[1] This translation of the moral rule into the legal rule has been expounded in the celebrated judgment of Lord Atkin in the civil case of *Donoghue* v. *Stevenson*, [1932] A.C. 562.

This striking divergence of law and morals is based perhaps on a respect for individual liberty. For while the law aims to protect the safety of the community and its members, in doing so it tries to strike a balance between the interest of the potential victims not to suffer harm and that of the potential wrongdoer not to have his liberty curtailed. The creation of any crime involves some limitation of liberty, since it restricts what may lawfully be done. But crimes of omission are much more restrictive than crimes of commission. If the law forbids me to do a certain thing, e.g. to kill, then it closes one avenue of action. If it goes further and commands me to rescue those in danger, then temporarily it closes all avenues save one; it forbids me to do anything else until I have rescued the victim. The interests of life, safety, and property have not, in the eyes of the law, merited the imposition of such fetters on individual liberty.

The exceptional cases where notice is taken by law of omissions tend to fall into two categories. Firstly, there are those cases where the need to preserve law and order outweighs the interest of personal liberty. In certain circumstances a private citizen has a duty to come to the aid of a police officer who calls upon him for assistance. The private citizen is under a legal duty to arrest someone who has committed a felony or dangerous breach of the peace in his presence. Failure to report a felony or treason constitutes the offence of Misprision, an offence rarely charged but still existing, as was recently affirmed by the House of Lords.[1]

The second category comprises cases within the law of homicide, where the existence of a special relationship between two people imposes a duty on the one to take care of the other. Parents owe such a duty to their very young children. Nurses owe such a duty to those patients whose care they have undertaken. If death results from an omission constituting a breach of this duty, the wrongdoer is guilty of homicide. In such circumstances the charge usually preferred is one of manslaughter, but if death was the intended result, the crime committed is murder.

In addition to these two types of case, recent years have witnessed the creation of a number of statutory offences consisting of omissions. The road traffic legislation provides several examples. If a person is alleged to have committed an offence of careless or dangerous driving, his refusal to give his name

[1] *Sykes* v. *D.P.P.*, [1961] 3 All E.R. 33.

and address to anyone with reasonable ground for demanding it amounts to an offence. Refusal to answer questions put by the police in their attempt to identify the driver of a vehicle who is alleged to have committed a driving offence is an offence. The best-known example is the offence committed by a driver who fails to report an accident in which he was involved and which caused damage to some person or vehicle other than himself and his vehicle.

(b) Acts not Intentions

An intention to commit a crime does not by itself suffice to make a person guilty of a crime. Here again law and morals diverge. Sins may be committed in thought and deed; crimes only in deed.

A reason sometimes advanced to justify this rule is the impossibility of proving intentions. 'The thought of a man is not triable', said Chief Justice Bryan in the fifteenth century; 'the devil himself knoweth not the thought of man.' This cannot, however, be a sufficient justification, since in many trials the only issue at stake is precisely this question of the state of mind of the accused. Did the accused act honestly? Did he intend to kill the night-watchman? These are the sorts of question which juries must decide every day. They base their decisions on the external behaviour of the accused, on what he says in the witness-box, and on what he may have said outside the court. It is true that without some observable behaviour it is impossible to discover a person's intentions, but this should not blind us to the fact that those societies that have considered it necessary to eradicate anti-social intentions and thoughts as well as anti-social actions have not lacked the means of forcing suspects to disclose what is in their minds.

The law's disregard of criminal intentions divorced from criminal conduct is based on an attitude shared by most civilized societies. The comparative harmlessness of mere thoughts and intentions by themselves is considered sufficient reason for not punishing them. The small degree of harm likely to result from such intentions is not thought to justify the interference with liberty which punishment would involve. The notion of thought-crimes is not consistent with that of a free society. English law takes the view that the mind is its own place.

Although mere criminal intention is not punishable, punishment is not reserved only for cases where the intention is fulfilled. Midway between the mere intention and the completed crime stands the inchoate crime of Attempt. We have already considered certain crimes which are in reality attempts to produce the harm prohibited by law. Larceny protects owners against permanent deprivation of their property, but the law does not wait for this to happen; it steps in to penalize the mere taking of property with such intent. Arson protects owners against the destruction of their property by fire, but once again the law does not wait till this result is achieved; it intervenes to prohibit the mere act of setting fire to the property. We must now consider the attempt to commit an indictable offence, which is itself an indictable offence, punishable as a common-law misdemeanour with imprisonment for life as a theoretical maximum.

Attempts to commit crimes

Despite the high sentence which is possible for attempts, courts normally award lighter sentences for attempts than they do for complete offences. In some instances statutes provide a lesser punishment for the attempt than for the full offence. The reason is no doubt the fact that less harm results from the former than from the latter. In fact, here the law would seem to be penalizing mere criminal intention, contrary to the general rule.

The justification for the exception made in the case of attempts may be sought partly on the ground of potential danger and partly on the principle of extra hazard. Criminal intent by itself may be a potential source of danger, but when it is accompanied by steps taken to carry it out, the risk of danger is increased. Moreover the existence of a penalty for attempts affords an extra hazard to the would-be criminal. The main deterrent is, of course, the penalty for the complete offence, since most criminals aim to succeed, but the penalty for the attempt provides an extra deterrent. Not only will he be punished if he succeeds, but also in the event of failure. Since the main deterrent is the punishment for the completed crime, and since less harm results from the attempt than from the completed crime, the lesser penalties for attempts may be justified on the ground that pain should be minimized. The infliction of a lighter penalty here will not detract from the deterrent force provided by the penalty for the full crime.

Considerable difficulty has been encountered in the search for a definition of attempting to commit crimes. In this context lawyers are faced with two difficulties which cannot be solved by the reflection on the ordinary extra-legal use of such words as 'attempt' and 'try'. For practical reasons judges are often obliged to give decisions about borderline situations as to which common sense and ordinary language give, and need to give, no answer. Secondly, in ordinary speech the words 'try', 'attempt', &c., are used mainly to mark a contrast between failure and success. To the lawyer, however, the all-important contrast here is the distinction between mere acts of preparation, which constitute no crime, and acts which have gone beyond this and amount to attempts and are therefore criminal. This difference of interest between ordinary language and legal language may be seen from comparing what an ordinary man would mean if he asked 'Was Smith attempting to kill Jones?' with what a lawyer might mean. The former would want to know whether this was Smith's purpose, whether Smith was really putting his back into the job, &c. But if the question arose in legal argument, the court might be trying to answer this question: 'Given that Smith loaded the gun, put it through the window, and was about to put the safety catch off, &c.; and given that he meant to kill Jones—as we know from his confession—does this in law amount to attempting to murder, or was it mere preparation?'

It is not surprising, therefore, that no completely satisfactory test has been elucidated to determine whether behaviour amounts to attempting. One rough test is to ask whether the accused has performed the last act dependent on himself. Such a test neatly covers cases where the accused fails to carry out his intention because of some external circumstance, e.g. the wind carries his bullet off the target. It breaks down, however, with regard to cases where the accused voluntarily abandons the venture. In law it is possible to arrive at a stage where there is no longer a *locus poenitentiae*, i.e. the accused has got so far that even if he goes no further he has committed an attempt. In such cases he has clearly not performed the last act dependent on himself. A recently applied test is to ask whether the accused's conduct, looked at objectively (and without regard to any subsequent confessions or admissions the accused may have made), can be considered as aimed only at the commission of a particular offence.[1] This test was suggested because of the curious case of *Robinson*.[2] Robinson staged a faked robbery on his premises and called in the police. His object was to prefer a fraudulent claim against his insurance company. He was acquitted, however, of attempting to obtain by false pretences, on the ground that he had not advanced beyond the stage of mere preparation. The new test would fit *Robinson*'s case, because his conduct could not be said to have been aimed at this particular fraud; there were several alternative purposes which he might have had. But the attraction of the new test is illusory. Suppose A fires a shot at B. Can this act be said to point unequivocally at only one end, or must we admit that A's intention might have been to kill, to wound, or perhaps only to frighten B? Yet if A admits that he meant to kill B (something the test tells us to exclude when considering whether the act points to the commission of one offence), he could certainly be found guilty of attempted murder.

Special difficulty has arisen over attempts to commit the impossible. To shoot someone with an unloaded gun is an impossibility, but if the accused is unaware that the gun is unloaded, there would be no hesitation in saying that he was trying to shoot his intended victim. Likewise it is impossible to steal money from an empty pocket, but the courts have felt little difficulty in convicting of attempted larceny where the accused was unaware that the pocket was empty. The difficulty arises in the case where the unattainability of the objective is due not to some circumstances as in these examples, but to the fact that objectives of the kind intended cannot be achieved by the type of means employed. Suppose X burns a wax effigy of Y, thinking thereby to cause Y's death. Here X's mistake is not a simple one of fact, but rather one as to the way that things behave, as to the laws of nature. Now if a person knows that the means employed is incapable of bringing about the end desired, we refuse to characterize his behaviour as attempting to achieve this end. If he knows that burning effigies of his enemy will not bring about the latter's death, then we refuse to consider such

[1] By Dr. J. W. C. Turner in *Modern Approach to the Criminal Law*, p. 278. This test was adopted by the court in *R. v. Miskell*, [1954] 1 All E.R. 137.

[2] *R. v. Robinson*, [1915] 2 K.B. 342.

burnings of effigies as attempts to kill, for in such a case we should not accept that he had an intention to kill. Where it is general knowledge that the means cannot produce the end, but the agent himself is ignorant of this, we tend to assimilate his case to that of the man who knows that the means cannot produce the end, and say of him too that this is not an attempt to kill. What little legal authority there is on this type of problem suggests that the law is that such cases would not count as attempts. This is what is meant by the distinction sometimes made in this context between relative and absolute impossibility.

Further problems arise with regard to attempts to commit crimes which are legally impossible. Since a boy under the age of fourteen cannot in law commit the offence of rape, i.e. he cannot be convicted of this crime, he cannot be convicted of attempted rape. For it would be a curious situation if acts committed by such a person in furtherance of rape were punishable as attempted rape, while the commission of the completed act was unpunishable. Similarly, attempts to steal property which is unstealable at law, e.g. a corpse in a grave, do not amount to attempted larceny. Academic controversy has raged over the problem whether there could be a conviction for attempted larceny in the case where X, intending to steal Y's umbrella, takes his own in mistake for that of Y. To this there is no authoritative answer. The problem might be approached in the following way. If X, through mistake of law, thinks that a certain object, e.g. a corpse, is capable of being stolen, and if he makes off with it, then his mistake of law is irrelevant. He must be judged by what the law is, not by what he thinks it is; and since the law does not in fact prohibit the act which he intends to perform and does perform, he should not be guilty of either stealing or attempted stealing. But if his mistake is one of fact, e.g. he thinks that the umbrella belonging to him belongs to Y, then he should be judged according to what he thinks the circumstances are. Accordingly he should be guilty of attempted stealing, since the law prohibits the act intended.

(c) Acts not Involuntary Behaviour

The criminal law's disregard of mere omissions and mere intentions would seem to be based upon a reluctance to encroach unduly on individual liberty. Its refusal to penalize involuntary behaviour together with mere states of body and mind appears to derive from a different principle, namely the moral principle that a man should not be punished for events beyond his control.

It is an accepted moral principle that commendation and condemnation must only be applied to matters over which the agent has control or ability to control. To blame a person for the colour of his skin or for the beatings of his heart would be quite out of accord with our ways of moral thinking. The proverbial example of an unjust law is, interestingly enough, a law commanding that all blue-eyed babies should be killed at birth. This, however, is drastic rather than discriminatory; for all babies are blue-eyed at birth. Part of the reason for this is the role played by moral words and judgments, by rewards and punishments in guiding actions. To praise or reward a man for some act encourages him to continue to behave in this way and encourages others to follow his example. To blame or punish him dissuades him from repeating his performance and deters others from following his example. But if the event in question is outside the subject's control and is something over which he has no choice, then praise and blame, reward and punishment fail to have any encouraging or dissuading effect. For where choice is absent there is nothing which can be guided. Accordingly, the withholding of blame and punishment for events beyond a person's control is linked up with the very meaning of blame and punishment. If we do utter unpleasant words about a person or inflict unpleasant things on him on account of the colour of his skin, our words cannot logically count as blame and our actions would not logically count as punishment.

But the fact that punishing a man for things beyond his control would be contrary to the logic of punishment and so would not qualify to be described as punishing must not blind us to the more important fact that 'punishments' are often inflicted for such things and that this is wrong. For whatever the logic of the term 'punishment', there is no lack of examples of people being punished openly for things beyond their power to control. Apart from the obvious example of the anti-Jewish legislation of Nazi Germany, we can find in our own law instances of such unjustifiable punishment. The best-known example is the celebrated case of *Larsonneur*.[1] According

[1] (1933), 149 L.T. 542.

to the law with regard to aliens it was an offence for an alien, who was refused permission to land in the United Kingdom, to be found in the United Kingdom. Larsonneur, having been refused permission and having been taken to Ireland, was subsequently brought back by police escort and detained in Holyhead police station. She was then found guilty of being found in the United Kingdom without leave to land in the United Kingdom. Despite the obvious intention of this regulation, which was to prohibit the entry of undesirable aliens, the court held that on a literal interpretation the rule extended to forced entries also. Had the court wanted to be really literal, it might have considered that Larsonneur was not *found* in the United Kingdom by the police as she was already known to be there.

The question arises why it is that it should be wrong to punish people for their racial origins and why it should be wrong to punish people in Larsonneur's position. The underlying principles seem to be these. To inflict injury or other unpleasant things on people is itself undesirable. To do this to a person may be tolerable, however, if it is done in order to deter certain sorts of behaviour or to reform the person himself, or to protect the public from him.

Now it is sometimes argued that what makes punishment for voluntary behaviour tolerable and punishment for involuntary behaviour intolerable is precisely that punishment for the former may have useful deterrent and reformative effects, so that the harm of the individual punishment suffered will be outweighed by the ultimate good produced. Punishment for involuntary behaviour it is said can produce no such good effects, because no deterrent and reformative effects can follow. This, however, is not entirely correct. So far as deterrence is concerned, a state of affairs may easily be imagined where the punishment of someone in Larsonneur's position may have very useful deterrent effects. All aliens about to land without permission would see that our laws regarding this were so strict that we even punish forced entries if made without permission. Seeing this they would realize that for voluntary entries there would be no mercy whatsoever and this would deter them all the more from carrying out their intention. Here the good produced might seem to outweigh the harm done. So far as concerns reform it could be argued that it is pointless to wait until a person with

criminal tendencies actually commits an offence before sub-
jecting him to reformative treatment. It might be better to take
measures of a preventive nature and improve his character
before he has a chance to commit any crime. His loss of liberty
through imprisonment might well be outweighed by the ultimate good produced.

But even if the punishment of involuntary acts or the treatment of mere potential offenders might be supported in some
circumstances, on the ground that the resulting good outweighs
the harm, there is still one serious objection to it. It is this
objection which no doubt underlies the criminal law relating to
punishing involuntary behaviour and which leads us to prefer
a system of punishment to a system of social hygiene. What
seems to make ordinary cases of punishment for the sake of
deterrence and reform tolerable is the breach of a rule which
the person being punished could have obeyed. Every person in
a society knows or can be expected to know the laws of the
society in which he lives. He can accept them and live in peace
with his environment, or he can violate them and pay the
penalty. It is because of his deliberate refusal to obey these
rules that he forfeits his right to his liberty and, having forfeited
this right, he may justifiably be punished in the interests of
society. But it is only when he deliberately refuses the terms
offered to him by society that he forfeits this right. Where he
cannot help acting as he does, it would not be right to take away
his right to freedom, even in the interests of the greater good of
the community. For each man should be regarded as an end in
himself; no one should be treated as a thing to be used for the
benefit of others.

With certain exceptions it is a correct generalization that the
criminal law is concerned with what people do, not with what
they are. States, conditions, and involuntary behaviour fall outside this ambit. Some quasi-exceptions to this can indeed be
found in the law relating to burglary and housebreaking. Among
the lesser offences connected with these two crimes is the offence
of being found by night in a building with intent to commit
felony therein, the offence of being found by night armed with
a dangerous weapon with intent to enter a building and commit
a felony therein, and the offence of being possessed by night
without lawful excuse of housebreaking implements. We have

also seen that it is an offence to be possessed without lawful excuse of certain explosives; to be found in enclosed premises at any time with criminal intent constitutes an offence against the Vagrancy Act, 1824.

But these are only quasi-exceptions. In all these cases though indeed the defendant is penalized for being in, or having possession, rather than for acting, yet he is not without choice in the matter. He could have chosen not to be in the building, not to be armed, not to carry explosives. Even if an example were concocted where a man was found in a building by night, without any choice of his, e.g. suppose he is carried into the building asleep, yet even here control and choice are not entirely lacking, for all these offences contain a reference to some mental element. The prosecution must prove that the defendant has the criminal intent required for the offence. Consequently, even if he was carried into the building asleep, he cannot be guilty of one of these offences, unless he also intended to commit a felony inside the building. Accordingly, though his entry may be involuntary, the formation of intention is within his control.

More important is the law relating to acts which are commonly within a person's control, but which in special cases turn out to be involuntary. The obvious case arises where a man's behaviour results from the application of some external physical force. Suppose A seizes B's hand and makes it hit C. Here the movement of B's hand is beyond his control and according to ancient authority B commits no crime.[1] The offence of battery is committed by A through use of B as an innocent agent. The act is not an act of B, but of A.

But lack of control may be due not to external compulsion. Some bodily movements are beyond the control of any normal human being. No one, for example, can direct the beatings of his heart or the circulation of his blood. Spasms, twitches, and automatic reflexes are all beyond normal powers of control, but since such activity rarely occasions harm to others, such matters do not form the subject of criminal offences.

More interesting are cases concerning bodily movements which are within the control of the normal person, but which are outside the control of the agent in question, owing to some peculiarity or abnormality. Examples of this are acts performed

[1] 1 Hale P.C. 434.

in sleep, under hypnosis, or as the result of epileptic fits. The rule that 'in sleep there is no sin' has its counterpart in criminal law. In the case of *Sergeant Boshears*[1] where the accused was charged with murder, the judge directed the jury that if the accused was asleep when he killed the victim, it was not a voluntary act and he would be entitled to be acquitted of murder. Accordingly, the accused was acquitted. Acts committed in the course of epileptic fits or as the result of epileptic automatism have been recently considered to some extent by the courts and the rule that emerges is that such acts do not involve the agent in criminal responsibility. In such cases the law takes the view that there is no act on the part of the person suffering from such a disability; as criminal lawyers put it, there is no *actus reus*.

This raises special problems with regard to driving offences.[2] Clearly the accused's inability to control his bodily movements makes it undesirable to hold him criminally responsible. On the other hand, there may be cases where he himself is to blame for letting himself get into such a state as to become a danger to others. For instance, while a man cannot control what he does in his sleep, it is obvious that a motorist who allows himself to fall asleep at the wheel is a menace to others. The difficulty of supporting a conviction of dangerous driving is that driving a car while asleep would not seem to be an act in the full sense of the word. What the driver ought to be punished for is not so much his bad driving while asleep, as his carelessness in allowing himself to fall asleep at the wheel. Since there is no specific offence of falling asleep at the wheel, such a driver must be prosecuted for dangerous or careless driving. If the time of driving is considered to be the time during which the motorist was asleep, difficulties arise as to whether there is any *actus reus* on the driver's part. If the time of the driving is taken to be the moment when he wrongfully allowed himself to fall asleep the difficulty is that though it may be dangerous to allow yourself to fall asleep at the wheel, to do so hardly seems to constitute driving in a manner dangerous to the public. Such a driver can, however, without difficulty be said to be driving at that time without due care, but this is, of course, a lesser offence than dangerous driving. Perhaps some special offence may have to

[1] *The Times*, 18 Feb. 1961.   [2] See *Hill* v. *Baxter*, [1958] 1 Q.B. 277.

be created to penalize the motorist who carelessly falls asleep at the wheel and to distinguish his case from that of the driver who is overcome without warning by somnolence or by a blackout.

There are cases where, although the person affected is in no way to blame for his condition, public safety demands that he ensure that he does not become involved in situations where his condition may constitute a source of danger to others. A man cannot be blamed for being an epileptic, but society can justifiably demand that he should refrain from activities where his condition may render him dangerous to others. Driving again affords the most obvious example. It is not surprising that the regulations prohibit the issue of driving licences to epileptics and so in effect debar epileptics from driving. This is not unduly hard on such people. While an epileptic does not choose his disease, he can choose whether to drive or not. A similar attitude could with fairness be adopted with regard to somnambulists who are aware of their tendencies, if they are liable to cause injury to others during sleep.

Sometimes it happens that a man's inability to control himself is such a potential source of danger that steps must be taken to protect the public. Here we are no longer concerned with punishment; at this stage we leave the criminal law and turn to the legal provisions for the care and detention of the mentally ill. Recent decisions have shown that where a defence of automatism is raised the accused is liable to be met by an argument from the Prosecution to the effect that his condition renders him legally insane within the M'Naghten Rules. Should this argument succeed, the accused, so far from being released, will be detained during Her Majesty's pleasure, i.e. until those in charge of him are satisfied that he is fit to be released. This is a sensible and obviously necessary rule, since otherwise an acquittal might put the community at the mercy of one who ought really to be kept out of harm's way.

In 1961 the question of the relation between the defence of automatism and that of insanity was raised in the House of Lords by the case of *Bratty* v. *Attorney-General for Northern Ireland*.[1] Charged with murder, the accused claimed to have acted under the influence of what he described as a 'terrible feeling'. Medical

[1] [1961] 3 W.L.R. 965.

evidence was adduced to show that he was possibly suffering from psychomotor epilepsy. The defence argued that the accused was not guilty because he was in a state of automatism, or alternatively that he was suffering from a defect of reason due to a disease of the mind so as to qualify as insane within the M'Naghten Rules. Medical witnesses agreed that psychomotor epilepsy is a defect of reason due to disease of the mind and the judge accepted this. Accordingly, the judge directed the jury that while it was open to them to accept a defence of insanity, the alternative defence of automatism was not open to them in this case. Rejecting the defence of insanity, the jury found Bratty guilty of murder.[1] Affirming the judge's ruling, the House of Lords laid down (i) that rejection of a defence of insanity does not necessarily rule out a defence of automatism, but (ii) before such a defence can go to the jury, the accused must lay a proper foundation for it by adducing evidence of sufficient substance to merit consideration by the jury. In *Bratty*'s case the evidence was insufficient since it consisted mainly of evidence by the accused himself—and this alone would rarely be enough —together with medical evidence that he was suffering from a defect of reason due to disease of the mind. His lack of volition, therefore, if there really was such a lack, depended on insanity, and consequently in this case there was no room for an alternative defence of automatism.

(d) Acts of the Accused not of Others

The principle that a person is responsible only for his own acts rules out liability for acts performed by others. If Smith kills Jones, Robinson is no more criminally responsible for Jones's death than if it had resulted from some non-human occurrence, such as an avalanche. So far as Robinson is concerned, the act of Smith and the occurrence of the avalanche are neutral.

The justification for this is partly the principle we saw underlying the refusal of the law to punish involuntary behaviour. One person as a rule has no control over the acts of others any more than he has over the occurrences of nature. Other reasons may be advanced which are related to the attitude of the law

---

[1] It should be noted that the defence of diminished responsibility does not exist in Northern Ireland.

towards omissions. In the example given above there is no casual connexion between Robinson and Jones's death. Consequently, there is no particular reason for fastening on him rather than on anybody else as the cause of the latter's death. Secondly, the law does not normally insist that one person should take positive steps to help others, and accordingly does not demand that someone in Robinson's position should take action to prevent Smith causing injury to Jones.

If, however, one person makes use of another's act or of some natural occurrence to further his own ends, then the law holds him as responsible as if he had brought about these ends by his own act. If A, wanting to poison B, puts poison in a drink which he knows C will give to B, A is as guilty of murder as he would have been had he handed the poisoned drink himself to B. In such a case C would be regarded as the innocent agent of A; for the instruments which people may use are not restricted to animals and inanimate objects. Likewise if X, wanting to bring about Y's death, lures Y into the path of an avalanche foreseen by X, X will be as responsible for Y's death as if he had personally engineered the downfall. As lawyers would say, intended consequences are never too remote.

The justification for departing from the normal rule is obvious. Where one man makes use of another's act or of some natural occurrence to bring about a result, he is no longer unconnected with that result. Secondly, there is no longer any lack of choice or control, since he could have avoided making the use he did of the act or occurrence.

But apart from these sorts of case there are certain other important types of situation where one man may be held responsible for the conduct of another. These are cases where one man becomes an accomplice to a crime committed by another.

The different parties to a crime

The law distinguishes four possible parties to a crime. The person who actually carries out the crime is the 'principal in the first degree.' Anyone who helps him by rendering assistance at the time of the commission is a 'principal in the second degree'. If A steals property from X's house, while B keeps watch and C detains X in conversation, A is the 'principal in the first degree' while B and C are principals in the second degree. Someone who incites another to commit a crime or who gives him help before the actual commission of the crime is an 'accessory before the fact'. If E had incited A to steal from X's house and F had lent A his car to carry out the enterprise, E and F would be accessories before the fact. Someone who helps another to escape from justice after the commission of the crime is an 'accessory after the fact'. If G hides A in his house after the theft, while the police are searching for him, G becomes an accessory after the fact.

The terms used above are in fact only used with regard to felonies. In treason and misdemeanour all parties are called 'principals'.

The difference in terminology is of little significance because the first three types of parties are all subject to the same penalty, whether the offence is treason, felony, or misdemeanour. The accessory after the fact, however, is treated differently in each type of offence. The accessory after the fact to a felony is subject to a maximum penalty of two years' imprisonment. The corresponding principal in treason is liable to the full penalty for treason. For a misdemeanour there is no party corresponding to the accessory after the fact. If in the example above A had committed a misdemeanour, e.g. false pretences, G would not be guilty as a party to A's crime. He may nevertheless be guilty of a conspiracy with A to defeat the course of justice.

Though the first three parties are all subject to the same penalty, the Homicide Act, 1957, has provided one important limitation here. Where two or more persons are parties to a capital murder, the death penalty may only be inflicted on those who cause the death, inflict grievous bodily harm, or use force on the victim. If, in the example given earlier, A's crime had been to murder X by shooting him, only A could be sentenced to death. B, C, D, E, F, and G would only be liable to life imprisonment.

A problem of some difficulty which arises with regard to accessories before the fact and principals in the second degree concerns the type of situation which occurs when the principal in the first degree commits an offence different in some way from that anticipated by the other two parties. Suppose A intends to steal money from a bank at night. B lends him his car for the purpose, and C acts as look-out. B becomes accessory before the fact and C principal in the second degree. Now suppose that in the course of the raid A overpowers the night-watchman and kills him. What is the responsibility of B and C in respect of the night-watchman's death?

Clearly we should not expect that any rule of law concerning accomplices would lay down that a person could only be guilty as an accomplice if the exact crime planned and expected were carried out. People who plan crimes have to improvise just as do their more law-abiding fellow citizens. Accordingly, if A changed his mind and broke into a shop next door to the bank, B and C would still be guilty as accomplices. On the other hand, the mere fact of supplying assistance to a person for the commission of one crime would not in any rational system of law be considered good ground for holding the assisting party an accomplice to every subsequent crime committed by the principal offender. Suppose while A is driving along to the bank in B's car and while C is keeping watch, A takes the opportunity to run over deliberately his old enemy D, the leader of a rival gang. It would be both odd and unjust to hold B and C responsible for this quite gratuitous act of A.

Between these two extremes, where common sense dictates the obvious answers, lie the cases which are difficult to assess. The test adopted by the law is as follows. If the crime committed is entirely different from that for which the other parties rendered their assistance, then they are not parties to this crime. If, however, the crime committed is one within the common purpose, then the other parties are responsible. In the problem posed the jury would have to decide whether it was part of the plan that A should overcome opposition by force. If there was a common plan to this effect, B and C will be guilty of murder as accessory before the fact and principal in the second degree. If there was no such plan, B and C are exempt from guilt for the murder.

Vicarious liability

Without being a party to the crime of another a person may still be held responsible for the offence. He may be vicariously liable. Such liability is by no means rare in history. In times of stress when law is not easily enforced, it is common practice to make use of collective responsibility. In early days England was divided for administrative purposes into districts known as 'hundreds', the men of each hundred being responsible for crimes committed within their district and fined for failing to prevent the commission of crimes. In modern times we have seen measures of collective punishment employed in Cyprus and other dependent territories.Akin to collective punishment is the practice of taking hostages, yet another kind of vicarious liability.

To punish one man for another's crime is often a most powerful deterrent. The knowledge that his relatives and neighbours may suffer is possibly one of the strongest deterrents that might dissuade a man from breaking the law. Moreover those liable to be held vicariously responsible have every inducement to ensure that potential law-breakers keep within the law. In some cases there may be no other means of stamping out rebellion.

Morally, however, vicarious responsibility in these cases is quite unjustifiable. All that may reasonably be asked of the citizen is that he should keep the law himself. He cannot fairly be expected to ensure that others keep it too. Visiting the sins of fathers on their sons, punishing the group for the offences of the individual, and penalizing the master for the crimes of his servant strike at the root of this element of fairness. Even though its deterrent force cannot be denied, the objection remains that it involves treating people as things rather than as ends in themselves.

Fortunately the incidence of vicarious liability in our criminal law is small, and is with one exception restricted to cases concerning masters and servants. The common law knew only of two crimes, public nuisance and libel, for which a person could be guilty for the act of his servant; and so far as the latter is concerned the Libel Act, 1843, provides that no one shall be liable for libels published by his servants in the absence of authorization or negligence on his part. In addition to these, statutes have created several offences where a person may be held vicariously liable. They fall for the most part into two categories. On the one hand there are the various offences against the Licensing Acts, where the licensee may be liable for the acts of his servants. On the other hand we find the same rule at work in many of the offences against the Food and Drugs Acts.

The exception referred to above is the useful provision which enables a magistrate to order that a fine imposed on a child be

paid by his parent if the latter's failure to control the child is
the cause of the delinquency.

2. THE MENTAL ELEMENT

Most of the offences which we have considered contain some
express reference to the state of mind of the accused. In murder he
must act with malice aforethought; in larceny fraudulently and
with an intent to deprive the owner permanently of the property;
in arson and malicious damage unlawfully and maliciously.
Generalizing from this fact lawyers have concluded that all
crimes can only be committed if the offender acts in a certain
state of mind. The venerable tag *actus non facit reum nisi mens
sit rea* epitomizes this generalization that an act does not render
a man guilty of an offence unless his state of mind is also guilty.
With scant regard for latinity lawyers proceeded to use the
words *mens rea* to denote the mental element required in a crime.
Thus the *mens rea* of murder is malice aforethought.

The difficulty of elucidating what is meant by *mens rea* in
general stems from the fact that it differs from crime to crime.
The basic notion is that unintentional wrongdoing is excluded
from criminal liability, just as part of the notion of *actus reus* is
that involuntary behaviour is excluded. Whereas the latter
exclusion allows for the defence 'I could not help it', *mens rea*
allows for the plea 'I never meant to do it.'

Some writers on criminal law have wanted to group these
two pleas together and suggested that the legal requirement that
the accused's act must not be involuntary is part of the notion
of *mens rea*. It is more correct, however, to keep these two aspects
quite separate and confine *mens rea* to the requirement that the
act must not be unintentional. There is legal authority to support this separate grouping.[1] Moreover, it is important in
connexion with offences of strict liability, offences where no
mens rea is required; for here the accused cannot be exonerated
because he acted unintentionally, but he can if he acted in-
voluntarily. To keep separate the plea 'I could not help it' from
the plea 'I never meant to do it' is to show an awareness of the
fact that lack of ability to control one's behaviour is something
more basic than mere lack of intention. While we may object to

[1] *R. v. Harrison-Owen*, [1951] 2 All E.R. 726.

penalizing unintentional acts, the idea of punishing involuntary acts is totally repulsive.

To describe what is entailed by the notion of *mens rea* we must distinguish three different types of crime. First are what might be termed 'simple crimes', e.g. battery and rape, where the *mens rea* consists in an intention to do the act prohibited by law. The second category comprises such crimes as murder, where the accused need not have the actual intention to produce the *actus reus*. Thirdly, there is a class of crimes such as burglary where the accused must commit the *actus reus* with some further purpose.

To take the first group of crimes—battery, rape, assault occasioning actual bodily harm, and various other offences—we may note that there is no reference to intent or foresight of consequences, no reference to any further intent or purpose. Here we may say that the mental element consists in the intention to do the unlawful act itself. In battery, for example, which consists of the unlawful application of force on another person, what is required for the defendant to be guilty is that he intended to apply such force. In other words in these offences the meaning of *mens rea* is that the defendant must act intentionally. Accordingly, this lets in certain defences which, if substantiated, show that the accused was acting unintentionally. For example, if A steps backwards and knocks into B, of whose presence he is unaware, A would be said to have knocked B by accident. Or suppose A is engrossed in some problem and forgets to look where he is going, he may knock into B inadvertently. Or again he might scratch B's foot, mistaking it for his own. Accidents, inadvertence, mistake, absentmindedness, and other factors are matters which render an act unintentional. What is meant by *mens rea* in relation to offences like battery, whose definition contains no express reference to any specific intention, is that no crime is committed if the act was done unintentionally.

The second class of offence consists of crimes like murder and malicious damage. Here the offender performs an act which produces harmful consequences and when he performs it he either intends to produce those (or similar) consequences or he foresees that his act will produce them. In murder the accused must either intend or foresee that death or grievous bodily harm will be the result of his act. Indeed we have seen that in certain circumstances murder can be committed without either intention or foresight of consequences, if the accused aims at the deceased an unlawful act which a reasonable man would realize to be likely to cause death or grievous bodily harm; this might be termed 'objective recklessness'. To commit malicious damage the accused must intend or foresee that his act will result in damage to the property. In these kinds of offence something less than intention amounts to *mens rea*. Mere recklessness is enough. If X plants a bomb in an aircraft, he knows that this will probably kill the occupants. Even though perhaps his intention is to destroy the plane and though he may fervently hope the passengers may escape, he commits murder if they are killed. For he has persisted in a course of action which he realizes to be fraught with serious danger to others. The rule that reckless-ness is as good as intent here means that the law will not allow one man to gamble with the life and safety of others. In this class of offence we may say that *mens rea* is either an intention to produce certain consequences or foresight of such consequences, while noting that the crime of murder allows for a third possibility.

The third class comprises those offences where there is a specific reference in the definition of the crime to some further intent or purpose which the accused must have in order to be guilty. Burglary, for example (or one form of it), consists in doing an act (breaking into a house) in order to do something further (commit a felony in the house). Very similar to this are other offences of dishonesty, stealing, false pretences, and receiving, where the accused does an act (takes the property) in order to achieve an objective (deprive the owner permanently of the property). In these cases it is the intention to do the further act or achieve the further objective that comprises the *mens rea* of the offence.

The notion of *mens rea* then is a complex one. The mental element may be some specific intention or purpose, as required by the definition of the offence. It may be the intention or fore-sight that certain consequences will result, i.e. here intention or recklessness is sufficient. On the other hand in some offences the mental element merely amounts to a requirement that the act should not be done unintentionally. In other words the charge may be defeated by a defence of accident, mistake, &c.[1]

---

[1] See on the notion of *mens rea* as a defeasible concept H. L. A. Hart, 'The Ascrip-tion of Responsibility and Rights', 49 *Proc. Arist. Soc.* (1948–9), 179.

The allowance for such defences and the doctrine of *mens rea* reflects a distinction we make when assessing moral culpability. Unintentional infliction of harm is less culpable morally than harm produced by conduct which is not unintentional. Moreover, one practical ground for treating unintentional conduct leniently is that the unintentional producer of harm is less of a menace to the community than one who pursues his own ends to the disregard of the law and of the interests of others.

This does not mean that the man who 'did not mean to do it' must always be exempt from blame. If the circumstances are fraught with serious risk of harm to others, special care may be demanded, and his plea may be met with the reply 'You should have taken more care'. In law such situations have led to the development of crimes of negligence, where the law lays down a standard of care. To avoid conviction here it is not enough for the accused to show that he neither intended nor was reckless. He must go further and show that the error, miscalculation, or misjudgement that led to the prohibited conduct (e.g. dangerous driving) was such as would have been made by any reasonable man in his position. He must show that he reached the standard of common prudence.

Strict Liability

There are today numerous offences in English law where there is no need for *mens rea*. In such cases a man may be convicted even though his act was unintentional and even though he was not behaving carelessly. (He will, however, escape liability if his behaviour is involuntary.)

With certain unimportant exceptions all such offences are statutory. In common-law crimes *mens rea* is essential; whether it is required in statutory offences depends on the wording of the statute as interpreted by the courts. An Act of Parliament could specifically exclude the defences of accident and mistake. Failing such express exclusion the courts generally presume that *mens rea* is required. Over the last hundred years, however, this presumption has been seriously displaced on many occasions. Offences of strict liability fall roughly into two classes. First there are certain serious offences against morality, notably abduction, carnal knowledge, and bigamy. The origin of the doctrine of

strict liability is to be found in *Prince's*[1] case, where the accused
was charged with offending against the Offences against the
Person Act, 1861, by taking a girl under sixteen out of the possession of her parents. His defence that he was mistaken as to
her age was rejected by the court, partly on the ground that
Prince knew in any case that what he was doing was immoral.
We have seen with regard to the offences of carnal knowledge
that mistakes as to the girl's age are irrelevant, and that the
interest of the girl is preferred to that of the man, who must act
at his peril. Bigamy too has produced a curious instance of strict
liability. It is a defence to this charge to show that at the time
of the second ceremony of marriage the first marriage had been
ended by the death of one of the parties or by divorce. The
Offences against the Person Act, 1861, provides that after seven
years' absence one may reasonably assume that the other party
is dead. In addition to this the court held in the case of *Tolson*[2]
that it was also a valid defence if the accused reasonably believed
her husband to have died, though the seven-year period had not
elapsed. But when in *Wheat and Stocks*[3] the court was faced with
an analogous problem concerning a party who reasonably
believed that his marriage had been ended by divorce, the
court unaccountably decided that reasonable mistake here was
not a defence.

The majority of strict offences are concerned with trades,
businesses, and certain other activities. Here the object is to
make the trader, businessman, or driver absolutely responsible
if anything goes wrong. The Food and Drugs Act, the Licensing
Act, and the Road Traffic Acts provide numerous examples of
such offences. Selling adulterated food, even without knowing
that it is adulterated; selling liquor to an intoxicated person,
even though he is not known to be intoxicated; failing to conform to a traffic signal—are examples of such offences. Here the
law is going beyond even the punishment of mere negligence, it
is even penalizing those whose ignorance was not even culpable.
How far *mens rea* is completely excluded, however, is nevertheless not clear. Suppose in the above example the accused claimed
that he had handed the customer an adulterated piece of cheese
by mistake for the pound of butter which he meant to give him;

[1] *R. v. Prince* (1875), L.R. 2 C.C.R. 154.
[2] *R. v. Tolson* (1899), 23 Q.B.D. 168.   [3] [1921] 2 K.B. 119.

that the publican gave the inebriate a bottle of beer by mistake for a bottle of lemonade; that the driver reasonably misunderstood the traffic signal. It is doubtful whether the accused in these cases could be convicted.[1]

The justification of strict liability in these cases, it is said, is that the public safety and welfare demand a very high standard of care by such people as food retailers; that in cases where there has been no fault on the part of the accused, nominal penalties may be imposed; and that in such cases it would be extremely difficult for the prosecution to prove that the accused had the necessary *mens rea*. These arguments are not wholly convincing. The need for a high standard of care is still compatible with absence of liability when there is no fault whatsoever on the accused's part. Nominal penalties, moreover, are by no means always imposed in such cases; in any event this leaves far too much to the discretion of the tribunal, which in such cases tends to be an unpredictable one—the Magistrates' Court. The argument about the difficulty of proving *mens rea* could be met by providing that it is for the accused to show that he was mistaken and that he was not negligent in being so mistaken. The chief argument against offences of strict liability is that it runs counter to moral principles to punish a person for breaking a rule, when there was nothing to suggest to him that what he is doing in any way violates that rule; he should be given a fair chance to conform to the rule. To punish a man for negligently infringing a rule is the utmost to which we can morally go. Absolute liability may serve its purpose in exacting a very high standard of care, by making the licensee, the retailer, or the motorist act at their peril. But this is only done at the cost of sacrificing the important principle that a man should not be punished unless he is at fault.[2]

---

[1] Examples suggested in Cross and Jones, *Introduction to Criminal Law* (4th ed.), p. 89.

[2] For a discussion of this topic see Glanville Williams, *Criminal Law* (2nd ed.), pp. 215 ff.

IV

DEFENCES

A PERSON accused of a crime may avail himself of a variety of
defences. It is open to him to forestall the attack by raising
certain preliminary points. He may on the other hand meet the
charge squarely by denying the facts alleged against him. Or he
may try to outflank the prosecution by conceding what is
alleged against him and introducing further factors which
negative or reduce his guilt.

Success on a preliminary point will constitute a bar to the
trial. If the accused shows that he has already been acquitted
(*autrefois acquit*) or convicted (*autrefois convict*) of the offence
charged, he cannot be tried again. Likewise if he shows that the
offence alleged is not in law a criminal offence, the proceedings
come to an end.

The commonest form of defence consists either in denials of
the accusation. For the most part such defences consist in the
straightforward denial of all or some of the facts alleged. The
accused may deny that the episode even occurred, i.e. he is being
'framed', or (as may happen in cases of indecent assault) the
prosecutrix's imagination has run away with her. Or he may
say that while the event may have taken place, he was not the
person involved. In some cases the defence may amount to a
denial of only some of the facts alleged. In a burglary trial the
accused might assert that it was not night-time when he was
seen doing the act, or that the building was not a dwelling-
house. If the prosecution fail to make out the presence of these
or any other constituent parts of the offence, he cannot be convicted of burglary.

Thirdly, there are certain special defences, where instead of
denying the charge, the accused alleges that there were special
circumstances in the light of which his action was justified or
excused. To justify an action is to show that there are circumstances such that the action, which might ordinarily be disapproved of, is in this case to be commended. To kill another
person is to do something prohibited by law. In certain circum-

stances in English law, however, the general duty not to kill is over-ridden by other more important duties, such as the duty of advancing or executing justice, the duty of preventing the commission of atrocious crimes. In other cases this general duty not to kill may be displaced by a right, e.g. the right to act in self-defence. Similarly, the duty not to use force against others may be displaced by a right to use reasonable force in the interest of self-help. These cases have already been considered in connexion with the lawful use of force. To excuse an action is to show that there are special factors which wholly or partly prevent it from being wrong. In English law the defences of accident, mistake, necessity, duress, and provocation operate in this way.

Some of these defences, such as accident, mistake, necessity, duress, and provocation, relate to the circumstances of the event. Others, such as infancy, insanity, diminished responsibility, and drunkenness, relate rather to some personal characteristic of the accused himself.

In this connexion we must note first that the common assertion that the law takes no account of motives is untrue. It is indeed natural that a system of law should be reluctant to allow its rules to be broken with impunity even for good motives. If the law prohibits stealing, then the activities of a Robin Hood amount to criminal offences. The citizen is not allowed to be wiser than the law and to substitute for the code laid down by law a private code of his own. Accordingly, mercy-killing and killing for revenge are equally criminal in English law. The relevance of the accused's motive, however, comes to the fore when sentence is about to be passed. It is at this stage that the court's discretion in sentencing can be used to adapt the penalty to the circumstances, so that crimes committed from good motives can be dealt with more leniently than those committed from the usual motives. In certain cases the question of the accused's motive may arise at an earlier stage, for it may be relevant to determining whether he is guilty or not. Where the definition of an offence includes words like 'fraudulently' or 'unlawfully', certain motives may operate to negative these words and so defeat the charge. If a man intentionally kills a dangerous criminal, this will not be murder if the criminal is a felon and is trying to escape from custody, and if there is no other way of keeping him in custody; for in such a case the killing is not unlawful. Even apart from such offences, which contain words connected with motives, the accused's motive is in any case of relevance if he can raise a general defence such as necessity or duress.

Secondly, it must be noted that it is a general rule that the prosecution must prove the prisoner's guilt; it is not for the accused to prove his innocence. This does not of course entail that the prosecution must negative every possible defence which may be open to the accused.

If X is charged with murdering Y, the prosecution need not in every case prove that there was no accident, no mistake, no provocation, and so forth. The accused bears what is known as the 'evidentiary' burden of proof, i.e. he must adduce sufficient evidence to raise these defences. Once he has raised sufficient evidence of any of these defences, however, the prosecution then bears the 'legal' burden of proof, i.e. they must satisfy the jury beyond reasonable doubt that the accused was not mistaken, provoked, &c. In some cases, viz. insanity and diminished responsibility, the accused bears not only the evidentiary but also the legal burden of proof. Not only must he adduce evidence sufficient to raise these defences, but he must also satisfy the jury that he was insane or suffering from diminished responsibility. Certain minor statutory offences also provide that the burden of proving innocence shall rest on the accused. Where the accused bears the legal burden of proof, however, his task is a lighter one than that normally incumbent on the prosecution. Whereas the latter must prove the accused's guilt beyond reasonable doubt, the accused in these exceptional cases need only establish his defence on a preponderance of probabilities. He need not, for instance, prove beyond reasonable doubt that he was insane at the time he committed the offence; it is enough to satisfy the jury of this on a balance of probabilities.

(a) Accident

The defence of accident applies to a variety of circumstances. It may mean that there was no *actus reus* in that the prohibited harm did not result from the act of the accused. For example, it may be in a murder case that the deceased died from a sudden heart-attack and not from the shot fired by the accused. The

defence would also apply where the accused acted unintentionally, e.g. if he pulled the trigger inadvertently. A further
example of this defence is where the accused simply does not
intend the consequence of his act, e.g. he shoots at a crow and
being a poor shot hits a pigeon. The defence of accident is
connected with the problem of causation, which has been considered earlier in the context of homicide.

(b) Mistake

There are two ways in which a man's mistake might lead him
to break a rule of the criminal law. He may not know that there
is such a rule, e.g. a motorist may not know that it is a crime
to drive when uninsured. Or he may know of the rule, but be
unaware that he is breaking it.

Mistake of law

Ignorance of law in English law is generally no excuse. This
severe rule is sometimes expressed by the fiction that everyone
is presumed to know the law. It is partly a rule of expediency
to avoid inquiry into the question whether each particular
offender was aware of the law on the subject. In many cases it
is justifiable. It is the citizen's duty to find out what the law is.
A motorist must find out the law relating to motor-cars. So far
as concerns serious offences of violence and dishonesty, the rule
is rendered palatable because such conduct is generally accepted
as immoral. In cases of burglary we do not stop to inquire
whether the accused had read up the latest decision in the
Court of Criminal Appeal on the meaning of 'breaking in'.

With regard to the numerous technical offences, where no
immorality is involved, the rule is less easy to justify. Here there
is no obvious moral rule to warn the accused that his behaviour
may be contrary to law. Sometimes it may be very difficult, and
even in some cases impossible, for him to know what the law
lays down. Special difficulty arises from the fact that in some
instances nothing short of a court decision will clarify what the
law means and show whether the conduct in question is a breach
of the law. Here, until a court has decided that the accused has
contravened the rule, no one could be certain whether the rule
has been broken. In such cases, although the court can impose
a merely nominal penalty, it is wholly unsatisfactory to stigma-

tize as guilty a person who cannot be expected to foresee what the decision of the court will be.

Offences of dishonesty provide an exception to the rule that ignorance of law is no excuse. If the accused honestly believed that in law he had a right to act as he did, he will be able to avail himself of a claim of right. If A promises to give B his watch, this promise by itself will not suffice to make B the owner, for the gift has not been completed by the delivery of the watch. Should B later take the watch, mistakenly thinking it is his, here he would have a claim of right due to a mistake of law. The rule as to ignorance of law is also dented by the rules relating to those who may avail themselves of a plea of obedience to superior orders. A soldier ordered by his superiors to do an illegal act cannot defend himself later by pleading that he was merely obeying orders. If, however, he had good reason to think that in the circumstances the act was lawful, this is generally considered a good defence; and when the order is not manifestly illegal, the fact that his superior ordered him to do act is good ground for his belief that the act was lawful.

Mistake of fact

Mistake of fact, on the other hand, usually affords a good defence. For while a man may be expected to find out the law, he cannot be required on all occasions to get the facts right. Such a mistake operates in offences like murder to negative the specific *mens rea*. If the accused did not know that the gun was loaded, he could not have intended or foreseen the fatal consequences of pulling the trigger. Or again suppose a soldier mistakes one of his officers for one of the enemy and kills him, here he has no intention to kill unlawfully.

Mistake of fact gives rise to two special problems. First, the mistake must be such that if the circumstances were what the accused thought, he would not be guilty of the crime charged. If X mistakes Y for Z and kills Y, this mistakes is no defence unless it would have been lawful to kill Z. In other words the accused must be judged on the facts as he imagined them to be. If a burglar breaks into the wrong house, he is still guilty of burglary. But suppose the burglar mistakes the time and thinks that it is not yet 9 o'clock. To judge him according to the facts as he imagines them would result in his conviction for house-breaking. Here, however, he is still guilty of burglary because on the facts as he imagined them he is not wholly innocent of the type of crime charged. It is not necessary for him to be wholly innocent on the imagined facts of any crime. If A shoots at B mistaking him for B's dog, he is not guilty of no crime at all in the imagined circumstances; he is guilty of malicious damage. But he is entirely innocent of any crime of homicide, and so is not guilty of murder. This differentiates his case from that of the burglar, whose mistake would not make him innocent of any crime of dishonesty, even if the circumstances were what he thought them to be. This sort of problem is related to the doctrine of transferred malice.

Secondly, there is a curious limitation on the doctrine of mistake, which has come to the fore in recent decisions on murder and in particular in *Smith*'s case.[1] While genuine mistake as to circumstance is a defence, genuine mistake as to the general way that things behave is only a defence in so far as such mistake would be shared by reasonable men. If A puts arsenic in B's tea, mistaking it for sugar, he has the defence of mistake. If he gives B arsenic not realizing that arsenic can kill, this is no defence because this property of arsenic is generally known by reasonable people. If, therefore, A knowingly gives arsenic to B, intending to drug B, but not knowing that he may kill him, B's death renders A guilty of murder. All the ingredients laid down by the House of Lords in *Smith*'s case are present: A commits a voluntary, unlawful act aimed at B which reasonable men would realize to be likely to kill or injure B. The attitude of the law here is that while people cannot always be expected to get particular facts right—for all of us are deceived by our senses from time to time—people are expected to find out the general rules about the world which are the fruits of common experience.[2]

(c) *Necessity*

The essence of this defence is that the accused does the prohibited act in order to avoid some greater evil. It differs from defences like self-defence and the advancement of justice in that there the duty not to injure the victim is negatived by

[1] See p. 31.   [2] See Holmes, *The Common Law*, p. 57.

the victim's own wrongdoing. Where necessity is pleaded, the victim is himself an innocent party. The defence of necessity has been written into the offences of Child Destruction and Abortion, which permit conduct normally prohibited if done to preserve the life of the mother.

Though the extent of the defence of necessity is far from clear, there is authority that in certain cases, where the harm done is something less than death, necessity is a valid defence. In the case of minor offences the police would usually use their discretion and avoid bringing a prosecution. In some offences terms like 'unlawfully' or 'fraudulently' may allow the accused to establish a defence without actually pleading necessity. In many cases reliance can be put on a plea of self defence or defence of one's property rather than on necessity.

Considerable doubt on this matter arose from the case of *Dudley and Stephens*.[1] Three sailors and a cabin-boy were shipwrecked in a small boat with no hope of rescue. To avoid starving, two of the sailors killed and ate the cabin-boy. On being picked up, they were brought back to England and tried for murder. Their plea of necessity was not allowed, though their sentence was commuted to one of six months' imprisonment.

This case established that necessity, will not excuse the deliberate killing of another. Quite reasonably, the court took the view that no one is entitled to prefer his own life to that of another innocent person. Textbook writers have suggested that a defence of necessity would hold good in certain cases even on a charge of murder. The stock example is that of two shipwrecked sailors on a plank only capable of supporting one of them. If one pushes the other off the plank to save himself, it is suggested that here necessity would be a good defence to a charge of murder. This case could be distinguished from that of *Dudley and Stephens*. In that case the accused used the cabin-boy's death as a *means* to their survival. In this case the survivor is not *using* the other person's death but is doing an act which produces two results, the survival of the one and the death of the other.

This brings into play what the theologians term the principle of 'double effect'.[2] According to this principle it is morally permissible to do an act which produces both a good and a bad

[1] (1884), 14 Q.B.D. 273.
[2] See H. Davis, S.J., *Moral and Pastoral Theology (A Summary)*, p. 3.

effect, provided that (i) the original act is not in itself immoral, (ii) the good effect, which is alone intended, either precedes the evil effect, which is not intended, or results as immediately as it, and (iii) the bad effect is not wholly disproportionate to the good effect. Its operation can be seen in the following examples. A soldier sees the enemy advancing over a bridge. To halt their advance he must blow up the bridge, and this may be morally permissible even though some innocent person standing on the bridge may be killed. On the other hand, suppose he sees them advancing towards a wounded soldier of his own side, who is possessed of information that would be of use to the enemy. To kill this soldier in order to prevent the enemy from getting this information would not be morally permissible. The distinction between the two cases is that in the first example the bridge is blown up to achieve a permitted end, though it will also bring about a consequence which is not desired; here the value of the end must be balanced against the incidental consequence. In the second example the soldier is killed in order to prevent the enemy obtaining information; and this is to use his death as a means to this end. According to the principle of 'double effect' the end cannot justify the means where the latter consists in a wrongful act.

(d) Duress

Duress is similar to necessity. The accused is faced with a choice of breaking the law or being injured by the person coercing him to break the law. It differs from physical compulsion, where the accused has *no* choice. In duress the accused's plea is that he had *no fair* choice.

Clearly it would not be desirable to excuse a man for the commission of any crime on the ground that the alternative was that he might suffer some injury at the hands of the coercing party. The seriousness of the injury threatened must be weighed against the gravity of the crime which he is coerced into committing. Authority is not very great on this topic, especially because where the crime committed is a minor one, the police may exercise their discretion not to prosecute.

The injury threatened must, it seems, be death or serious physical injury. Moreover, the accused must have had an immediate fear of such injury. Threatened damage to property is insufficient.

Duress is not a valid defence to a charge of murder. No threat is sufficient to excuse the killing of another person. The defence of duress has succeeded, however, in cases where the accused was charged with certain forms of treason and kindred offences. It has been admitted also as a defence to charges of malicious damage and receiving.

Originally a married woman was in a special position in that if she committed a crime (other than treason or murder) in the presence of her husband, she was presumed to have acted under his coercion and was accordingly free from guilt. Since the Criminal Justice Act, 1925, this presumption has been abolished. Today a married woman would have to show that she was acting under such coercion. What is not entirely clear is whether threats which would not amount to duress against other people would constitute coercion of a wife by her husband.

(e) Provocation

Provocation is not strictly a defence. It is a mitigating factor to be taken into account when the accused is sentenced. In murder, however, where the penalty is fixed, provocation cannot be taken into account in this way, and special rules were developed to allow provocation to reduce the charge to the lesser charge of manslaughter where the judge has a discretion as to the penalty to award. In such a case the accused is guilty of Voluntary Manslaughter.

The essence of the defence is that the accused had to contend with special difficulties, which were such that any ordinary person might have given way. It is a concession to human weakness.

First, the accused must show that he was provoked to kill the victim. This a question of fact for the jury. To decide it they must consider whether the murder followed straight upon the provocation or whether there was an interval during which the accused's temper had time to cool down.

Secondly, the jury must be satisfied that a reasonable man would have been provoked to do what the accused did. Prior to 1957 the law was that mere words were not enough to constitute provocation, because a reasonable man would not be provoked by mere words. The Homicide Act, 1957, has provided that the question whether a reasonable man would have been provoked in the accused's position (whether by acts or words) is a matter entirely for the jury. In deciding this matter the jury has to weigh the provocation with the retaliation. They may think that a blow from a fist might provoke a reasonable man to return it in kind but not to stab the victim to death.

Difficulty arises in connexion with the notion of 'the reasonable man'. Some such notion is needed in order to provide an objective standard. The concession afforded by the defence of provocation must obviously be confined to such loss of control as one might reasonably expect from anyone in the accused's position. Without such an objective standard the result would be to allow hot-tempered people easily provoked by trifles to defend themselves on the grounds of provocation; and this would be to set a premium on hot temper. On the other hand, in considering whether it was reasonable for the accused to give way to the provocation, the jury must take into account all the circumstances of the case. They must consider what a reasonable man in the accused's position would have done. Otherwise they would be considering the hypothetical behaviour of a reasonable man isolated from the very circumstances which give rise to the provocation.

The problem is what is meant by putting the reasonable man in the accused's position. Clearly the jury cannot be asked to consider what a reasonable man would have done if he had *all* the characteristics of the accused, i.e. if he *was* the accused, because then the objective test would fall to the ground. On the other hand, there may be certain circumstances which it would be unjust not to take into account. A blow may provoke more readily if the accused suffers from some disease which makes such injuries excruciating. To jeer at a man on the ground of his illegitimacy may more easily provoke someone who is illegitimate than someone who is not. In *Bedder's*[1] case (1954) the accused, who had the misfortune to be sexually impotent, was convicted of the murder of a prostitute, His defence was provocation. Amongst other things the deceased had jeered at Bedder's impotence, and the defence claimed that in assessing what the reaction of a reasonable man would have been the jury should consider the reaction of a reasonable man who was impotent. The House of Lords, however, refused to allow the hypothetical reasonable man in this case to be invested with Bedder's physical

[1] [1954] 2 All E.R. 801.

peculiarity. The difficulty is to evolve a test to exclude certain characteristics like hot temper, irritability, and drunkenness, things which the accused must fight against and for which he may be responsible, and yet to allow in certain physical or mental idiosyncrasies in fairness to the accused. At the present the law would seem to be that the jury can put the reasonable man into the shoes but not into the skin of the accused.

SPECIAL CATEGORIES OF PERSON

We come now to consider cases where criminal responsibility is negatived or reduced, not by virtue of any special features relating to the circumstances surrounding the act, but by virtue of some special characteristics relating to the agent himself. In this section it is proposed to deal with Infancy, Insanity, Diminished Responsibility, and Drunkenness.

(a) Infancy

The case of children provides an example of considerable departure by the courts from the principle that everyone is equal before the law. The rules of criminal law contain special provisions relating to the age of criminal responsibility; the rules of procedure lay down that charges against children must be investigated in special courts; the age of an offender places restrictions on the kinds of punishment which he can be made to undergo. In this chapter we are concerned only with the substantive rules regarding the age of responsibility. As the law now stands no child under eight years old can be convicted of a criminal offence. A child between the age of eight and fourteen years cannot be found guilty of an offence, unless he can be shown to have understood that what he was doing was seriously wrong. There is a presumption in favour of such a child that he is incapable of committing a crime, but this presumption can be rebutted by showing that he knew that his act was wrong. In such a case his knowledge makes up for his lack of age.

Clearly, no one would wish to subject young children to the full rigours of the criminal law. Many young children have not sufficiently developed and acquired the ability to distinguish between right and wrong. Moreover, the publicity of proceedings in an ordinary Criminal Court and the kinds of punishment to which ordinary criminals are subjected may not be the best way of ensuring that a potentially delinquent child should develop into a good, law-abiding citizen. In a child's early years the responsibility for ensuring this should rest, most people would agree, primarily on his parents. This attitude of the criminal law appears to be based primarily on the child's inability to distinguish right and wrong. It is not entirely clear what is meant by 'wrong' in this context; whether it means that the child must know that what he is doing is legally wrong, or that he must know that it is morally wrong. The latter would seem to be, on the whole, a preferable interpretation.

While the lack of such knowledge is one very good reason for exempting a young child from responsibility, there would seem to be another ground which is entirely ignored by the law. We do not normally expect young children to resist temptation to the same extent as we expect adults. Children should be allowed time, not only for their knowledge of right and wrong to develop, but also for their ability to do what is right in the face of temptation. English law, however, makes no provision for this.

In the opinion of many people eight years is far too low an age to hold a child guilty of crime and label him as a criminal. In many countries the age of responsibility is higher. In France it is thirteen, in Germany and Austria fourteen, in Denmark and Sweden fifteen. The *Ingleby Committee*[1] on considering this question recommended in 1960 that the age should be raised to twelve. By this they did not intend that people under twelve should be able to commit crimes with absolute impunity. Even children under eight, as the law stands today, are not in this position. A child of six or seven who is found stealing cannot be prosecuted for this, but the circumstances may enable him to be brought before a Juvenile Court as being in need of care or protection, or as being beyond control. This non-criminal jurisdiction of the Juvenile Courts is more aptly dealt with in connexion with the constitution and procedure of such courts.

One curious provision of English law is that a person attains an age on the day preceding his birthday. If, for instance, a boy was born on 1 January 1950 we should say that he was eight on 1 January 1958, but for legal purposes he reaches this age on 31 December 1957.

[1] October 1960, Cmnd. 1191.

(b) Insanity

Insanity raises for the lawyer the problem of reconciling the principle of equality before the law with the need to protect society and indeed the insane themselves against their insanity. The civil law contains special rules relating to the legal capacity of lunatics to make valid wills and to enter into binding agreements. The Mental Health Act, 1959, provides for the detention of the mentally ill under certain conditions. In criminal law the insanity of the accused is relevant in three different respects. It affects his fitness to stand trial, his fitness to undergo punishment, and his responsibility for the commission of a crime.

One essential requirement for a fair trial is the ability of the accused to understand and follow the proceedings. An accused who is found to lack this ability cannot in English law be tried, but must be detained until he is fit to plead. The question whether a defendant is fit to plead is a matter which must be decided, if it arises, as a preliminary point by the jury. A person charged with a comparatively minor offence would be unlikely to raise the matter, as he might well prefer a short prison sentence to indeterminate detention. Even in the case of a more serious accusation a defendant might be reluctant to claim that he was unfit to plead, as there might be good evidence to show that he was not guilty. A problem not yet finally decided is whether, if it appears to the court that the defendant may be unfit to plead, this matter must be determined first regardless of the defendant's wishes; or whether the defendant by refusing to claim that he is unfit to plead must be permitted to try and secure an acquittal on the substantive charge. The first solution would seem logically preferable, but savours of injustice in so far as it debars a possibly innocent defendant from disputing the main charge.[1]

A defendant's inability to follow the proceedings will usually arise from insanity. It might, however, stem from mere inability to communicate, as would be the case of a deaf-mute with whom contact were impossible. The case of *Podola* (1959)[2] established that retrogressive amnesia was not a factor which

---

[1] In *R. v. Roberts* (1953), 37 Cr. App. Rep. 86, it has been held that the general issue could be considered without reference to the question of the defendant's fitness to plead. In *R. v. Beynon*, [1957] 2 Q.B. 111, however, Byrne J. refused to follow this case and held that the question of fitness to plead must be considered first.

[2] *R. v. Podola*, [1960] 1 Q.B. 325.

would render a defendant unfit to plead. Podola, accused of the capital murder of a policeman, claimed that he was suffering from amnesia such that he was entirely unable to remember the incident in question, and that accordingly he could not properly instruct his lawyers and make a proper defence. The court's ground for ruling out this plea was that, even if the jury had believed the accused, he was still able to understand and follow the trial. The apparent harshness of trying a man whose lack of memory may prevent him from raising valid defences of accident, self-defence, or provocation, is mitigated by the fact that a jury which believed him to be suffering from amnesia would no doubt be directed by the judge to exercise extreme caution and to take account of the possible existence of defences which the accused himself could not substantiate.

The relevance of a prisoner's insanity to the question of his treatment is due partly to the fact that any penal system which attaches any importance to the aim of reforming the criminal must consider the mental state of a prisoner in order to decide on the most suitable treatment for him, and must also take account of the effect on ordinary prisoners of having insane inmates confined in the same institution with them. Under our prison system any convicted prisoner diagnosed by the prison medical officer as a lunatic or mental defective must be certified and removed as soon as possible to an appropriate institution. The need to treat such people differently and separately from ordinary criminals has been recognized in the Mental Health Act, 1959, which empowers a court, in any case other than one involving a fixed penalty, to authorize the detention and admission of a mentally ill defendant to a mental hospital. Magistrates' Courts have this power in trials for offences punishable by Magistrates' Courts with imprisonment.

The restrictions due to insanity on the punishment which can be inflicted is well exemplified in the rule which provides that a person under sentence of death cannot be executed while insane. Instead, he must be detained until he recovers, but in fact will not be executed if he does. There are many possible reasons which can be adduced to support this rule. The prisoner's insanity might prevent him from clearing himself by some new evidence at the very last moment. On religious grounds there is the strongest objection to executing a man incapable of preparing himself properly for death. On moral grounds there seems to be something repellent in the idea of punishing a person who no longer appreciates what is being done to him. Such reasons justify the existence of the Home Secretary's power to appoint a statutory inquiry to determine the sanity of any prisoner under sentence of death and to substitute, if necessary, an order that the prisoner be confined in Broadmoor or be reprieved.

Most interest has naturally centred on the relevance of the accused's insanity to the question of his criminal responsibility. Here we are concerned with the accused's state of mind not at the time of trial or punishment, but at the time he committed the offence. If the accused succeeds in making out a defence of insanity, he is acquitted but is ordered to be detained at Her Majesty's pleasure in Broadmoor, a mental hospital in Berkshire, until he is fit for release. Since this means that he may be locked up for ever, a defendant will usually raise such a defence only where it is worth his while, e.g. when the alternative is the death penalty; and his advisers may not raise it without his consent. At one time it was thought that the prosecution was debarred from raising the question of insanity. The recent development of the defence of automatism ('my act was involuntary, therefore there was no *actus reus*') and the introduction in 1957 of the defence of diminished responsibility, have led judges to direct that where the defence rests on either of these bases, the prosecution may lead evidence as to the accused's insanity.[1] Since automatism would result in acquittal and since diminished responsibility would give the judge a discretion as to sentence, it is only reasonable that in the public interest a person suffering from either of these misfortunes should, if he is also insane, be dealt with as insane and confined in Broadmoor.

It is unfortunate that the jury's verdict in such cases is expressed as 'guilty but insane', because this obscures the fact that in reality the defendant is being absolved from blame. The reason for this form of words is purely historical. Originally the verdict was 'Not guilty because insane' but was altered at the wish of Queen Victoria. The present form of the verdict does not, however, alter the fact that it is an acquittal, and so a verdict from which there is no appeal by either side.

The rules for determining whether a defendant is to be

[1] *R. v. Kemp*, [1957] 1 Q.B. 399; *R. v. Bastian*, [1958] 1 All E.R. 568.

exonerated on the ground of insanity were laid down by the judges in answers given to questions put to them by the House of Lords. One M'Naghten, labouring under the delusion that he was the victim of persecution, tried to terminate his misfortune by assassinating Sir Robert Peel, and in mistake for the Prime Minister killed the latter's secretary, Drummond. The widespread dissatisfaction aroused by his acquittal led to a debate in the House of Lords, which resulted in the formulation in 1843 of the M'Naghten Rules.

The Rules lay down first that everyone is presumed sane unless the contrary is proved. This means that (except in the two cases referred to above) it is for the defendant to prove that he is insane. He need not, however, establish this beyond reasonable doubt, but need only show that the balance of probabilities is that he is insane.

Secondly, the Rules describe the categories of person who may be exonerated on the ground of insanity. The defendant must at the time of the crime have been suffering from a defect of reason due to a disease of the mind, such that he either did not realize the nature and quality of his act or did not realize that the act was wrong. If the defendant was suffering from a partial delusion, his responsibility must be assessed in the light of the facts as he imagined them to be.

The Rules do not provide tests of insanity. They provide extra tests to determine whether an insane person shall be exonerated. Before the further tests as to knowledge of the nature or wrongfulness of the act can be applied, it must first be shown that the accused was suffering from a defect of reason due to a disease of the mind. Accordingly, it was often said that the class of legally insane was a sub-class of the medically insane. This proposition is no longer accurate in the light of the case of *Kemp* (1956).[1] Accused of causing grievous bodily harm to his wife, the defendant pleaded that he was suffering from automatism resulting from arterio-sclerosis. The judge, directing the prosecution to put before the jury evidence to show that the accused came within the M'Naghten Rules, instructed the jury that the words 'disease of the mind' did not mean that only mental diseases could qualify to put the accused within the Rules, but that these words were there to exclude defects of reason due to 'brutish stupidity'. Today, therefore, it may well be that the class of legally insane for this purpose includes some who would not qualify as medically insane. What is not clear is whether it would include persons whose mental development has been congenitally arrested or retarded. While dementia and psychosis appear to be within the Rules, amentia from inherent causes, e.g. the case of the idiot, imbecile, and feeble-minded, is not clearly included.

The M'Naghten Rules, with their emphasis on reason and their entire disregard of emotion, reflect the times in which they were formulated. Despite the advances made in psychiatry and the increase in our knowledge of the workings of the human mind, the criminal law relating to insanity is wedded to a scientific conception at least a century out of date. Nothing makes this more evident than does the failure of the Rules to provide for the case of the man whose insanity prevents him neither from understanding what he is doing nor from realizing that his conduct is wrong, but whose emotional disturbance results in his no longer having complete control over his behaviour. Many have advocated that the law of insanity should be altered to take account of irresistible impulse.[1] Medical objection to this suggestion is largely based on the view that this would only allow for acts done on the spur of the moment, whereas an amended law of insanity should also provide for acts which are not impulsive in this ordinary sense but which result from a continued state of emotional disorder. Objection has also been raised by psychiatrists on the ground that every criminal act is impulsive and that all that is meant by saying that it results from irresistible impulse is that the impulse is not resisted. But the idea of the suggested defence of irresistible impulse is that the accused gave way to an urge which a sane man could have resisted, but which the accused could not, because of his insanity, resist. To say that the impulse was irresistible is to claim more than just that it was not resisted. Over and above the fact that the urge was not resisted, other evidence can be given to show that the accused lacked the ability to resist it. Such evidence might consist in the fact that he had very good reasons for not acting as he did, e.g. because a policeman was standing beside him; that he had no good

[1] See *Report of Royal Commission on Capital Punishment* (1953), Cmd. 8932, pp. 79–81, 82–83, 87–88, 93–96, 105–12.

reason for acting as he did, e.g. he was already plentifully
supplied with articles like the ones he stole; that in the past he
had in similar circumstances given way to the impulse; that
before committing the crime in question he had said that he
felt just such an impulse and could not resist it. These and other
things are the matters relevant to the question whether the
impulse was irresistible. The defence of irresistible impulse by
no means involves us in drawing the unjustified conclusion that
it was irresistible merely because it was not resisted. Provision
for irresistible impulse has in fact been made by the defence of
diminished responsibility, introduced by the Homicide Act,
1957.

Of the two tests laid down by the M'Naghten Rules the first
is such that it is doubtful whether it would apply to anyone.
The accused must be suffering from a defect of reason due to
a disease of the mind such that he did not know the nature and
quality of his act. The examples usually given of this are the
case of a woman sawing off her child's head thinking it is a loaf
of bread, and the case of a man strangling a woman thinking
he is squeezing a lemon. According to the leading authorities on
medical jurisprudence the existence of such forms of insanity is
nothing but a legal fiction.[1]

The second test, however, provides for the case of the man
who realizes what he is doing, but whose insanity prevents him
from realizing that his act is wrong. Originally, when formulat-
ing the rules, the judges were reluctant to suggest that the
defendant's responsibility should depend on whether he realized
that his act was contrary to the criminal law, because this would
mean that knowledge of the criminal law would be a necessary
prerequisite of his guilt. Ignorance of law is in general irrelevant
to criminal responsibility; and indeed it would be an odd result
if a man were to be exempt from guilt and placed within the
M'Naghten Rules if, for example, he looked up the law on
murder but misunderstood it because of his want of reason.
What the judges seem to have had in mind was the case of the
insane man who, without knowing the law, realizes that the
act is morally wrong. Such a man's ignorance of law would no
more entitle him to make out a defence of insanity than the
sane criminal's ignorance of law entitles him to escape legal

---

[1] Taylor's *Principles and Practice of Medical Jurisprudence* (11th edn.), p. 578.

punishment. Accordingly, the judges stated, in answer to the Lords, that if the insane man was conscious that the act was one which he ought not to do, and if the act was contrary to law, he was punishable. What they did not fully consider was the case of the man who realizes that his act is contrary to law but does not think that it is morally wrong. We have seen that the law will not allow the citizen to substitute for its provisions his own private code; the citizen is not allowed to be wiser than the law. Whether this principle should apply to debar, for example, the lunatic who thinks that in breaking the law he is acting in obedience to divine voices, from raising a defence of insanity is questionable. That it does so apply, however, is established by the case of *Windle* (1952).[1] The accused, a feeble-minded man, killed his wife by giving her a large number of aspirins, realizing that this was contrary to law but thinking that it was beneficial for her and therefore not morally wrong. It was held that in such a case the defendant's own notions of right and wrong are irrelevant; his knowledge that his act was legally wrong prevented him from coming within the M'Naghten Rules. It seems then that the defendant will be outside the Rules if he knows that his act is morally or legally wrong. To hold fully responsible for their actions mentally abnormal people who break the law in obedience to the dictates of their own warped consciences is, in the writer's view, wholly unjustifiable.

The rule relating to insane delusion has been a frequent target for criticism. In the first place medical experts deny the existence of partial insanity, and claim that a disease which interferes with the workings of the mind in one respect will also affect the subject's motives and emotions generally. Secondly, there is obvious ground for objecting to a rule which ordains that a man suffering from an insane delusion must be judged as if the facts were what he imagined them to be. According to the rule, the accused would escape responsibility for killing a man whom he insanely imagined to be putting him to death by electronic waves; for if the facts were as imagined, the accused could make out a plea of self-defence. If, however, he killed the deceased because he insanely imagined that the deceased was depriving him of his reputation by magic, he would not come

---

[1] *R. v. Windle*, [1952] 2 Q.B. 826. The Australian High Court refused to adopt this rule in *R. v. Stapleton*, [1952] A.L.R. 929.

within the Rules; for here he would have no defence even if the
facts had been as imagined. Yet in both the examples given
above the defendant is equally insane and equally lacking in
responsibility for his behaviour. To differentiate between them
seems totally unjust. As the law stands, the Rules demand that
the accused show method in his madness. It has been well said
that he must be reasonable in his unreason, sane in his insanity.[1]

A further criticism often levelled by medical men at the lawyer's
attempts to grapple with the problem of insanity is that the diag-
nosis of mental illness is far too complex and difficult for a jury
of non-medicals to comprehend, and is a matter totally unsuited
to the partisan procedure of the English criminal trial with its
ritual of examination, cross-examination, and re-examination
of expert witnesses. On the other hand, where life and liberty
are at stake, the accused has by law a right that his responsibility
should be decided by a jury. Experts may give their opinions,
but only the jury may decide. Unless popular feeling were content to hand this matter over to a panel of experts, the procedure
must remain. At present there would seem to be little support
for what is termed 'trial by doctors'.

(c) Diminished Responsibility

The unduly antiquated and restrictive nature of the M'Naghten Rules was a cause of widespread dissatisfaction. In one context provision had been made for mental unbalance which
would not amount to insanity within the Rules. The creation of
the crime of *infanticide* by the Infanticide Act, 1922 (now replaced by the Infanticide Act, 1938), enabled a verdict of guilty
of infanticide to be returned whenever a woman, accused of the
murder of her child, being under twelve months, was suffering
at the time of the crime from disturbance of her balance of mind
as a result of the birth or of lactation. This new offence was
made punishable to the same extent as manslaughter.

In 1957 the Homicide Act, section 2, introduced into English
law a defence already well-established in Scots law, the defence of
diminished responsibility. This is a defence only to a charge of
murder and operates to reduce the offence to manslaughter,
enabling the judge to pass any sentence up to the maximum of
life imprisonment instead of being obliged to pass the fixed

[1] Maudsley, quoted by Glanville Williams, *Criminal Law* (1st edn.), p. 333.

sentence for murder. As in the defence of insanity, the burden
of proof lies on the defendant, but diminished responsibility is
in other respects more attractive to him than insanity. If he
is found guilty but insane he faces the possibility of lifelong
confinement in Broadmoor, whereas if he escapes on a plea of
diminished responsibility, he is liable at the most to life imprisonment,which in fact means on the average nine years, though
the practice of releasing after nine years will in all probability not
apply to those sentenced for life under this section of the Act.
This is by no means satisfactory so far as the public interest is
concerned, because whether the defendant's mental illness
brings him within the M'Naghten Rules or not, he may be
equally dangerous if left at large. Accordingly, where the defence is diminished responsibility, the judges have ruled that
the prosecution may adduce evidence to show that the accused
is within the M'Naghten Rules.

   To succeed in making good this defence the accused must
show that he was suffering from 'such abnormality of mind
(whether arising from a condition of arrested or retarded development of mind or any inherent causes or induced by disease
or injury) as substantially impaired his mental responsibility' for
his behaviour. Clearly this defence extends to *amentia* (arrested
or incomplete development of mind from inherent disease or
injury) and to *dementia* (structural damage, disease, or degener-
ation of the brain and nervous tissue). Whether it also extends
to *psychosis* (functional insanity, impairment of contact with
reality, not due to defect or structural damage) and to the case of
the psychopath would seem to depend on whether the words in
parenthesis are taken to be exhaustive of the types of abnormality
of mind to which the defence refers. In the event, however, the
courts have avoided interpreting the section in a narrow sense.
In *R. v. Byrne*[1] the defence of diminished responsibility was held
to apply in the case of a sexual psychopath, who had strangled
a girl while under the influence of violent perverted sexual desires. The court asserted that the words 'abnormality of mind'
mean a state of mind so different from that of ordinary human
beings that the reasonable man would term it 'abnormal'; and
that they are wide enough to cover not only the perception of
physical matters and the ability to form a rational judgment as

[1] [1960] 2 Q.B. 396.

to whether an act is right or wrong, but also the ability to exercise will-power to control physical acts in accordance with that rational judgment. Furthermore, the court declared that inability to exercise will power, due to abnormality of mind from one of the causes specified in the parenthesis, is sufficient to entitle the accused to the defence of diminished responsibility; and that difficulty in controlling his physical acts, depending on the degree of difficulty, may be sufficient.

In practice this new defence has enjoyed considerable success. It has been calculated that in the first twenty-seven months of its operation it was raised in seventy-three cases and succeeded in fifty-three of these.[1] Juries, therefore, have shown no reluctance to find that a defendant is suffering from diminished responsibility. The retreat which this defence involves from the purely intellectual criteria of the M'Naghten Rules, however, has been strongly criticized.[2] Three main criticisms have been levelled against the new defence. In the first place it is said that the lack of criteria of responsibility independent of the actual commission of the offence results in a vicious circle, whereby we argue from the fact that a horrible crime was committed to the conclusion that the culprit must have been lacking in responsibility to commit it. We are also, it is urged, involved in making a leap in the dark from the fact that the accused did not control himself to the unwarrantable assertion that he could not control himself. Secondly, the practice whereby the worse the defendant's past record, the more likely he is to succeed in a defence of diminished responsibility, is held up as a paradoxical exception to the normal rule that the worse the record, the heavier the sentence. Finally, it is suggested that in the event the public is liable to be insufficiently protected if the more dangerous the criminal is, the more likely he is to succeed in this novel defence.

The first criticism is by far the most interesting as well as the most misconceived. The new defence is contrasted with the old defence of insanity, under which the accused had to show either that he did not know the nature and quality of his act or that he did not know that the act was wrong. These tests of responsibility are claimed to be independent of the commission of the offence in a way in which the tests under the Homicide Act, section 2, are not. The argument is that, in trying to show under

[1] e.g. Barbara Wootton, 76 *L.Q.R.* 224 (1960).　　　[2] Ibid.

section 2 that he suffers from an abnormality of mind such as substantially impairs his responsibility, the accused relies partly on the very fact that he committed the crime and possibly other similar crimes. Once this is allowed, it is open to any murderer to deny responsibility for his crime by claiming 'I must have been beside myself to do a thing like that'. In fact, however, the defence in such cases does not rely solely on the fact that the accused committed the crime. Considerable other evidence is adduced as to the accused's previous mental history, his behaviour on other occasions, together with what he said before and after the event. The sort of evidence which is likely to substantiate a defence of diminished responsibility is evidence that the act was performed in circumstances where the agent had nothing to gain and everything to lose from its performance. This would be some evidence of abnormality since generally human beings do not act in a manner directly contrary to their own interests. Further evidence of relevance would be that in similar circumstances on previous occasions the accused had given way to impulses to which ordinary people do not give way. The attack on diminished responsibility, like the objection to irresistible impulse, obscures the distinction between the merely wicked and those who cannot help themselves, e.g. between the habitual thief and the kleptomaniac. The difference between the thief and the kleptomaniac is that the latter continues stealing in circumstances where the former would desist, e.g. where he is already plentifully supplied with the goods, where the theft cannot escape detection, &c.

Nevertheless, it is claimed that we are still making a leap in the dark. The fact that an impulse was not resisted by no means warrants the assertion that it was irresistible, and evidence that on several occasions the accused failed to control himself does not prove that he was unable to do so. While behaviour is observable, culpability is hidden from our view. This is in reality a facet of a well-known sceptical position in philosophy about the problem of other minds. Whether we can ever really know what goes on in another's mind, and if so how, is a central problem for philosophers. Sceptics have frequently stressed that thoughts are not observable like actions. However clear it may seem that Smith thought the money was his, intended only to keep it if it was his, and so on, we may be deceived; perhaps his whole life has been a lie. In everyday practical affairs, on the other hand, we are continually forced to decide questions involving problems about what other people know, feel, think, or intend. Juries have to determine whether the accused meant to kill the deceased, whether Smith really thought the goods he took belonged to him, whether Jones broke into the house with intent to commit a felony inside. In such cases they answer these questions after considering the evidence; they look at what the defendant did, what he may have said (especially when caught by the police), and they consider how an ordinary innocent person would have behaved in the defendant's position. Though it is often far from easy to decide these questions, and doubt has to be resolved in favour of the accused in English law, no one has seriously suggested that all the juries throughout the country are deciding the undecidable. Again, many of the defences which we have considered are open to criticism from the sceptic but have caused no serious misgivings in practice. If a plea of provocation is advanced, the jury must decide whether the accused actually was provoked; on a defence of duress, whether he was really in fear of the coercer; on a defence of mistake, whether he was really unaware that the facts were as they were. The seemingly straightforward defence of physical compulsion is in the same case. A may establish that B seized his arm and applied force to it and that the arm then struck C. But where is the proof that A tried to resist? Even the defence of insanity within the M'Naghten Rules raises the same difficulty. The defendant may act just as if he did not know the nature or quality of his act and all the doctors may agree that he comes within the Rules, but perhaps he was fooling them all the time. Whether or not he really knew is hidden from all but divine eyes.

The defence of diminished responsibility then, though imposing a hard burden on the criminal jury, is not based on a complete misconception, nor need it in practice give rise to any more sceptical doubts as to unjustified leaps in the dark than do the defences of provocation, duress, mistake, and many others. But the paradox still remains that the worse the defendant's record is, the more likely is he to succeed in the defence of diminished responsibility. This means that a murderer who can show that throughout his life he has been given to attacks of violence may get a lighter sentence than one who has hitherto led a blameless life, and this runs counter to the general practice, which is surely right, that the worse the record, the heavier the sentence. After all, the first offender is usually treated more leniently than the habitual criminal. Yet the paradox is dissolved if we reflect that there may be no good reason to demand that the same scheme of things which operates within the ambit of crimes committed by the mentally normal should also apply to those committed by the mentally abnormal. The practice of imposing a heavier sentence on the old lag in the normal case can be justified on several grounds. By persisting in crime he has shown that his previous punishments were insufficient to deter him and failed to effect a reformation, while his persistent flouting of the law is more culpable morally than one isolated offence. But if the persistent violation of the law could be shown to result from some abnormality of mind, then it would clearly be outrageous to apply the usual rule of practice to the case. Where mental abnormality impairs responsibility, treatment of the abnormality and incarceration to protect the public are admissible, but to punish the offender as though he were fully responsible would be quite unjustifiable.

Whereas the penalty for murder is either death or life imprisonment, a defendant who makes out a defence of diminished responsibility is convicted of manslaughter. This means that the court has a discretion to impose any sentence up to life imprisonment. In practice the courts have frequently imposed lighter sentences. In thirty-six of the fifty-three cases previously referred to, where the defence was successful, a lesser sentence than life imprisonment was imposed. From this it appears that those more likely to commit crimes are liable to be returned to the community more quickly than those with less fixed criminal propensities, and the protection of the public suffers. Provided, however, that the courts are careful to take into account the question of the protection of the public—and judges have not been notorious for overlooking this factor—there is every reason to expect that the most dangerous of those convicted under section 2 will be detained the longest.

(d) Drunkenness

Drunkenness was always regarded by moralists as one of the deadly sins because of its being a fertile source of other sins. At

one time in English law it was a separate offence by itself,
punishable by the stocks. Later, after it ceased to be an offence, it
was considered an aggravation of other criminal offences. Today
there is a tendency to think that drunkenness should count
as an excuse. In English criminal law, however, drunkenness is
generally no defence.

A distinction must be made, however, between voluntary and
involuntary drunkenness. If a man's friends make him drunk
for a joke, then his subsequent conduct can hardly with justice
be laid at his own door. The law has always taken the view that
intoxication in no way due to the defendant's own fault exempts
him completely. Quite what is covered by involuntary drunkenness, however, is not certain. Intoxication resulting from the
acts of others, as in the example above, is clearly within this
category.

When the defendant's intoxication is due to his own fault, generally it will afford him no defence. There are, however, two types
of situation where even this voluntary drunkenness may serve to
acquit an accused. Where alcohol reduces him to a condition
in which he is wholly unable to appreciate what he is doing (as
with delirium tremens), his case is treated on the same footing
as the case of insanity. Should the defendant convince the jury
that on account of intoxication he was temporarily insane, then
he is entitled to a verdict of guilty but insane, resulting in detention in Broadmoor. The result of the success of this plea explains
the rarity of its incidence.

Secondly, it may be that though the accused was not so intoxicated as not to know the nature and quality of his act, yet he
was unable to form the specific intent required by the crime in
question. To take another man's property, while under the influence of alcohol, may fall short of larceny if the accused is acting
in a drunken haze and has no real intent to deprive the true
owner permanently of the property. Such an intent to defraud
or to deceive is the type of intent whose formation may most
often be prevented by drink. It may also be that the defendant
acted under a mistake which he would not have made had he
been sober. Intoxication may lead him to mistake a helping hand
for a brutal attack and to retaliate by way of self-defence. In
such a case the defendant's responsibility would have to be
decided in the light of the facts as he imagined them to be.

On the other hand, intoxication is no excuse in law for loss of control. If the defendant's drunkenness led him to give way more readily to his anger than he would have done if sober, intoxication is no defence. The reason is that in the defence relevant to this type of case, viz., provocation, the accused must satisfy the jury that a reasonable man would have done the same as he did in the circumstances. Clearly if a reasonable man would have been provoked to do what the accused did, then his inebriation is of no account. On the other hand, if a reasonable man would not so have acted then it does not avail the accused to argue that a reasonable man would so have acted if he had been intoxicated; for the law does not allow the concept of 'the reasonable drunk'. In such a case the defendant gets drunk at his peril.[1]

Moreover, the Inebriates Acts, which relate to 'habitual drunkards' and 'inebriates', empower the courts to take special measures in respect of persons whose intemperate drinking renders them a danger to themselves or others, and to order them to be detained at 'inebriate reformatories'. This, however, is outside the scope of this work.

[1] *R.* v. *McCarthy*, [1954] 2 Q.B. 105.

V

THE CRIMINAL LAW AT WORK

THE rules of criminal law so far discussed limit the activities of the citizen. The rules of procedure and evidence now to be considered limit the activities of those institutions of society which are concerned with the prevention of crime. For the rules governing the procedure to be followed in criminal trials and the powers of the police in the matter of investigation and arrest set boundaries to what may lawfully be done by policeman, prosecutor, and judge.

Important though it is to prevent crimes, we should not expect a society to pursue this objective to the complete disregard of all other interests. The aim of crime prevention in a free society is part of the larger aim of producing a society in which the citizen can fulfil himself in the pursuit of his individual happiness, free from want, disease, and external interference. The pursuit of this aim naturally entails some measure of state interference with individual liberty. But unless a society is careful to keep a check on the measure of interference, it may end by losing more in the way of liberty than it gains in freedom from want, disease, and crime.

The war against crime has been waged for a much longer time than those against want and disease. It is not surprising, therefore, to find in existence a whole variety of rules which serve to protect the interests of the individual and to ensure that in its pursuit of the narrower aim of crime prevention the state should not forget the wider objectives outlined above. These rules may be examined under three broad headings. First there are those rules which protect the liberty of the individual by setting limits to the jurisdiction of the criminal law and by restricting the powers of police and other investigators. The second group of rules serves to secure a fair trial for an accused person and to prevent miscarriage of justice. The third set of rules is concerned with ensuring that the authorities should treat all people, whether suspected, accused, or convicted, in a humane manner and should not fall below standards of behaviour dictated by civilization and respect for human dignity.

Before examining these rules, however, we must first consider briefly the course of criminal proceedings, starting with the moment when it is decided to launch a prosecution and ending with the sentencing of the defendant.

I. THE COURSE OF CRIMINAL PROCEEDINGS

Once it has been decided to prosecute a person, the first problem is to secure his appearance before a court. In England there are three ways of securing the defendant's attendance. The method most frequently employed is to apply to a magistrate for a *summons*. The prosecutor appears before a magistrate and 'lays an information' orally or in writing; in other words he informs the magistrate of the name of the defendant and of the offence which he is alleged to have committed. Thereupon the magistrate, if he thinks fit, will issue a summons directed to the defendant ordering him to appear before a Magistrates' Court on a certain day and informing him of the offence with which he is charged. If the offence is so serious that the defendant cannot be trusted to appear in answer to a summons, or if the defendant refuses to answer the summons, the magistrate will issue a *warrant* for his arrest. The prosecutor lays an information in writing and on oath, whereupon the magistrate will issue a warrant directed to all the police officers within his jurisdiction ordering them to apprehend the defendant and bring him before a Magistrates' Court on a certain day to answer the charge specified in the warrant. In some cases it is imperative to act immediately and arrest the defendant without a warrant, and the police and even private citizens have power to effect such arrests under certain circumstances which we shall consider later. This constitutes the third method of securing the defendant's appearance before the court.

Once the defendant is before the court, the question arises where he is to be tried. Certain very serious offences, such as murder, rape, and crimes involving special legal difficulty, must be tried before a jury on indictment in a higher court. The majority of offences can only be dealt with summarily in a Magistrates' Court. In between these two categories comes a third category where the defendant may either be tried by the magistrates or by a jury. Many indictable offences, such as larceny, have been allowed by law in the interests of expedition to be tried by magistrates if the accused consents. On the other hand, all summary offences which can be punished with three months' imprisonment or more, must, if the accused wishes, be tried by jury in deference to the principle that no one should suffer loss of liberty without being tried by his peers.

In this third category of offences, therefore, the defendant has a choice of being tried by the magistrates or being tried on indictment. The advice usually given by lawyers to their clients in such cases is that there is more chance of an acquittal in front of a jury, but that the sentence awarded by a magistrate will probably be less than that awarded by a higher court, since magistrates have only limited powers of sentence. The maximum sentence they can inflict is one of six months' imprisonment, though a client with a bad record should be informed that if a Magistrates' Court considers on conviction that the case justifies a heavier penalty, they may commit the defendant to Quarter Sessions for sentence.

By far the greatest number of offenders are tried in the Magistrates' Courts. In 1960 out of a total of 1,035,212 recorded convictions 1,007,382 were recorded by Magistrates' Courts. Such courts consist of non-lawyers appointed for each county and for most large towns by the Lord Chancellor on the recommendation of local committees. Unqualified and unpaid, they rely for legal advice on their clerk, a qualified lawyer. In London and many of our larger cities stipendiary magistrates have been appointed to sit full-time. These are qualified lawyers, usually barristers of seven years' standing; they are paid, and unlike lay magistrates they sit alone and not as a bench of magistrates. The chief magistrate, who has exclusive jurisdiction over questions of extradition and certain other matters, sits in Bow Street, the successor of the Fieldings.

Since 1957 an amendment in the law has provided for the defendant's presence to be dispensed with in certain cases, in order to increase the speed of proceedings and to save the defendant unnecessary trouble.[1] This amendment relates to offences which cannot be tried on indictment and to which the defendant wishes to plead guilty in his absence. In such cases the summons is accompanied with a statement of facts which the prosecution intends to put before the court. If the defendant

[1] Magistrates' Courts Act, 1957, s. 1.

sends the court written notice of his intention to plead guilty without appearing, the case may proceed in his absence.

Normally, however, the defendant is present before the court and the procedure is as follows. The clerk reads the charge to him, and the defendant thereupon pleads guilty or not guilty. A plea of guilty shortens the proceedings greatly. The prosecution or prosecuting lawyer outlines the facts of the case to the court and puts before them the defendant's previous convictions if any. The defendant is allowed to cross-examine the officer who has given evidence of his record, and may then give evidence himself or say anything he wishes to the court. The court thereupon passes sentence, or remands the defendant in order to make further inquiries, or, as we saw, may commit the defendant for sentence to Quarter Sessions.

A plea of not guilty forces the prosecution to prove its case. Each witness is sworn, examined by the prosecution, cross-examined by the defendant or his legal representative, and re-examined by the prosecution. At the close of the prosecution case the defendant can give evidence on oath, he can call witnesses, and the same procedure of examination, cross-examination, and re-examination applies. The defendant may, however, if he wishes, say nothing; or he may make an unsworn statement from the dock, on which he cannot be cross-examined. After the close of the defence's case, and after speeches by each side (the rules relating to which are too complex to warrant discussion here) the court comes to its decision. A bench of lay magistrates decides according to the majority vote. In the event of the votes being equally divided, the case must be reheard by a new bench. If the court finds the defendant not guilty, he is discharged. If he is convicted, the court hears the evidence as to his past record and anything which the defendant may wish to say in mitigation, before passing sentence.

Proceedings in the Magistrates' Courts are quick and informal. As often as not the parties appear in person. The prosecutor, usually a police officer, conducts the prosecution case and the defendant is his own advocate. Both sides can, however, be represented by counsel, and, unlike in the higher courts, by a solicitor. Even where there is legal representation, the proceedings are accompanied by none of the ceremonial trimmings to be found at Quarter Sessions and Assizes, such as wigs and gowns.

If the offence is to be tried on indictment, the duty of the Magistrates' Court is to hold a preliminary investigation. This differs from the procedure just discussed in several ways. In the first place the court is not concerned to decide whether the defendant is guilty or not, but merely whether there is enough evidence to justify his being sent for trial. For this reason the defendant is not asked to plead to the charge. Secondly, the evidence of each witness must be taken down in writing, read over to him, and signed by him in the presence of the court and the accused. At the end of the hearing all the depositions so taken are signed by one of the magistrates. Should the court decide that there is enough evidence to warrant committing the defendant for trial, they will commit him, if the case is a serious or difficult one, to Assizes, and in other cases to Quarter Sessions. In this case the depositions will be forwarded to the appropriate court, copies being supplied to the prosecution and defence, and the witnesses bound over to appear at the trial. If the Magistrates' Court is not satisfied that the defendant has a case to answer, they will refuse to commit and will discharge the prisoner.

Before the institution of regular police forces the preliminary investigation fulfilled the function now performed by police inquiries. Today, however, its purpose is to sift out cases where the evidence justifies the trial of the defendant from the cases where there is insufficient evidence against him to warrant committal. Since Magistrates' Courts are loath to refuse to commit for trial, the value of such proceedings is doubtful. The amount of time devoted to recording evidence, all of which must be given again at the trial, imposes a heavy burden on Magistrates' Courts. The publicity sometimes aroused at the investigation makes it difficult to obtain a fair trial before an impartial jury. The main result of this system is that the defendant in a trial on indictment has advance notice of all the evidence which the prosecution intend to call against him, while the prosecution is left in the dark as to the defence which he means to raise.

On committing the defendant for trial, the magistrates remand the defendant in custody or release him on bail, and authorize the prosecution to prefer a bill of indictment. The indictment is a written (or printed) accusation against the defendant at the suit of the Crown—hence the name of a criminal case on indictment begins with the words 'The Queen v.——.' It contains a statement of the offence or offences charged, together with particulars thereof. In difficult cases the indictment may be drafted by solicitor or counsel, and it is signed by the Clerk of Assize or Clerk of the Peace (i.e. Clerk of Quarter Sessions), as the case may be. The importance of the indictment is that, with certain exceptions, the trial is confined to the offences contained in it. If the defendant is indicted for arson he cannot be found guilty of some other offence such as robbery or burglary.

The most serious indictable offences must go to the Assizes. An Assize Court consists of a commissioner, usually a High Court judge, appointed by letters patent. The country is divided into circuits, Assizes being held in each county and in some large towns on the circuit. In London the Central Criminal Court in the Old Bailey is the permanent Assize Court. Lesser offences are triable at Quarter Sessions, which are held in each county and in many larger towns. County Quarter Sessions consist of county magistrates sitting in Quarter Sessions, usually presided over by a legally qualified chairman, who is paid for his services. Borough or City Quarter Sessions consists of a legally qualified recorder, who sits without other magistrates and is remunerated. Recorders and legally qualified chairmen are usually practising barristers, who perform these public duties part-time. In London, Liverpool, and Manchester, however, there exist permanent sessions, where the judges are full-time officials.

The proceedings begin with the clerk's reading the indictment to the defendant, who then pleads guilty or not guilty. The majority of cases consist of pleas of guilty. The procedure is very similar to that following a plea of guilty in a Magistrates' Court, except that the prosecution must be represented by counsel, since, except for the defendant, who may always be his own advocate, only barristers have the right of audience in these courts. If the defendant pleads guilty to a crime carrying a fixed penalty, such as murder, nothing remains but for sentence to be passed. In all other cases the court must listen to the prosecutor's summary of the facts, to evidence of the defendant's record and character, and to his or his counsel's speech in mitigation.

A plea of not guilty is followed by the empanelling of the jury.[1] Sitting at the back of the court are the jurors in waiting, the

[1] See Lord Devlin, *Trial by Jury.*

men and women who have been summoned for jury service.
The clerk selects the names of each juror one by one, usually by
drawing each name from a receptacle, and calls out each juror
in turn. As each comes forward, the defendant has a right to
challenge the juryman, i.e. he can object to his presence on the
jury. This is known as the challenge 'to the polls'. A defendant
has seven peremptory challenges, that is he may object in seven
cases without giving reasons; thereafter he must support his
objections with reasons and his objection may be overruled.
The prosecution, too, may challenge a juror, but has no peremptory challenge. In England little time is devoted to selecting
the jury, in contrast to the procedure in certain of the United
States, where this is one of the most important tasks which an
advocate has and where many hours are devoted to questioning
the prospective jurors as to their religious, political, and other
beliefs, as to their background and economic circumstances. In
English courts the empanelling and swearing of the twelve jurors
rarely takes more than a quarter of an hour.

Counsel for the prosecution then opens the case by informing
the jury of the charge against the defendant and summarizing
the facts of the case. Counsel thereupon calls his witnesses who,
after being sworn, are examined, cross-examined, and re-examined. The important differences between each of these three
stages will be considered later.

At the end of the prosecution case the defence have a variety
of courses open to them. Earlier we considered the different
kinds of defence of which a defendant could avail himself. Here
we are concerned not with differences in law but differences in
tactics. The defence may submit that there is no case to answer
because there is not sufficient evidence to go before a jury. It
may be that there was never sufficient evidence and there should
never have been a committal; or it may be that the prosecution
witnesses give less damning evidence at the time than they gave
at the preliminary investigation. After hearing the argument
of the prosecution, the court may either uphold the submission
and direct the jury to acquit the defendant, or may overrule the
submission, in which case the defence must present its case. One
great problem confronting the defence is whether to call
the accused as a witness and submit him to the dangers of a
searching cross-examination. Another problem is whether the

defence should call witnesses other than the accused, and so lose the 'right of reply', for when only the accused is called, the closing speech for the defence follows that of the prosecution, but where other witnesses are called, the order is reversed. If the defence call no evidence, defending counsel merely addresses the jury and the prosecution has no final speech.

After the speeches, the judge, recorder, or chairman as the case may be, sums up to the jury, directing them on points of law and considering the evidence for them. The jury then consider their verdict, usually retiring in order to do so. Their verdict, which they arrive at in the secrecy of the jury-room and for which no reasons need or can be given, must be their unanimous verdict. Failure to agree will entail the discharge of the jury and the defendant must be tried before a new jury. An acquittal results in the defendant's discharge; a conviction is followed by evidence of the prisoner's record and a speech in mitigation, as in the case of a plea of guilty.

At this point it is convenient to consider the question of appeals.

A person convicted by a Magistrates' Court may appeal against conviction or sentence to Quarter Sessions. His appeal is heard by the appeal committee or in Borough Quarter Sessions by the recorder sitting alone, and it takes the form of a retrial. A defendant will be advised to appeal to Quarter Sessions, therefore, where the defendant or his advisers consider that the magistrates were misled by the witnesses against him. From the decision of Quarter Sessions both sides may appeal to the High Court on a point of law and the case is heard by three judges of the Queen's Bench Division. On a point of law both sides may appeal likewise straight from the Magistrates' Court to the High Court, so by-passing Quarter Sessions. Since 1960 there exists a further right of appeal from the High Court to the House of Lords, provided the High Court or the House of Lords gives leave to appeal.

A person convicted on indictment may appeal against conviction or sentence to the Court of Criminal Appeal, where his case is heard by three judges. One notable defect in the law here is that the Court of Criminal Appeal must either allow the appeal and quash the conviction or must dismiss the appeal. It often happens that because of some defect in the trial below the conviction must be quashed although the jury may have been justified in convicting. What is badly needed by the court is a power to order a retrial before a different judge, but this power is not included in the provisions of the Criminal Appeal Act, 1907, which is the governing statute in this context. From the decision of the Court of Criminal Appeal either side may appeal to the House of Lords, provided that leave to appeal is granted either by the Court of Criminal Appeal or the House of Lords.

2. AMATEURS AND PROFESSIONALS

English law is remarkable for the role it assigns to the ordinary citizen in the working of the machinery of justice.[1] At times he is seen in the part of policeman or prosecutor, and it is he for the most part who, as magistrate or juror, determines the question of an accused's guilt. This is partly due to the Englishman's distrust of experts and his preference for the amateur, partly the result of historical factors. On the other hand, as society develops, amateurs tend to give way to professionals. Professional police, professional magistrates, like professional politicians and professional sportsmen, displace their lay predecessors. Moreover the Crown exercises very real control over criminal proceedings through the law officers, the judiciary, and the Home Office. The English criminal system today presents a picture into which the function of the layman and the central authority's control exercised through professionals are neatly dovetailed.

(a) Investigation and Arrest

Until the nineteenth century there existed in England little in the way of institutionalized means of investigation of crime and apprehension of suspects and offenders. The towns were served by unpaid officials such as the parish constable and the night watch, amusingly caricatured for us in *Much Ado About Nothing*. To assist in the fight against crime the ordinary citizen might be called upon to serve on a grand jury, which was composed of representatives from each county. Their duty was to present suspected offenders to the sheriff in his court. Originally they acted on their own knowledge, but in later years they merely listened to the evidence against a suspect in order to decide whether to send him for trial on indictment. Meanwhile their task of

[1] See Lord Devlin, *The Criminal Prosecution in England*.

investigation had fallen into the hands of Justices of the Peace. The practice of assigning 'good men and true' in each county to keep the peace arose in the fourteenth century. The justices had the threefold duty of investigating offences, arresting suspects, and detaining them until the royal judges arrived to try their cases. In due course the creation of the police force ended the need for the justices, or magistrates, to investigate offences themselves, and with the abolition of the grand jury in 1932 the magistrates took over the task of holding the preliminary investigation to decide whether to commit a defendant for trial on indictment.

The lack of organized professional means of law-enforcement cast a heavy burden on the ordinary citizen in his private capacity. He was bound to report to the authorities any felony which came to his notice, and failure to do so is still today the offence of Misprision of Felony. At one time the discovery of a felony laid the citizen under the duty of raising the 'hue and cry', whereupon a general pursuit of the offender ensued and all taking part had the same powers of arrest as would be granted today by the issue of a warrant. Though the hue and cry is no more, the citizen still retains his duty to prevent the commission of felonies or dangerous breaches of the peace in his presence, and must if necessary effect an arrest to fulfil this duty. If lawfully called upon for aid by a police officer attempting to prevent a breach of the peace, he is obliged to render assistance. In addition to these duties he has a right at common law to arrest without warrant any person who commits a felony or dangerous breach of the peace in his presence, and any person whom he reasonably suspects of committing a felony, if a felony has actually been committed. Statutes have added to these common-law rights. For example the Prevention of Offences Act, 1851, authorizes anyone to arrest without warrant any person found committing an indictable offence by night.

Today, however, the task of investigation and arrest is primarily that of the police. Our modern police force originated with the creation in 1829 by Peel of the Metropolitan Police Force. The formal creation of the Criminal Investigation Department followed in 1878. To Peel's proposals there had originally been considerable opposition. The existence of a police force could well lead to the creation of a police state and constitute a dangerous threat to the freedom of the citizen.

To prevent the emergence of a police state, a unified command of the police force was avoided. In England there is not one but many police forces, in fact over a hundred; all counties and many large towns have their own police forces. Of these the largest is the Metropolitan Police Force, the head of which is appointed by the Home Secretary, and which comes under the direct control of the Government. The local forces are each headed by a locally appointed chief constable under the control of the local police authority. The chief constables of the counties are appointed by a Standing Joint Committee, consisting partly of county councillors, partly of Justices of the Peace. The chief constables in the towns are appointed by the Watch Committee, consisting of the mayor and some of the town councillors. Concentration of control of the police forces in local hands, however, is not an unmitigated benefit. This may be seen from the difficult situation which arose in 1959, in Nottingham, where the chief constable's investigation into the activities of certain city councillors led to such strained relations that the Watch Committee suspended him. Clearly if the police are to be able to perform their duty objectively without fear or favour, some check on the powers of the local authorities is necessary. Such a check, in fact, is provided by the control of the Home Secretary. The appointment of a chief constable needs the approval of the Home Secretary. Moreover, any police officer can appeal to the Home Secretary against his dismissal by the local committee. Furthermore, the Home Secretary is empowered to make regulations concerning the discipline, remuneration, and conditions of service in all police forces. Lastly, the Central Government exercises very real control through holding the purse strings. The police are paid by the police authorities out of funds, half of which come from a grant from the Central Government.

The freedom of the individual has also been protected by the peculiar position of the police officer, who in England has never become a special person immune from the ordinary process of the courts. In law a policeman is merely a private citizen with a particular duty to keep the peace, and his powers are merely the ordinary citizen's powers enlarged. For wrongful excess of these powers he must answer in the Criminal and Civil Courts, where he may be liable for assault, trespass, and false imprisonment.

(b) Prosecution

Although prosecutions are undertaken on behalf of the Crown, any individual may lay an information and prosecute. Indeed even when the prosecutor is, as in most cases, a police officer, he prosecutes in virtue of his right as a private citizen. This may be seen from the way of naming summary cases, for example. If P.C. Smith prosecutes Jones for speeding, the case would be referred to as *Smith* v. *Jones*, just as would a civil action between the two parties. We have seen that cases on indictment are described differently because an indictment is an accusation at the suit of the Crown. Nevertheless even in such a case a private citizen may prosecute, though he will, of course, have to brief counsel since he himself will have no right of audience at Quarter Sessions or Assizes.

The effect of this private right of prosecution is seen in many different aspects. First, there is the considerable part played by private prosecutors. Ordinary citizens and corporate entities frequently bring criminal proceedings. R.S.P.C.A. and N.S.P.C.C. inspectors appear to prosecute in cases concerning cruelty to animals and children. Another example is the Dental Board, which prosecutes contraventions of the Dental Act. There are certain cases where only the person aggrieved may institute criminal proceedings. The most notable example is that of common assault, the reason in this case being that a decision in a criminal court is a bar to subsequent civil proceedings. It is only fair, therefore, that the victim of the assault should have the choice of prosecuting or suing.

Secondly, it means that the police enjoy considerable discretion as to the question of prosecution. Though this may result in undesirable discrepancies in the treatment of offenders in different areas, such discretion is desirable to enable the police to use common sense and avoid undue oppression in trivial cases. No one would wish the police to be forced to prosecute automatically, for instance, every young child found stealing apples from an orchard

In this way England differs from many countries, where, once the police have concluded their investigation, the matter is placed in the hands of a national or local prosecuting authority, such as the procurator-fiscal in Scotland or the well-known district attorney in the United States. In England the decision whether to prosecute rests normally with the local police force. Nevertheless in criminal proceedings the Crown has considerable control which it does not possess with regard to civil proceedings. In the first place there is considerable restriction on the private right of prosecution. For certain offences, e.g. offences against the Official Secrets Act, prosecution may not be commenced without the consent of the senior law officer, the Attorney-General. Prosecutions for certain other offences, e.g. offences against the Bankruptcy Act, require the consent of the Director of Public Prosecutions. This office was created in 1879, the director's function being to act as the Crown's solicitor in criminal cases. The prosecution of the more serious indictable offences, such as murder, and of offences of general public interest, such as conspiracy to defeat the ends of justice, must be undertaken by the director. Secondly, even in any private prosecution, it is open to the director to intervene and take over the conduct of the case, if he thinks fit.

Thirdly, once a prosecution has been launched, the prosecutor is not at liberty to drop the proceedings, as is the plaintiff in a civil action. Criminal cases do not admit of settlement at the will of the parties, for the reason that the prosecutor, even in a private prosecution, is regarded as conducting the case on behalf of the Crown. It often happens, however, that the prosecution may wish to drop a charge. For example, the defendant may be indicted for burglary, stealing, and receiving, but the evidence on the first two charges may be very slight. If he indicates that he is prepared to plead guilty to the third charge, the prosecution may quite properly, in the interests of time and expense, propose to drop the first two charges, of which the defendant might in all probability be acquitted. In such a case the prosecutor's course is to offer no evidence on the charges, and, subject to the court's permission, to withdraw them. But besides the court's controlling power in this matter, there is also this further check, that all cases which are withdrawn or not proceeded with must be reported to the director.

On the other hand, while the private prosecutor is not wholly free to compromise a criminal action, the Crown has power to stop any proceedings on indictment, regardless of the wishes of the prosecutor. This is done by means of a *nolle prosequi*, an order issued by the Attorney-General directing that the case be stopped. Such a direction is not applicable to summary trials in the Magistrates' Courts. These could be stopped by the Director of Public Prosecutions intervening, taking over the prosecution, and offering no evidence. In addition to the power of stopping criminal proceedings, the Crown also has an absolving power and can grant a free pardon to a person convicted of an offence, the legal result being the same as if he had been acquitted.

(c) Magistrates

The Justice of the Peace Act was passed in 1361 to assign good and lawful men to keep the peace in the different counties. Today magistrates are appointed by the Lord Chancellor on the advice of local advisory committees and hold office by virtue of having their names on the Commission of the Peace for the county or borough. Any man or woman residing within fifteen miles of the county or borough is eligible for appointment, apart from special disqualifications relating to bankrupts and convicted felons. Besides appointed magistrates, certain persons are *ex officio* magistrates. High Court judges and privy councillors are national justices of the peace and are on every commission of the peace. Mayors and chairmen of county and district councils are *ex officio* magistrates during their terms of office. As we have seen, the magistrates have a threefold function with regard to the criminal law. They issue summonses and warrants; they hold preliminary investigations to decide whether to commit for trial; they try cases without juries in the Magistrates' Court, and in County Quarter Sessions they try cases with a jury. At one time they had vast jurisdiction in civil matters, and it was true to say that the whole of local government was in their hands. They still retain considerable civil jurisdiction, the best-known example being the hearing of matrimonial cases and the granting of licences under the Licensing Acts.

The Magistrates' Courts are not without their critics. The selection of justices is not always thought satisfactory, undue weight being given to political considerations. It is doubtful whether mayors and council chairmen should become magistrates automatically. The time needed to perform this service tends to exclude from the bench professional and business men, leaving us with benches drawn from the ranks of the relatively leisured rather than being generally representative of the community. On the other hand, the more representative the bench, the more susceptible it is to local and economic prejudices. This is very noticeable in the case of the staple diet of Magistrates' Courts, driving offences, which tend to be differently treated according to whether or not the bench is drawn from the ranks of motor-car owners. This, together with the newly appointed magistrate's complete lack of training and experience, has led to some diminution in respect for lay magistrates and to a desire for qualified stipendiaries to replace them.

The two great factors in favour of retaining a system of lay magistrates is its cheapness and the association of ordinary citizens with the administration of justice. To replace all benches with paid magistrates would cost a considerable amount, while it would deprive the citizen of the opportunity of playing a valuable part in local affairs. The lack of legal training is of little importance. Most of the cases turn on questions of fact, while the clerk is there to advise the magistrate on the law. All told, the lay benches provide an inexpensive and highly successful popular court for minor offences.[1]

(d) The Jury

The 'mother of Parliaments' apart, no English institution has been so extolled as the criminal jury, and no right is more valued by the Englishman than his right to be tried by jury—a right which, we have seen, he possesses in the case of any offence for which the penalty on conviction is three months' imprisonment or more. This committee of twelve is drawn from the ranks of property-owners or householders of either sex between the ages of twenty-one and sixty. Many persons, however, such as clergymen, professional men, and others are exempt from jury service. The result of these exemptions, together with the property qualifications (low as they are), is that today juries are less representative of the community as a whole than of a small section of the community. Lord Devlin has aptly described the modern jury as predominantly 'male, middle-aged, middle-minded and middle-class'.[2]

---

[1] For an assessment of the lay magistrate see John A. F. Watson, *The Child and the Magistrate*, ch. xvi.   [2] Lord Devlin, *Trial by Jury*.

The selection of the jury proceeds in two stages. First from a list of persons eligible for jury service the sheriff selects a panel to form the jury in waiting and attend the Assizes or Quarter Sessions in readiness to serve. In former times, when sheriffs were not averse to packing the jury with members drawn entirely from persons of one political persuasion, the defendant often needed to exercise his valuable right of challenging 'to the array', i.e. he could challenge the whole jury. Today this right is not needed and is never exercised. The second stage is the selection by lot or ballot by the clerk of the court of the twelve jurors from the list of the jury in waiting. This procedure together with the defendant's right of challenge 'to the polls' has already been discussed.[1]

In a criminal trial it is the jury who constitute the judge of fact. It is their verdict, arrived at in secrecy, unanimous and unsupported by reasons, which decides the guilt or innocence of the defendant. At one time juries were locked up without food and drink until they decided upon their verdict. Moreover, verdicts contrary to the wishes of the judge rendered the jury liable to punishment. The jury that acquitted William Penn in 1670 on a charge of preaching to an unlawful, seditious, and riotous assembly was heavily fined. In default of payment they were imprisoned, but the judges of the Court of Common Pleas held the imprisonment to be unlawful, thus establishing the independence of the jury.[2] Today, however, no such restraint on the freedom of the jury would be tolerated. In 1959 a conviction was quashed by the Court of Criminal Appeal in a case where a jury, which was taking considerable time in reaching a verdict, convicted the accused six minutes after being informed by the judge that he had power to keep them under lock and key until they arrived at their verdict.[3] The jury are free to return their verdict without threat or restraint, and the judge is bound to accept their final verdict. A perverse conviction can, of course, be quashed on appeal; an acquittal, however perverse, must stand. This is the jury's sovereign right of acquittal.

Nevertheless the jury is subject to very real control by the

---

[1] At pp. 151-2.   [2] *Bushell's Case* (1670), Vaughan 156.

[3] *R. v. McKenna*, [1960] 1 All E.R. 326, where the Court of Criminal Appeal pointed out that a jury is not in fact locked up in the jury room all night, but is accommodated in an hotel.

presiding judge. Not only does he sum up the evidence to them at the end of the case, but it is he who directs them on points of law. We have seen that murder committed in the course of a theft is capital murder. In a trial for this type of murder it would be for the jury to decide the question of fact whether the accused killed the deceased in the course of a theft; it would be for the judge to direct them as to what in law could count as 'in the course of a theft'. Another powerful restrictive weapon in the judge's hands concerns the admission of evidence and the withdrawal of issues from the jury. While the jury decide the case, they can only decide it on the evidence put before them, and where disputes arise as to the admission of evidence, it is the judge who decides whether the evidence can be put before the jury. Secondly, the jury cannot give a verdict for which there is no evidence whatsoever. They can always give a general verdict of acquittal, as we have seen, however contrary to the weight of evidence this may be. This is the necessary result of making the jury the final arbiter of the defendant's guilt; it is not open to the judge to insist on a verdict of guilty. But this does not run counter to the proposition that the jury cannot give a verdict for which there is no evidence, because in criminal law the golden rule is that the prosecution must prove its case beyond reasonable doubt. Accordingly, an acquittal does not have to be based on defence evidence; it can rest on the jury's view that there is not enough evidence against the accused, and that is a matter entirely for them. Although the judge cannot remove from the jury the right of returning a general verdict of not guilty, he can withdraw from them the right to pronounce a special verdict, e.g. guilty but insane, if there is not sufficient evidence to support it. Likewise, if there is insufficient evidence against the accused, the judge can direct there is no case to go before the jury and can discharge the defendant.

The jury system is not without defects. For the ordinary citizen jury service involves loss of time and money. The length of a trial is undoubtedly increased if it has to be explained to a lay jury unfamiliar with the law and procedure of the courts. Indeed for this reason the jury has largely disappeared from the Civil Courts. Juries are open to prejudice. Extensive reports of preliminary investigations sometimes render it difficult to secure a fair trial before an impartial jury. Juries are often unduly influenced by evidence which is prejudicial rather than conclusive. In murder trials, for instance, the judge sometimes refuses to allow the jury to see photographic evidence of the corpse, for fear that it might prejudice them against the accused. The case of *Steinie Morrison*[1] affords an example of a jury which may have been unduly prejudiced against the defendant by evidence that he had previous convictions for criminal offences. In that case the judge himself seems to have been unhappy about the defendant's conviction for murder, and his subsequent reprieve would indicate that these doubts may have been echoed in the mind of the Home Secretary.

These defects are wholly outweighed by the value of the jury as a protection of freedom. Although the judiciary in England are independent and in no way subservient to the Crown, this was not always so; and the right to be pronounced guilty only by a lay jury constitutes a defence against any move by a government to encroach on the liberty of the subject. Any potential tyrant would have to cross swords with this body sooner or later in order to enforce his laws. Even as it is, though the judiciary is not in the pocket of the Crown and though the Government is not bent on establishing a totalitarian state, the jury still provides actual protection against both judges and governments. For the former's familiarity with criminal courts breeds an understandable contempt for defences and leads often to 'prosecution-mindedness' on the part of the judge. The jury, to whom everything is new and who see the inside of the court for the first time, counterbalance the judge's tendency by leaning if anything too heavily in the defendant's favour.[2] Meanwhile, even a democratic government may pass laws repugnant to the community. Persistent acquittals by juries in driving offences, even on occasions in the face of overwhelming evidence, show clearly that the majority of jurors feel reluctant to regard such offences as on a par with crimes of violence and dishonesty. Regardless of the rights and wrongs of this problem, it is obvious that the jury system is a powerful obstacle to the enforcement of unpopular laws.

Apart from these considerations there is great wisdom in

---

[1] *Famous Trials* (3rd series, 1950 ed. J. Hodge).
[2] It is a well-known fact that juries serving to try several cases begin by acquitting and end by convicting.

entrusting the decision to a jury rather than to a judge. Criminal cases mostly turn on the question which side is to be believed. The ordinary people who sit on juries are experienced in their own callings in deciding on people's reliability. In their ordinary dealings and business they learn from results and from mistakes whether their trust has been well placed. Judges, drawn from the ranks of barristers, are trained and experienced in testing the veracity of witnesses by cross-examination. They do not, however, have the experience of having to impose reliance themselves on other people as part of their professional work; nor do they enjoy the opportunity of judging of people's reliability by subsequent results. A jury composed of ordinary men of the world is in all probability a better test of honesty and reliability, and better able to give a satisfactory decision on the merits of the case.

3. RESTRICTIONS ON THE SCOPE OF THE CRIMINAL LAW

Important as it is to prevent crime, this is by no means the only aim of a civilized society, and in England the pursuit of this aim is subject to various limitations. In the first place there are various restrictions on the scope of the criminal law to prevent its use as an instrument of oppression and to ensure that zeal for law enforcement does not lead the enforcing agents to fall below the standard of treatment demanded by respect for the individual as a human being. Respect for the dignity of human personality rules out many things which might undoubtedly be of use in society's battle against crime, and lays down a minimum standard of treatment for all, guilty as well as innocent. It is this principle which underlies such matters as the illegality in England of torture, the practice of issuing a summons rather than a warrant for arrest in the first instance, the gradual abolition of corporal and capital punishment. Under this head we shall consider limitations on the jurisdiction of the Criminal Courts in respect to territory, persons, and time; the principle of legality; the rules against double jeopardy and self-incrimination.

(a) Limits to Jurisdiction

The aim of the criminal law is to prevent conduct injurious to society or its individual members. Acts performed outside a state's territory will in general fall outside this category. If Brown assaults Dupont in Paris, no harm is done to England or its countrymen. On the other hand, if the crime were committed in London, the breach of the peace would be an injury to our community and the assault would be an injury to a person whom the Crown should temporarily protect. English law in general adheres to a territorial principle of jurisdiction, assuming jurisdiction over all offences, by whomsoever committed, on English territory. English territory for this purpose includes Wales, but not Scotland, Ireland, the Isle of Man, and the Channel Isles, and it is extended by law to afford the courts jurisdiction over offences committed within British territorial waters, on British ships on the high seas, and on British aircraft. The extent of territorial waters is at present the subject of acute international controversy.[1] For the purpose of the criminal law the extent is that recognized by consistent British practice, a three-mile belt.

Crimes committed outside these limits are in general outside the jurisdiction of our criminal law. It would be a quite unwarranted piece of oppression and interference for English courts to require that the behaviour in other countries should conform to the canons of English law. To seek to penalize, for example, French nationals for activity in France contrary to English law would be as officious as it would be unnecessary. What happens within the territory of a state is the prime concern of that state, which would be quick to protest if any infringement of its sovereignty arose by virtue of some other state assuming jurisdiction over acts committed there.[2]

Complete adherence, however, to the territorial principle is not necessary in all circumstances, nor does it exist in English law. Increased development in communications between countries makes states more and more dependent on each other, so that the order and welfare of one state tends to become a matter of concern for others. Piracy has long been recognized as an international offence, punishable by our courts wherever committed. In recent years international conventions have been concluded to outlaw such matters as trafficking in drugs and

---

[1] The Geneva conference on the law of the sea in 1958 failed to reach agreement on the question of the breadth of the maritime belt.
[2] See Starke, *Introduction to International Law* (4th ed.), pp. 176 ff.

counterfeiting currency, whereby each party undertakes to punish persons found guilty of such conduct. Yet, on the whole, convenience demands that a crime should be investigated in the place where it was committed, where the witnesses are most likely to be. Accordingly, most states have concluded treaties with other states to provide for the extradition of offenders from the state to which they have escaped to the state in whose territory the offence was committed. Since 1870 this country has concluded such treaties with most states, though in most cases extradition is only allowed for serious crimes, while it is refused for offences of a political or religious nature. Within the Commonwealth a similar arrangement exists under the Fugitive Offenders Act, 1881.

Departures from the territorial principle of jurisdiction relate in English law mainly to treason and kindred offences, where the crime consists of a breach of a duty of allegiance and where acts committed abroad, as for instance by Casement and Joyce, are clearly harmful to this country. Offences by British subjects against the Official Secrets Act are, for similar reasons, within the jurisdiction of English courts, even though committed abroad. A curious departure from the territorial principle has been made in the cases of murder and bigamy. If either of these crimes is committed by a British subject, English courts have jurisdiction regardless of the place of commission. The reason and justification for this rule are far from clear.

Acts begun outside England but creating their harmful effect within English territory also come within the jurisdiction of the courts. If X, from a ship outside British territorial waters, shoots and kills Y on a ship within territorial waters, the homicide for the purposes of jurisdiction is regarded as taking place where the deceased was when he was attacked.[1] Accordingly in this case the courts would have jurisdiction. Likewise if A in France obtains money from B in England as a result of a false pretence made in a letter sent by A, it seems that the courts in England would have jurisdiction to try A (if he came to this country) for obtaining money by false pretences.[2] This doctrine to the effect that jurisdiction extends to acts resulting in harmful effects within English territory would seem to be restricted to acts causing direct physical harm or loss of property. Acts committed

---

[1] *R.* v. *Coombes* (1786), 1 Leach 388.   [2] *R.* v. *Oliphant*, [1905] 2 K.B. 67.

abroad resulting in loss of reputation, for example, to this country or to individual Englishmen in England, even if the acts constituted criminal libel, would not be within the jurisdiction. In this respect English law is in accord with internationally accepted practice. When the Mexican authorities in 1887 prosecuted *Cutting*,[1] a citizen of the United States, while temporarily present in Mexico, for publishing in Texas an article libelling a Mexican citizen, this being an offence against Mexican law, the United States objected strongly and these objections have been widely supported by the majority of states. Some states have at times assumed jurisdiction over offences committed outside their territory and injurious to their nationals.[2] In the celebrated *Lotus*[3] case in 1927 the French ship *Lotus* collided with a Turkish ship on the high seas with resulting loss of life to Turkish nationals thereon. The French officer responsible was prosecuted in Turkey for manslaughter on the ground that the effects of his act were produced on a Turkish vessel, which for legal purposes was part of Turkish territory. The Permanent Court of International Justice at The Hague held that this was not contrary to any rule of international law, but the Geneva Convention on the Law of the Sea (1958)[4] has adopted the rule that in such cases only the authorities of the flag state of the offender or the state of which the offender is a national shall have jurisdiction.

As far as concerns acts committed within the territory of this country, the rule is that our courts have jurisdiction to try such offences whether committed by a British subject or by an alien. If A murders B in London, the crime is not rendered less injurious to the interests protected by the criminal law by the fact that A is an alien. There are, however, certain categories of person who are immune from the jurisdiction of the Criminal Courts. The courts have no jurisdiction over the person of the reigning monarch, as a consequence of which principle the trial of Charles I was illegal. Similar immunity is accorded to foreign sovereigns in the interest of the peace and harmony of nations. The immunity does not extend to deposed or exiled sovereigns,

[1] (1887) Moore's *Digest of International Law* (1906), ii. 228.
[2] The Eichmann trial is the obvious example in recent times.
[3] (1927), P.C.I.J. Ser. A, No. 10.
[4] Geneva Convention on the Law of the Sea, Art 11.

such as, for example, Mary Queen of Scots, whose trial could not be challenged on this ground. Diplomatic envoys from foreign states are also immune from criminal jurisdiction, though this immunity can be waived by the foreign government in respect of its representatives.[1] Such immunity also protects acts performed within foreign legation premises, except where such premises are used for subversive purposes. If a foreign diplomat commits an offence, the normal practice is either for his immunity to be waived or for him to be sent home for trial in his own courts. In 1954 a Dominican diplomat who committed murder in the Dominican embassy was taken back to stand trial in the Dominican Republic.[2]

In civil proceedings there exist strict rules barring actions which are brought after the expiration of certain time-limits. It is generally recognized that some limit must be set to exclude stale claims and to allow a man to order his affairs with some certainty. Moreover, delay in bringing an action prejudices the defendant, because his witnesses may have died and his records may be destroyed. In criminal law, however, time does not run against the Crown. A lapse of nineteen years was no bar to the prosecution of Governor Wall for murder in 1802.[3] To this harsh general rule certain exceptions have been made. Certain types of treason must be prosecuted within three years, offences against the Riot Act must be prosecuted within twelve months, and summary offences must be prosecuted within six months. In the case of certain driving offences no prosecution can be brought unless the defendant is either warned at the time that the question of a prosecution will be considered or unless he is within fourteen days served with a summons or notice of intended prosecution. In practice also the authorities use their discretion not to prosecute for offences committed a long time previously, except in the case of very grave crimes.

(b) The Principle of Legality

This principle is summed up in the maxim *nulla poena sine lege*, according to which no one should be punished by law except for a breach of law.[4] According to this maxim judges and

---

[1] *R. v. A.B.*, [1941] 1 K.B. 454.
[2] *The Times*, 12, 13, 15 July 1954. See *B.Y.I.L.* 1958, p. 373.
[3] See p. 29.   [4] Glanville Williams, *The Criminal Law*, (2nd. ed.), p. 575.

tribunals should not have power to penalize conduct merely because it is in their view immoral, anti-social, or in some way undesirable. The kind of guardianship of morals exercised by the Star Chamber could not on this view be tolerated.

The principle of legality demands that the citizen should be ruled by law and not by the decisions of individual men. The reasons for this are obvious. In a liberal community the rules of criminal law should be written down in black and white, so that the citizen has a chance to ascertain what the rules are and to conform to them. Without this we lose any objective standard and uniformity with regard to what is to constitute criminal conduct; for what one judge today thinks unimpeachable another court tomorrow may consider anti-social and therefore criminal. Moreover, quite apart from the desire for objectivity and uniformity in the interest of certainty, the idea of one person's life and liberty being entirely in the hands of another, albeit clad in ermine, runs counter to the whole idea of a free community.

This principle has particular relevance to the question of retrospective legislation. According to the doctrine of *nulla poena* no one should be penalized for conduct which is contrary to a legal rule that only came into existence after the performance of that conduct. Only contraventions of existing legal rules should be punished. It is the regard for this principle which underlies the misgivings about the Nuremberg Trials and the Eichmann Trial. Although the latter's conduct was utterly reprehensible, at the time it took place there was no state of Israel and no Israeli law which Eichmann could be said to have violated. Whatever justification can be advanced for the trial, it cannot be overlooked that the bringing of Eichmann 'to justice' has entailed on Israel's part a sacrifice of one very important principle.

The objection to retrospective criminal legislation is not wedded to any theory as to the aims and objects of punishment. A deterrent view of punishment might seem to rule out the punishment of conduct not criminal at the time of commission, on the ground that subsequent penalties not then envisaged could not operate to deter the offender. Yet a severe law-maker might in enacting a new law make use of the punishment of such conduct in order to provide extra deterrence for future would-be offenders. A reformative theory might seem to commit us to the view that only those who break an existing rule should be reformed. Yet here again it could be argued that if a man does some anti-social act which is later made a crime, the fact that his conduct preceded the prohibition does not prevent him from being a danger to society; his anti-social tendency should be treated before he commits an actual offence. The objection to retrospective criminal law is simply that it seems unfair to punish someone unless he has a chance to know the law and conform to it. This view underlies the reluctance of the law to hold young children and the insane as criminally responsible, for they are denied this chance. Young children, of course, often have to learn how to behave by an empirical method of tuition, being punished each time they misbehave. This too is the only way of training animals. But ordinary adult human beings need not be treated in this fashion. Due respect for their human dignity demands that they should be informed beforehand what may and may not legally be done, together with the penalties for breach of the law. With Bentham we may object to a system whereby the individual is treated by the law as a dog is treated by his master.

The principle of legality has been adopted by many states as a fundamental rule. France, Germany, Belgium, Portugal, Italy, Brazil, Chile, Colombia, Uruguay, and the United States have all adopted it. It has been written into international law in the Universal Declaration of Human Rights (1948), and in the European Convention of Human Rights (1950). English law, however, has never accepted the principle as a rule of law. Although the practice of passing acts of *attainder*—to punish people for acts not illegal prior to the act of attainder—fell into disuse in the eighteenth century, two factors combined to exclude the principle from finding a resting-place in English law. The criminal law, like the rest of the common law, is largely the child of judicial creation. As need arose, so the courts created new offences. But in English law judicial decisions are always retrospective in that the decision relates back to the facts and circumstances which led to the trial. This is obscured by the fiction that judges do not make law but only declare and apply existing law. But the fact remains that wherever there is a judicial extension of the criminal law, this results in the punishment of a defendant for an act which could not before the conclusion of the trial have been known to be criminal. The possibility of the courts' discussing the abstract question whether such conduct is criminal, without reference to any particular defendant, is ruled out by the fact that English courts (apart from the Privy Council) are precluded from deciding merely academic matters. The adoption of any principle forbidding the creation of retrospective criminal law would have stifled judicial development of the law in this field.

The second factor excluding the principle of legality is the English doctrine of parliamentary sovereignty. In English law there are no fetters on the sovereign to make what laws it likes, provided only it enacts them according to the procedure required by law. But this law itself, like any other law, including such venerable corner-stones of our legislation as Magna Carta and the Bill of Rights could be as easily repealed (so far as the legal requirements are concerned) as could the Dogs Act.[1] This being so, any statutory formulation of the rule against retrospective legislation would have no particular legal force. If Parliament does not mean to create such law, the prohibition is unnecessary; if it was bent on retrospective legislation, the prohibition would be useless. Acceptance of the prohibition as a legal rule to restrict the legislature is of value chiefly in the framework of a constitution which contains organic laws which are either by law irrepealable or only repealable with great difficulty.

English law does not, however, completely ignore a fundamental principle so widely accepted. The courts rarely exercise the power to create new crimes, leaving this to the democratically elected representatives of the community, although the case of *Shaw* v. *D.P.P.*[2] displayed a remarkable revival of the judicial creative power in the realm of criminal law. So far as legislation is concerned, it is not present practice to pass retrospective criminal statutes. Moreover, when interpreting criminal legislation, the courts are guided by the presumption that Parliament does not intend to legislate retrospectively in this sphere.

(c) *The Rule against Double Jeopardy*

An important restriction on the operation of the criminal law is the rule that no man shall be put in peril twice for the same

---

[1] Per Lord Birkenhead L.C. in *McCawley* v. *R.*, [1920] A.C. 691 at p. 704.
[2] See p. 8.

offence. Once a man has been tried and either convicted or acquitted, he cannot be tried again for that offence. If he were prosecuted, he could raise the defence of *autrefois convict* or *autrefois acquit*, the proof of which would be a complete bar to further proceedings.

The reason for this rule with regard to a defendant who has already been convicted is obvious. English criminal law is based on the idea that once a person has been convicted and sentenced and has undergone the punishment imposed upon him, he has paid the penalty. To allow the authorities to prosecute him again in order to seek the imposition of some further punishment would be unduly oppressive. The law permits the accused, by serving his sentence, to wipe the slate clean and start again; and this he could not do if he were perpetually liable to further prosecutions for the same offence.

Less obvious are the reasons for the defence of *autrefois acquit*. The mere fact that a defendant has been acquitted is no proof of his innocence. The prosecution may subsequently obtain fresh evidence conclusive of his guilt, or they may be able to demonstrate that the defence succeeded by perjury and conspiracy to defeat the ends of justice. In such a case, there would be something to say, in the interests of truth and justice, in favour of allowing the defendant to be tried again. But the discovery of what actually happened in a given case and the bringing of the defendant to justice are not allowed to override all other considerations. Once a man has been acquitted, it is felt that it would be too harsh to allow the prosecution further bites at the cherry. The defendant must be allowed to order his affairs with some certainty. This means of course that occasionally the guilty slip through the net, and nothing can be done about it. This disadvantage is outweighed, however, by the gain in freedom from oppression, which the possibility of perpetual exposure to prosecution would entail. Moreover, if the practice were allowed, not only those wrongly acquitted but those who were actually innocent would be at the mercy of the potential tyranny of a prosecutor.

The rule against double jeopardy only applies where the defendant actually has been in peril in respect of the same offence. A man accused and acquitted of murder cannot subsequently be tried for manslaughter arising out of the same facts, because on a charge of murder it is open to the jury to bring in a verdict of guilty of manslaughter; accordingly the accused was in peril as regards manslaughter. But a man accused of unlawful wounding may, whatever the verdict, be subsequently tried for murder if the victim dies, because it was not open to the jury to return a verdict of guilty of murder at the first trial, so that the defendant was never in peril with regard to murder. Where he was in jeopardy, but was acquitted, the prosecution cannot get round the rule by altering the charge in some minor details. A man acquitted of murdering his wife on 1 January 1961 could not be prosecuted subsequently for murdering her on 2 January if it is clear that this second charge relates to the same event as the first.

For the defendant to avail himself of this rule he must be able to show that the first trial ended in a final verdict of guilty or not guilty. A disagreement by the jury is not a final verdict, and the accused can be tried again. In practice after two disagreements the prosecution usually withdraw the charge. A refusal by the magistrates to commit a defendant for trial is not a final verdict. As a general rule their refusal to commit puts an end to the matter, but if there is sufficient evidence to warrant the defendant's committal, the prosecution may appear with the depositions before a judge of the High Court, who can, if he thinks fit, commit the defendant for trial.

The rule against double jeopardy is also seen at work with regard to appeals. Only the accused can appeal against the decision; the prosecution has no right to appeal against an acquittal, for this would result in jeopardizing the defendant twice. To this rule there are certain exceptions. The prosecution can appeal from a decision of the Court of Criminal Appeal to the House of Lords, the reason being that the point of law at issue is of public importance and requires final settlement. From the defendant's point of view, however, it would seem unduly harsh, and indeed in capital cases the authorities have occasionally preceded the appeal by informing the House of Lords that the accused will not be executed if the Lords reverse the decision. This seemingly merciful approach has allowed the House to come dispassionately to decisions from which it might have recoiled had the prisoner's life been at stake and to frame a harder law for future prisoners than for the prisoner whose case is being decided. The need to settle points of law is also the reason for the right of the prosecution in summary cases to appeal from a decision of the appeal committee of Quarter Sessions or straight from a decision of the Magistrates' Court to the High Court.

4. THE LIBERTY OF THE SUBJECT

The rules designed to protect the liberty of the subject against excessive zeal on the part of the police and the authorities operate chiefly in the sphere of pre-trial investigation. By these provisions the citizen is safeguarded against questioning, searching, and arrest. Here the private individual's interest conflicts with the public interest that crimes should be detected and punished, and the rules now to be considered represent a compromise between these two competing interests.

(a) Questioning

One of the most important parts of the task of anyone investigating a crime is interviewing and questioning all those who can furnish information on the matter, including, of course, any possible suspects. Now although the citizen has in certain cases a duty to assist the police, to prevent the commission of felonies, to report such felonies as come to his notice, and indeed in many other ways to promote the interests of justice, yet when we turn to look at the legal position of a person being questioned by the police (or by any other investigator), we find a rule curiously conflicting with these other duties. In law a person is not obliged to answer any questions put to him. The main reason for this is the principle well established in English law that no one is bound to convict himself out of his own mouth. In civil cases the position is quite different. One party to a civil action may deliver questions, known as 'interrogatories', which his opponent may be bound to answer, failure to do so resulting in his losing his action and possibly being imprisoned for contempt of court.[1] In criminal cases the citizen is protected from self-incrimination. He need say nothing to the police; if charged, he must be warned that he has a right to say nothing; at his trial he has a right to refuse to give evidence. This rule resulted from the popular dislike of the procedure in the Star Chamber, when

---

[1] In a civil case one party may even call his opponent as a witness.

suspects were examined by the court on oath, but it is also connected with the requirement of English law that the prosecution must prove its case; the accused is not bound to prove it for them. In recent years it has sometimes been suggested that this rule should be abolished or modified, but it is doubtful whether any change would be popularly acceptable.[1]

The rule against self-incrimination is not the only basis for the citizen's right not to answer questions. For it may be that the citizen is innocent and has nothing to hide. Yet he too is entitled not to say anything, even though there is no question of his incriminating himself, and this would seem to arise partly from the law's concern to protect the citizen's privacy against intrusion.

In theory the citizen's right not to co-operate with the police could make their job impossible. A police officer has generally speaking no right, for example, to obtain from any person his name and address, even though he sees him commit a crime for which he intends to prosecute. The suspect may refuse to answer, or he may give a false name and address. Withholding information or giving false information, though it may hamper the police, does not amount to the offence of obstructing the police, since this seems to require some element of physical prevention of their carrying out their duty. The limit to which this offence has been extended is the case where survivors of a motor accident falsely informed the police in answer to inquiries that the vehicle had been driven by a passenger who died in the crash. In this case, however, the police had a legal right to true information.

Statutes have made inroads on the citizen's right to withhold information. The Public Order Act, 1936, provides that if any person attending a public meeting behaves in a disorderly fashion, any policeman present at the meeting may through the chairman request that person's name and address and that failure to comply with this request is a criminal offence. Under the Road Traffic Acts any driver is legally bound to produce his licence to a police constable on demand. A police officer who

---

[1] See, for example, the suggestion of John Foster, Q.C., that accused persons should be required to give early notice of their defence in Report on 'Preliminary Investigations of Criminal Offences' in *Justice* (Dec. 1960). See also Glanville Williams, *The Proof of Guilt*, pp. 37–73.

sees a driver driving recklessly, dangerously, or carelessly is entitled to demand the driver's name and address or licence and is entitled to arrest any driver who refuses to comply. Where a driver of a vehicle is alleged to be guilty of a driving offence, the owner of the vehicle and other persons involved in the matter are legally bound to answer truthfully any questions concerning the identity of the driver. Such provisions, however, are exceptional and the general rule remains that if a policeman sees a person committing some trivial offence for which there is no power of arrest, he has no power legally of compelling the offender to disclose his name and address.

It may be thought that the law leans too heavily in favour of the individual at the expense of the interests of the community and that the restriction on the powers of the police with regard to searching, entry, and questioning could well make it impossible for any investigation to succeed. That the police are not unduly hampered in their inquiries is partly due to the fact that the desire to prevent crime is shared by most innocent members of society, who are, accordingly, willing to give the police every assistance. This means that in practice the right of the accused to withhold and conceal evidence is less effective than might be imagined, since refusal to assist the police is itself an indication of guilt. Moreover, the majority of citizens remain blissfully unaware of their right to keep silent.

(b) Search and Entry

The power of the police to search suspects and to enter and search premises is similarly restricted. The interest of privacy and liberty demands some limitation on the activities of the authorities in this regard. So far as concerns searching the person of a suspect, the general rule is that no one is bound to submit to being searched and if the police forcibly search him, they commit the crime of assault as well as rendering themselves liable in damages for the tort of assault. On the other hand, if a thief could hide the stolen goods in his pocket and remain immune from search, the detection of crime would be utterly frustrated. Accordingly, the law provides a right of searching any suspect who has been arrested. He may lawfully be searched either for material evidence or if he is suspected of carrying a weapon with which he might do violence.

So far as concerns entry and search of premises, the Englishman's home is still his castle to the extent that the police have no general right to enter premises without the occupier's consent or to remain there against his will. If they do so, they become trespassers. But clearly the inability to follow the criminal into his house and to look there for the goods he might have stolen would stultify any efforts to combat crime. Here too, therefore, a balance must be struck between the individual's right of privacy and the public's right that crime should be punished. At common law a police officer may enter any premises to effect an arrest, to prevent the commission of a felony, or to prevent a breach of the peace. In *Thomas* v. *Sawkins*[1] police officers who attended a public meeting held to discuss the possibility of dismissing the local chief constable, and who, on being requested to leave, refused to do so, were held to be within their rights in remaining on the premises, since they had good reason to anticipate a breach of the peace, which it would be their duty to prevent. In addition, where stolen goods are thought to be concealed in the premises of a person convicted of dishonesty, the chief constable can authorize his subordinates to search such premises. Secondly, the case of *Elias* v. *Pasmore*[2] decided that where police officers lawfully enter premises for one purpose (e.g. to effect an arrest) they may lawfully seize any documents which constitute evidence that a crime has been committed. Apart from these cases, the police may only search premises by virtue of a search warrant issued by a magistrate. At common law a magistrate can issue a warrant to the police within his jurisdiction to search premises for stolen goods, and this power has been supplemented by statute in certain cases. But the magistrates have no general power of issuing search warrants except in these cases, and in any event the discretion of issuing the warrants rests with the magistrates.

When we come to discuss the question of confessions and admissions of guilt obtained from a defendant by illegal means, we shall see that such statements cannot legally be admitted as evidence and put before the jury. It might have been expected that the courts would have taken a similar view of evidence obtained as the result of an illegal search. The position here, however, was summed up in the words of a nineteenth-century

---

[1] [1935] 2 K.B. 249.   [2] (1934), 50 T.L.R. 196.

judge who asserted 'it matters not how you get it, if you steal it even, it would be admissible in evidence'.[1] Accordingly, in *Jones* v. *Owen*[2] where a police officer illegally searched the defendant and discovered a salmon in his pocket, this evidence was admitted on a charge of unlawfully fishing. In such cases, however, the court has a discretion to exclude such evidence if its admission would be contrary to justice.

(c) Arrest

The most important safeguard of the liberty of the subject are the rules which protect him against arbitrary arrest. In the first place the power of the police to arrest suspects is limited by law. In addition to this the law has laid down certain conditions which must be fulfilled if an arrest is to be lawful. Thirdly, provisions have been made to protect the interest of a person who has been arrested.

We have seen that the ordinary citizen has the right to arrest without warrant anyone who commits a felony or dangerous breach of the peace in his presence and anyone whom he reasonably suspects of having committed a felony, provided such a felony has actually been committed. A police officer has the additional right of arresting without warrant any person whom he reasonably suspects of committing a felony, even if such a felony has not actually been committed. To these common-law powers various statutes have added. Beyond these limits an arrest cannot lawfully be made without a warrant issued by a magistrate. The police have no power, for example, to detain a suspect for questioning, unless the case comes within these provisions.

The chief requisite of a lawful arrest is that the person arrested should be informed of the reason for his arrest. A warrant will specify the charge alleged and must be shown by the police officer to the prisoner at the time of arrest or as soon as possible

[1] See Cross, *Evidence*, p. 264.

[2] (1870), 34 J.P. 759. Cf. *Kuruma* v. *The Queen*, [1955] A.C. 197, where the Privy Council held that the evidence given by two police officers that they had searched the appellant and found on him ammunition, contrary to the Emergency Regulations, 1952, of Kenya, was rightly admitted, even if the officer, being below the rank of assistant inspector, had no legal power to search the appellant. The test, the court held, is whether the evidence is relevant to the issue being tried, though in cases where admission of illegally obtained evidence might work unfairly against an accused, the judge has a discretion to exclude it.

thereafter. In the case of an arrest without warrant, there is no document informing the prisoner of the charge alleged against him, but the House of Lords laid down in *Christie* v. *Leachinsky* (1947)[1] that in such a case the prisoner must be informed at the time of the arrest by the officer making the arrest the true reason for such arrest, and that failure to inform the prisoner will render the arrest unlawful. If the reason for the arrest is obvious, e.g. where the prisoner is arrested in the act of committing a felony, or if the prisoner makes it impossible for the officer to inform him of the reason, e.g. by running away, then failure to inform him will not prevent the arrest from being lawful.

A police officer who arrests a man without warrant is bound to bring him before the magistrates as soon as possible. Meanwhile the inspector or other officer in charge of the police station must inquire into the case, and unless the case is a serious one, may release the prisoner on bail. He must so release him if he cannot be brought before the magistrates within twenty-four hours. These provisions ensure that no person shall be detained for long periods by the police without a specific charge being brought.

Once brought before the magistrates, the prisoner has the right to ask for bail, i.e. to be released on condition that he appears when called upon to answer the charge against him. The magistrates generally fix a sum of money which the prisoner will forfeit should he fail to surrender to his bail, and further they often refuse bail unless some other parties are willing to stand surety, i.e. to guarantee that the prisoner will appear and to forfeit sums of money if he fails to do so. To refuse bail wrongfully is a violation of the Habeas Corpus Act, 1679, and the Bill of Rights, 1689, which latter statute lays down that bail (i.e. the sum of money to be forfeited) must not be excessive. Against the refusal of the magistrates to grant bail the prisoner may appeal to a High Court judge. In serious cases the magistrates will not grant bail, and in cases of treason they have indeed no power so to do.

To obviate the possibility of lengthy detention of prisoners without trial, the law requires that they must be brought to trial speedily. A prisoner committed for trial to Assizes must either be tried at the first practicable Assize or be released on

[1] [1947] A.C. 573.

bail, and if his case is not heard at the second Assize he must be discharged. A prisoner committed for trial to Quarter Sessions may, if his case is not heard at the next Quarter Sessions, apply to Assizes to be tried there or discharged.

The great remedy for a person who is wrongfully detained is to apply for a writ of habeas corpus. The applicant (usually the prisoner himself) applies to the High Court for an order directing the person to whom it is addressed and who will be the person having custody of the prisoner, to bring the prisoner before the court and state the cause of his detention. Should he fail to satisfy the court that there is valid cause for the detention, the court will order the prisoner's instant release. Part of the force of this writ lies in the breadth of its scope. It can be issued against any subject of the Crown, whether police officer, prison governor, or government minister such as the Home Secretary.

Having secured his freedom, the prisoner can then pursue his other remedies. In wrongfully arresting and detaining him the police (or other authorities) commit the torts of assault and false imprisonment, for which the person wronged can recover damages in the Civil Courts as compensation. In addition, they commit the crimes of assault and false imprisonment, for which they can be prosecuted and punished.

5. ENSURING A FAIR TRIAL: EVIDENCE

A corollary of the respect for liberty and the prohibition of arbitrary deprivation of freedom is the need to ensure that, before anyone is convicted and punished for an offence, it is fairly established that he has committed the offence. Some obvious and elementary conditions must be fulfilled to ensure that a suspected offender has a fair trial. First the tribunal must be impartial. Secondly, both sides must be free to present their case. But the bulk of the rules of English law in this context consist of rules prescribing how evidence is to be taken and what evidence can be received.

In England the impartiality of the tribunal is doubly secured. The idea that no one should be a judge in his own cause, but that the judges should keep aloof from the arena and thereby hold the balance between the contestants, led to the separation of the functions of judge and prosecution. Not since the abolition of the Star Chamber has there been in England a court which acted as a judge and prosecutor combined. Over and above this, the jury system has created a division of labour whereby the judge decides the law and the jury the facts.

The result of this division is that if the judiciary were too sub-servient to the Crown or too anxious to secure a conviction, the defendant would still have the protection of the jury. On the other hand, if the jury's feelings ran away with them and their anger or revulsion at what happened led them to convict against the evidence, the judge and the Court of Criminal Appeal could afford the defendant a protection against the jury.[1] This division of functions does not formally exist in the Magistrates' Courts, though in the majority of courts where the bench is composed of lay magistrates, the magistrates decide the facts and rely on the clerk for the law. It is true to say, therefore, that in England in almost all cases a defendant can only be found guilty by his fellow countrymen, the ordinary non-professional magistrates or jurymen.

That both sides should be heard and allowed to present their case would seem obvious enough today. Indeed the prosecution has never really been in difficulty on this score, being sufficiently equipped with the wherewithal to engage legal representatives. The accused, on the other hand, was at one time denied the benefit of legal representation. This either meant that because of his lack of knowledge of law and his inexperience in advocacy he was unable to defend himself properly, or it meant that in fact his defence was undertaken by the judge, who in many cases carefully presented the arguments in favour of the accused. This was often more advantageous to the accused than if he had been defended by counsel, but it was not calculated to promote the interests of justice if the presiding judge stepped down, as it were, from the bench to assume the brief for the defence. Today not only may an accused person be legally represented, but any defendant who is unable to afford to engage lawyers can be granted free legal aid under the Poor Prisoners' Defence Act, the costs being paid out of a special fund. Legal aid, however, can-not be foisted on an accused against his will, for the accused has

[1] As happened in the case of *R. v. Matheson*, [1958] 2 All E.R. 87, where the peculiarly horrible features of the accused's actions so affected the jury that they refused to accept against all evidence his defence of diminished responsibility. On appeal his conviction for murder was quashed and a verdict of manslaughter sub-stituted.

the right to defend himself as and how he wishes. The defendant also has the right of choosing from the dock any counsel robed and present in court (apart from the prosecutor), to defend him provided he pays the fee of £2. 2s. The number of 'dock briefs' has declined since the introduction of legal aid. Though often a means whereby the younger barrister made a start, it was extremely onerous for senior members of the profession, since a barrister chosen to undertake a dock brief could not relinquish it and hand it over to another barrister, although it clashed with other more important and remunerative cases. The one exception was that a dock brief could be 'returned' if counsel was briefed to appear in the House of Lords.

For a long time, though the accused was allowed representation, he was not allowed to be heard, in the sense that he was debarred from giving evidence. Originally the parties to civil and criminal trials were excluded from the witness-box on the ground that they were likely to be biased. The prosecution was not excluded, because in law the Crown was the opposing party. The accused, however, the one person who really knew what had happened, was the one person not permitted to tell his story in court. Until 1898 the accused was not in general a competent witness. He could, however, make from the dock an unsworn statement not subject to cross-examination, as did for example Florence Maybrick[1] in her trial for the murder of her husband. A judge might also question the accused and elicit his story in this way. In 1898 the Criminal Evidence Act of that year allowed the accused to go into the witness-box and give evidence on oath subject to cross-examination. Consequently the defendant today has three alternatives: to say nothing, to make an unsworn statement, or to give evidence on oath. The addition of this last alternative, the denial of which seemed such a monstrous injustice, has proved a mixed blessing to defendants. No longer able to shelter behind their inability to give evidence and leave the jury with the impression that if only they had been able to give evidence all the evidence against them could have been explained, they are expected today, if an explanation is called for, to go into the box and submit to the hazards of cross-examination. Failure to do so may lead to unfavourable comments from the judge and adverse decisions by the jury. The extension to

[1] *Famous Trials* (3rd series, 1950, ed. J. Hodge).

the accused of the right to give evidence has tended to deprive him of his other right, his right to keep silent.

We now come to the rules governing the course of the criminal trial. Here we are chiefly concerned with the law of evidence, a curiously unsystematized and unrationalized branch of English law, which has for the most part grown up almost unnoticed, being added to from time to time by *ad hoc* decisions. In this chapter it is proposed only to note briefly some of the more important rules applicable to criminal and civil trials and some which relate only to criminal cases.

The rules of evidence are mainly rules of exclusion. They debar certain persons from giving evidence. They exclude certain matters from being given in evidence. They prohibit counsel from putting certain types of question.

Anyone is competent to give evidence who is capable of understanding and taking the oath. In fact non-believers and people whose religion forbids them to take the oath are allowed instead to make a solemn affirmation. Very young children may be allowed to give unsworn evidence if the judge is satisfied that they appreciate the duty to tell the truth.

In criminal cases, however, there are two people who are not competent as witnesses for the prosecution. These are the accused himself and his wife (or husband). The significance of the exclusion of the accused can be seen where two or more defendants are tried together, for the result of this rule is that the Crown cannot call one defendant as a witness against the other. If the prosecution wish to call 'Queen's evidence', they must either arrange for separate trials, or else before giving evidence the witness must have pleaded guilty so that his trial has come to an end. In either of these cases he would not then be a co-defendant and would therefore be a competent witness. The defendant's wife cannot in general testify against her husband, the law attaching more importance here to the closeness of the marriage tie than to the need to convict the guilty. To this rule there are certain necessary exceptions, where a wife can give evidence for the prosecution against her husband. An obvious example is where the husband is accused of a crime of violence against his wife.

Witnesses who are competent are normally compellable, that is, they may be made to give evidence even against their will.

The party wishing to call an unwilling witness can issue a *subpoena* ordering him to appear and testify, disobedience to which constitutes contempt of court as well as a civil wrong against the party wishing to call the witness. The accused, however, cannot be compelled by anyone, not even his own legal advisers, to go into the witness-box. Nor can one defendant be forced to give evidence on behalf of any other co-defendant tried with him. The wife (or husband) of an accused cannot be compelled to give evidence for the defence or for the accused's co-defendant without the accused's consent. Apart from the defendant and his wife, there are certain other privileged categories of persons, such as the reigning monarch, foreign sovereigns, and persons with diplomatic immunity.

Although English courts frequently consider documentary evidence and 'real' evidence, i.e. objects actually produced in court (e.g. the weapon found at the scene of the crime) the bulk of evidence consists of oral testimony. Such evidence may be direct, e.g. where the witness states that he saw the accused commit the offence; or it may be circumstantial, e.g. different witnesses produce pieces of evidence which make it highly likely (though not certain) that the accused committed the crime. Circumstantial evidence falls short of conclusiveness, since it is always possible that there is an innocent explanation for all the evidence against the accused. Direct evidence is conclusive, but is in many cases not forthcoming (since many crimes are committed in secret). Moreover it suffers from the defect that it is not always trustworthy. If circumstantial evidence may mislead, witnesses giving direct evidence may lie.

Because evidence may be false and facts can mislead, English lawyers have developed a system of examining witnesses in three stages. This procedure is one of the distinctive features of English legal procedure and one of its finest contributions to the technique of judicial investigation. First each witness is examined by the lawyer who calls him—his examination-in-chief. At this stage the court wants to hear the witness tell his story in his own words. Accordingly, leading questions, i.e. questions which put the answer into the witness's mouth, are excluded. Counsel cannot for example say to the witness, 'Did you see the accused kill the deceased?' If this sort of question were allowed, all the court would have would be the witness's monosyllabic assents to a tale told by the lawyer calling the witness. The second and most dramatic stage is the cross-examination. In some countries the reliability of a witness's evidence is tested by confronting him with conflicting witnesses. In England this is done by the opposing lawyer, who questions the witness, probing the reliability of his memory, the accuracy of his observations, and the honesty and impartiality of the witness himself. Here, since the witness is being attacked, contradicted, or asked to modify his evidence, leading questions are necessary and are allowed. The third stage is the witness's re-examination, where the lawyer who called him into the box tries to re-establish the witness and repair the damage done by cross-examination. Questions are confined to matters arising out of cross-examination and leading questions are barred.

The overriding rule as to what evidence may be allowed in a trial is that all relevant evidence may be admitted. Irrelevant evidence would only protract a trial and confuse the jury and is therefore excluded. Certain matters, however, which might seem to qualify as relevant are also excluded. Under this heading come hearsay and opinion evidence and evidence as to the defendant's character.

(a) Hearsay Evidence

The rule against hearsay evidence means that a witness cannot report in court another person's statement of fact as proof of that fact. If the accused is charged with murder, a witness X cannot testify that Y told him that he saw the accused commit the murder; only Y can give this evidence; X is restricted to evidence of what he himself observed.

It does not follow, however, that a witness may never report another person's words. It may be that such words are not statements of fact but verbal performances. For instance if a man says, 'I give you this money', this is not an account of what he is doing; it is part of the act of giving, and can accordingly be reported in evidence. In such a case evidence that X said, 'I give you this money' would be not hearsay but original evidence.

Sometimes even statements of fact too can constitute original evidence. Words accompanying and forming part of a transaction may be admissible as original evidence, since otherwise the report of the transaction would be incomplete. In a murder trial, for example, where the accused is alleged to have strangled the deceased, a witness would be allowed to testify that while the accused and the deceased were struggling, the latter had cried out, 'You're hurting me'.

Akin to this example are reports of what another person says with regard to his bodily feelings or his state of mind. If the charge were murder by poisoning, it would be permissible for a witness to testify that shortly before he died the deceased had said that he felt very ill. Though such evidence would consist of another person's reports of fact, these cases are in a special category, because what a person says to a witness about his feelings is not a mere report of fact but is, like a cry of pain or a wince, one of the only indications available to the witness of such internal events.

Sometimes, however, even second-hand reports of externally observable facts are admissible as original evidence. If a defendant seeks to defend himself on a charge of murder by shooting, on the basis that he did not know that the gun was loaded, evidence that a third person told him that it was unloaded could not be admitted to prove that it was unloaded, but it would be admissible to show that the accused had reason to believe it was unloaded.

The reason for the exclusion of hearsay evidence is its unreliability. Apart from any other considerations it is common knowledge that stories alter as they pass from hand to hand. Moreover, the original statement of fact is less reliable than firsthand evidence given in court in two respects. The original statement was not made on oath, so that its maker had no special reasons to be accurate. Secondly, he was not subject to cross-examination, so that the original statement cannot be tested for accuracy, honesty, and so forth.

In some exceptional cases, however, the lack of oath and cross-examination is made up by other factors and hearsay evidence is admitted. Public documents, such as marriage registers, are admissible as proof of the information they contain, the method of their compilation being sufficient guarantee of their accuracy. Depositions taken at a preliminary investigation may in certain cases be put in evidence at the subsequent trial, e.g. if the witnesses whose evidence they contain are dead or too ill to travel. In the case of 'dying declarations' the solemnity of the occasion is regarded as a substitute for the oath. What this means is that in trials for homicide evidence may be given of the victim's statement as to the cause of his death, provided he made the statement under a settled, hopeless expectation of death. So if the victim just before expiring says, 'It was John who stabbed me', this would be admissible; for the expectation of death is considered to remove all motives for lying and to constitute a strong reason for him to speak the truth. A curious exception to the hearsay rule concerns complaints made by the victims of sexual offences. If for example the victim of an indecent assault informs her parents shortly after the incident of what happened, her parents may give evidence of what she said. But such evidence is admissible only to show that the prosecutrix has consistently told the same story.

By far the most important exception to the hearsay rule concerns the admissibility of *admissions* and *confessions*. If a party to a trial has made some admission against himself, this can be put in evidence. Accordingly, if the accused on being apprehended by the police says, 'It's a fair cop', the police officer can put this statement in evidence. The fact that the statement was not made on oath is outweighed by the fact that people do not usually make admissions against their own interest unless they are true. The fact that the person making the admission was not subject to cross-examination is made up for by the fact that the accused, being in court, can deny, explain, or modify the statement, leaving the jury to draw their own conclusions.

In ninety-nine cases out of a hundred where a man is convicted on indictment of a criminal offence, part of the evidence against him consists of some admission or confession he has made. *Rouse*[1] and *Timothy Evans*[2] provide examples of defendants who talked themselves into being convicted. An admission is an informal statement in some way admitting guilt. A confession is a formal written admission made to a person with authority over the case, e.g. the police officer in charge.

The danger of such evidence is threefold. In the first place it would be only too easy for the police to fabricate evidence that the accused admitted his guilt. Secondly, there is the danger that

---

[1] The story is well told in Sir Patrick Hastings's *Cases in Court*, p. 191.
[2] The fullest account of this case is to be found in Ludovic Kennedy's *Ten Rillington Place*.

threats or inducements may lead the accused to make a false
confession. A promise of bail, a promise not to prosecute the
defendant's wife, threats of violence, and so on may induce a
man to confess falsely to a crime of which he is innocent. Thirdly,
confessions and admissions are such useful items of evidence that
there is a danger that a defendant might be deprived of that
right which we have already discussed, his right to keep silent.

To avoid these dangers the law provides that no confession
may be admitted unless it is voluntary. Accordingly, confessions
made as a result of threats or inducements held out to the
accused by those in authority over the case are excluded. In
addition to this requirement the judges drew up in 1912 rules
for the guidance of police officers questioning suspects. The
Judges' Rules[1] provide amongst other things that if a suspect is
in custody or if the officer has decided to charge him, the suspect must first be cautioned that anything he says may be given
in evidence and must be informed of his right not to say anything. If these rules are violated, the judge has a discretion to
exclude the evidence. In many a trial the most important task
of the defence is to prevent the accused's confession or admission
from being admitted in evidence. The admissibility of such
evidence is a matter for the judge, who usually hears arguments
in the absence of the jury.

(b) Opinion Evidence

In English law witnesses are not in general allowed to give
their own opinions in evidence. The principle is that it is for the
witness to relate the facts and for the jury to draw conclusions
from them. A statement of opinion by a witness would not only
be irrelevant, it would usurp the functions of the jury. If, for
example, a motorist is charged with careless driving, witnesses
may tell the magistrates what happened, but they may not assert
that in their view he drove carelessly. One interesting application of this rule is that if an incident gives rise to both civil and
criminal proceedings, the outcome of the criminal trial is irrelevant to the decision in the civil trial and vice versa. If as a
result of the same accident a motorist is charged with careless
driving and sued for negligence, the finding of the Magistrates'

[1] For a full statement of the rules see Archbold, *Criminal Pleading, Evidence and Practice* (34th ed.), p. 422, para. 1118.

Court is, so far as the civil court is concerned, purely the opinion of a third party (and vice versa). Each court must make up its own mind independently.

Though the fundamental distinction between fact and opinion is clear, at times the dividing-line becomes blurred. Many seemingly straightforward reports of observation involve a mixture of fact and opinion. Descriptions of a person's appearance (smart, untidy, unwell, &c.) are a combination of observed factors and conclusions drawn therefrom. Identification, whether of persons, handwriting, objects, or places, similarly involves a mixture of observation and conclusion. Many descriptions entail a measure of assessment. Any statement as to size, distance, speed, weight, volume, brightness, temperature, and many other measurable factors, contains an element of opinion, unless actual measurements with instruments have been made. Nevertheless a description of a man as tall, a road as wide, a vehicle's speed as fast,[1] a sack as heavy, and so forth, would not be ruled out on the ground that it was opinion evidence. If it were, then little would remain which could be admitted as evidence.

Besides these simple cases where even the ordinary witness is permitted to give what is partly opinion evidence, opinion evidence is allowed to be given by expert witnesses. Handwriting and fingerprint experts, doctors, pathologists, psychiatrists, and many other scientists are constantly employed to give the courts the benefit of their opinions. In such cases the law accepts opinion evidence because it would be difficult for the court or jury unaided to draw conclusions from observed facts. Nor is there any question of the expert usurping the function of the jury, because the latter is not bound to accept the view of any of the expert witnesses. While psychiatrists may give their opinion as to the mental state of the defendant, the question whether he is insane within the M'Naghten Rules or whether his responsibility is substantially impaired, &c., can be decided only by the jury. The problem which is arising today, with increased scientific knowledge, is whether the ordinary method of trial before laymen conducted by examination, cross-examination, and re-examination is really conducive to fruitful investigation of such complicated matters as a man's mental state. The alternative, however, involving a surrender of certain

[1] See p. 193.

technical matters to boards or panels of experts, would not at present attract much support.

(c) *The Character of the Accused*

If it were found that money had been stolen from a purse and it were known that the thief must be one of say three different persons, most people would think it highly relevant if one of the three was known to have previously stolen money. For a person who has stolen once has shown that he is the sort of person who is likely to steal again. English law, however, will not allow the prosecution to give evidence like this merely to prove that an accused is the kind of man likely to commit the crime charged. The prejudice which such evidence would raise against the accused in the minds of the jury greatly outweights its probative value, so that the general rule is that such matters must be excluded.

On the other hand, a defendant is always at liberty to prove that he has a good character and has never been convicted, in order to show the jury that he is not the sort of man who is likely to have committed the offence. If he does put his character in evidence, however, the whole of his character must go in. That is to say, he cannot tell the jury of points in his favour, such as his good war record, while concealing points against him, such as his previous convictions. Consequently an accused with no previous convictions will always put himself before the jury as a person of unblemished character, while a defendant with previous convictions will say nothing about his character. Experienced jurors come to realize the significance of a defendant's silence on this score.

There are cases, however, where the prosecution may give evidence of the defendant's convictions even though he does not claim to be a person of good character. An ordinary witness can always be attacked as to his character in order to show that he is not to be believed. Had the defence in *Evans's*[1] case been able to show the jury what sort of a man the witness Christie was, it is hardly likely that his evidence would have been believed. The defendant, however, cannot normally be attacked in this way, since this would be to infringe the rule stated above. But if the defendant attacks the character of the prosecution witnesses,

---

[1] See p. 187, n. 2.

then, if he himself gives evidence, the prosecution can reply in kind and attack the defendant. Or if the defence is that the prosecution are conspiring to 'frame' the accused, it is thought only right that he should be open to cross-examination as to his criminal record so that the jury may know the character of the man who makes these allegations. In *Steinie Morrison's*[1] case the attack by the defence on the character of one of the prosecution witnesses laid the defendant open to counter-attack by the prosecution which may have swayed the jury to convict. Similarly, where two or more defendants are tried together, if one in his own defence gives evidence against the other (a 'cut-throat' defence), that other can attack the character of the first.

While, apart from these exceptions, the prosecution cannot give evidence of the defendant's previous convictions merely in order to show that he is not a reliable witness or to prove that he is the sort of person likely to have committed the offence alleged, yet in certain cases evidence of previous convictions may be relevant and admissible if it goes further than this. Evidence of acts committed on other occasions (whether or not the accused has been convicted as a result) may be relevant to show that the accused has been working according to some system or method, and to negative a plea of accident or mistake. In the case of *Smith*,[2] who was charged with murdering his wife shortly after their marriage and after he had insured her life, by electrocuting her in a bath, evidence that he had disposed of former wives in similar circumstances was admitted to negative any suggestion of accident. Here the evidence of what had occurred on other occasions showed that only on the assumption of an extraordinary coincidence could Smith be innocent of the crime charged. Such evidence may serve to identify the accused as the person responsible for the offence, if there are special features common to this offence and to others which he is known to have committed. In *R. v. Straffen*[3] the defendant, an escaped Broadmoor patient, was accused of the murder of a young girl by strangling her. The body was found lying unconcealed near a road and there were no signs of sexual interference. Evidence was admitted that he had killed two other girls in very similar

---

[1] See p. 163, n. 1.
[2] The celebrated 'Brides in the bath' case: (1915), 11 Cr. App. Rep. 229.
[3] [1952] 2 Q.B. 911.

circumstances, since this showed that he had a disposition not merely to commit crime but to commit acts of a highly exceptional nature. In such a case, however, the judge has a discretion to exclude such evidence if the prejudice that it will create outweighs its probative value.

(d) Presumption of Innocence

Criminal trials differ from civil proceedings in one very important respect. Since the outcome of a criminal trial may result in the defendant's loss of liberty or even life, the courts evolved a rule which casts upon the prosecution a heavy burden of proof. No rule of criminal law is of more importance than that which requires the prosecution to prove the accused's guilt beyond reasonable doubt. In the first place this means that it is for the prosecution to prove the defendant's guilt and not for the latter to establish his innocence; he is presumed innocent until the contrary is proved. Secondly, they must satisfy the jury of his guilt beyond reasonable doubt. In civil cases where a plaintiff sues a defendant, he who shows that on a balance of probabilities the evidence is in his favour wins the day. In criminal cases, however, the Crown cannot succeed on a mere balance of probabilities. If there is any reasonable doubt whether the accused is guilty, he must be acquitted. An acquittal therefore either means that the jury believe the accused and are satisfied of his innocence, or that, while not satisfied that he is innocent, they do not feel sure of his guilt. In England there is no middle verdict such as the Scottish verdict of 'not proven' to cover this sort of situation; 'not guilty' is the only alternative to a conviction.

In certain cases, however, the burden of proving his case rests on the accused. We have already seen that in law everyone is presumed to be sane. If, therefore, a defendant puts forward a defence of insanity, the onus is on him to establish that he comes within the M'Naghten Rules. The same holds true of the defence of diminished responsibility. Here too it is for the defendant to prove that his responsibility was substantially impaired by mental abnormality. In certain statutory offences Parliament has laid down too that the burden of proving innocence shall rest on the accused. For example the Road Traffic Act, 1960, provides that a motorist shall not be convicted of certain offences unless he was either warned at the time of commission that he would be prosecuted or was within fourteen days served with a notice of intended prosecution; but the Act further provides that this rule shall be presumed to have been complied with by the prosecution unless the defendant proves the contrary.

Where the burden of proof is on the defence, as in insanity, diminished responsibility, and other special cases, the burden is a lower one than the burden of proof borne in normal cases by the prosecution. The defence need not prove its case beyond reasonable doubt, but only on a balance of probabilities. On a plea of insanity for example the onus on the defence is merely to establish that the probability is that the accused was insane. If, therefore, X is charged with murder and sets up a plea of insanity, the jury would first have to be sure beyond reasonable doubt that X committed the murder; lack of such certainty would result in an acquittal, because any doubt would have to be resolved in favour of the accused. But if the jury were sure of this, then X would merely have to satisfy them that it was probable that he was insane; lack of reasonable certainty would not automatically result in their dismissing the defence, because here it is not the case that any doubts on the matter would have to be resolved in favour of the prosecution.

The heavier burden of proof required in criminal trials can also be seen to operate in the rules which provide that in certain cases corroboration is necessary. In some instances the rule is one of law and the absence of corroboration is a bar to conviction. For example, the unsworn evidence of a child must be corroborated. A jury cannot convict on such evidence alone, for the law does not consider it sufficiently reliable to warrant a conviction. In a charge of perjury the jury may not by law convict the accused on the uncorroborated evidence of one witness alone. The falsity of the defendant's evidence cannot be established by the evidence of only one witness, for if this were allowed, it would be merely a case of oath against oath. Another well-known example of an offence where corroboration is required concerns prosecutions for speeding. The Road Traffic Acts lay down that no one may be convicted of speeding on the uncorroborated opinion evidence of one witness, because it is obviously a difficult matter to estimate speed. The evidence of one witness who measures the speed with instruments, however, will suffice, because here the court is not relying on opinion evidence.

In some cases the rule requiring corroboration is merely one of practice. The judge is bound to warn the jury that it is extremely unsafe to convict without corroboration. This rule applies to prosecutions for sexual offences, where the jury must be warned of the danger of convicting on the uncorroborated evidence of the victim, for in these cases people's imaginations are only too prone to invention and fantasy. Similar warnings must be given with regard to the evidence of accomplices, because clearly the testimony of a person who by his own admission was involved in the crime is unlikely to excel in reliability. In all these cases, although a jury can convict without corroboration, if the judge fails to warn them of the danger of doing so, the Court of Criminal Appeal will quash the conviction.

The rule as to corroboration is not such an obstacle for the prosecution as it might appear. Where corroboration is needed, all that is necessary is some other evidence implicating the defendant in some material way and connecting him with the crime. Such evidence may consist not only of testimony of other witnesses, but of statements made by the accused himself or of documentary evidence. Nevertheless the rule exemplifies the higher standard of proof required in criminal trials.

VI

PUNISHMENT

1. THE PROBLEM OF PUNISHMENT

COMPARED with other aspects of the criminal law, the question
of punishment is one of peculiar difficulty. For the lawyer it is a
question which presents special problems for a variety of reasons.
In the first place, although the task of imposing penalties is that
of a subsection of the legal profession, the punishment of a
criminal is a combined operation of Parliament, the courts,
and the administration. The range of penalties which may be
imposed is in most cases set by the legislature, which fixes the
maximum sentences for different offences. In exceptional cases
there may be a fixed or fixed minimum penalty. For the vast
majority of offences, however, only the maximum penalty is
prescribed by law, so that the court is left free to select in each
actual case the appropriate sentence. After the court has selected
what sentence seems suitable, the carrying out of this sentence
falls to the lot of those who administer the penal system: prison
governors and prison officers, those who are in charge of borstal
and other detention institutions, and probation officers, all of
whom work under the aegis of the Home Office. Consequently,
the part played by the courts is only one part of the whole operation of punishing the offender.

One result of this is that once sentence has been passed, the
courts are no longer concerned with the offender's fate; their
task is concluded. This means that the effect of the sentence can
be seen less by the courts themselves than by those whose function it is to see that the sentence is carried out and by those who
study the social effect of punishment. For this reason those who
actually pass sentence on the offender must to some extent work
in the dark, unless they are willing to accept the guidance of
those who study the effects of punishment. This has been recognized by the Streatfeild Committee, which investigated the
problem of the business of the Criminal Courts and which suggested in 1961 that it would help the courts if they were provided by the Home Office with a booklet on sentencing. Such

a booklet, which they suggested should be periodically revised, could serve as a textbook for sentencing and could assist the courts to select the punishment best suited for each different offender and each different offence.[1]

Another difficulty confronting the lawyer in this field is that the problem of selecting the appropriate sentence is not one which can be solved by normal legal techniques. In fact it is not the typical sort of legal problem, which lawyers learn by training and experience to tackle. The problems with which the lawyer has to deal fall roughly into two classes. Purely legal problems he must tackle by threading his way through statutes, reported cases, and so forth in order to discover the legal rules relevant to his problem. The meaning of these rules must be established, and the rules must be applied to the facts of the problem in hand. In contrast to this the lawyer spends a great part of his time in making a quasi-historical inquiry, in order to establish what the actual facts in a given case are. This involves him in putting forward, testing, and weighing evidence, and in drawing inferences from such evidence. But the selection of the appropriate sentence cannot be made by either of these methods.

What sentence should be passed cannot be decided merely by looking up rules, because in the first place English law has very little in the way of rules regarding sentence. Certain offences indeed carry a fixed penalty; in practice murder is the only important crime of this category. There are, too, certain motoring offences for which Parliament has fixed minimum penalties of disqualification or imprisonment. There are also regulations concerning the increasing of penalties if the prisoner has been previously convicted and has reached a certain age. Apart from these provisions, however, the law has been content with setting a maximum penalty—normally grossly in excess of any punishment inflicted[2]—and with leaving the courts free to impose any lesser sentences which they think fit.

---

[1] 30 Dec. 1960, Cmnd. 1289.

[2] See the report by *Justice* on Legal Penalties (1959). It should be noted that when a prisoner pleads guilty to or is convicted of more than one offence, the sentences imposed in respect of each offence may be ordered by the court to run concurrently or consecutively. It should also be observed that frequently a prisoner convicted of one crime asks the court to take into consideration other offences with which he has not been charged but which he admits. If these offences are taken into consideration by the court, the accused will not in practice, though he could in theory, be afterwards prosecuted for them.

Nor can the selection of the appropriate sentence be made purely by reference to the past facts of the case, for in sentencing an offender the court is attempting at least in part a measure of social control. Whether such control will be achieved can only be calculated by reference to existing evidence as to the effects of different sorts of punishments both on the offender himself and on the rest of the community. A court passing sentence, therefore, should have its eye to the future, as compared with the advocate in the trial, who is concerned not with what will happen, but with what did happen.

As a result, the stipendiary magistrate, recorder, or judge, though well trained and experienced in deciding points of law and in inquiring into questions of fact, receives no formal training for this most difficult and important task of selecting the appropriate sentence.[1] The law student learns little about punishment except to note that four offences carry the death penalty and that he must distinguish between capital and non-capital murder. The practising member of the bar, though he is frequently engaged in pleading in mitigation for an offender, rarely has to argue as to the suitability of one particular sentence rather than any other; and this is partly due to the fact that in English law it is no part of the function of prosecuting counsel to press for any particular penalty. Regular attendance, however, at the criminal courts does give the practitioner an insight into the factors which lead judges to impose different sentences.

Though it is wise on account of the uniqueness of every case to leave the ultimate selection of sentence to the judge, who, unlike Parliament, has heard the case and is aware of all the facts, yet as a general rule of justice we should expect to see like cases treated alike, and the similarity between different cases would lead us to suppose the existence of some general principle regulating the operation of sentencing. Indeed observation of the courts at work does reveal certain features of a general pattern. The sentences passed tend to reflect the grading of offences in the substantive law according to the intention of the offender and the extent of harm caused. The more deliberate the offender's act, the heavier the sentence, while temptation, provocation, drink, and such factors tend to lessen the penalty. Again, the greater the harm done, the greater the

[1] For magistrates' need of training in such matters see Watson, op. cit.

punishment; a trivial peculation is treated more leniently than a theft of thousands of pounds. Moreover, the courts are not content merely with fitting the punishment to the offence. They go further and try to fit it to the offender himself. So we see the prisoner's past history and previous convictions being taken into consideration, together with his background and future prospects. An old lag with no settled way of life will receive less mercy than a first offender with a home and employment waiting for his return.

Such general features resulting from the application of rules of thumb do not, however, add up to a coherent sentencing policy. Nowhere is there to be found even the most general judicial statement of the factors to be taken into account by courts in passing sentence. There are many things which courts may, but none which they must, take into consideration in this matter. Accordingly, sentences vary from court to court. One judge, looking to the future, will attach great weight to the fact that the accused has a job to return to and will impose only a light sentence. Another, looking rather to the past, will be impressed more by the harm the prisoner has done and will pass a heavy sentence. More alarming, however, is the inconsistency in the approach of the courts to different offences. Driving offences, which may make one court 'see red', may appear to another tribunal as mere technical crimes without any intrinsic immorality. Or again, a prisoner guilty of gross indecency may find in one court that the judge's repugnance for his conduct finds expression in a heavy sentence of imprisonment, while in another he may see the judge proceeding by the use of conditional and absolute discharges to implement in his own court the recommendations of the Wolfenden Committee. A textbook such as that envisaged by the Streatfeild Committee would go far to remedy these defects and ensure a uniform sentencing policy. Meanwhile, one may question what at present is treated as axiomatic, the entrusting to one and the same person the two very different functions of presiding over the trial and of passing sentence.

Much of the difficulty surrounding the problem of punishment, however, arises from a lack of agreement as to the purpose of punishment. Such disagreement can be seen in the evidence put before the Royal Commission on Capital Punishment, in the debates on capital punishment, and in the evidence put before the Advisory Council on the Treatment of Offenders with regard to the question of corporal punishment. Moreover, in criminal cases one finds at times a conflict of attitude between the judiciary on the one hand and probation officers, psychiatrists, and social workers on the other. The problem is bedevilled by a dispute both as to the ultimate end of punishment and as to the immediate use of punishment as a means to this end.

Before turning to the question of the purpose of punishment, however, it is worth examining shortly what is entailed in the notion of punishment and considering what the acceptance of a penal system commits us to.

The notion of punishment

Punishment might be roughly defined as the authoritative infliction of suffering for an offence.[1] There are then three major elements involved in the notion of punishment. The first element is that it is imposed by someone in authority over the person punished. So, for example, a parent may punish his child, but the child cannot be said to punish his parent; for in this case the child's lack of authority over the parent would prevent his action being described as punishing. Secondly, punishment involves the infliction of something unpleasant on the victim, whether consisting of positive physical pain or of deprivation of something which the victim desires such as his liberty. Curing offenders with kindness, therefore, does not, by virtue of lacking this feature, qualify as punishment.

Thirdly, and most important, the notion of punishment entails the actual or supposed commission of an offence. This is one side of the retributive nature of punishment: punishment in the abstract is meaningless; punishment can only be inflicted for an offence. In the usual case the person punished and the offender are one and the same. There are, however, cases which diverge from the standard case and where the two are not identical, as in the case of collective punishment, the punishment of scapegoats, and cases of vicarious liability. But there is always this limit that for anything to qualify as punishment, it must be

---

[1] The literature on this topic is vast. Recent discussions include J. D. Mabbot, *Mind*, 1939, p. 153; D. J. B. Hawkins, 7 *M.L.R.* 204; H. L. A. Hart, *Proc. Arist. Soc.* (1959–60), p. 1.

inflicted on account of some actual or supposed offence committed by someone. Though one can punish an innocent man
whom one wrongly imagines to have committed an offence, one
cannot logically punish a man when it is known that no offence
whatsoever has been committed; for this would not qualify for
the description of punishment. A system whereby suffering was
inflicted without reference to any offence, though the infliction
need not necessarily be made at random, would not be a system
of punishment as we know the term. Accordingly, prophylactic
measures, preventive justice, and systems of social hygiene, involving the treatment of potential offenders before they commit
actual offences, would differ from a system of punishments in
this very important respect.

The logic of a concept, however, is not the justification of its
acceptance. The mere fact that other ways of dealing with anti-
social conduct fail to qualify for the description of 'punishment'
does not prove them inferior to a system of penalties awarded
for offences. But there are certain moral and practical grounds
for supporting adherence to this system instead of adopting
some other approach. There would be little disagreement as to
the necessity, whatever system of treatment were adopted, of
ensuring that it should be administered by authority. A society
which allowed blood-feuds, vendettas, self-help, and private
measures of justice, would find itself overrun by anarchy.

As regards the second aspect of punishment, viz. that it must
be unpleasant, at least two reasons may be advanced in support
of it. First there is the obvious practical need to discourage
criminal conduct. While the best cure for a man who persists in
driving away cars without the owners' consent might well be to
provide him with a car of his own at state expense, this might
positively encourage others to follow his example. Undue emphasis on reclamation and reformation of offenders tends to
overlook the importance of the potential offender and obscures
the ambivalent nature of punishment, which is concerned not
only with the person in the dock, but with the rest of society also.
Secondly, there is the fact that pampering the offender may
result in injustice if he obtains advantages denied to those who
are guiltless of crime.[1] In the above example, even supposing
the rest of the citizen body were so honest as not to be spurred

---

[1] See p. 237.

to emulate the 'joy-rider' by seeing him provided with a free car, nevertheless the provision of a free car to the offender would be unjust to all the other citizens whose want of means had not led them to make free with the property of others.

The third feature of punishment is the requirement that it may only be administered for an offence. One reason for preferring this to some system whereby potential offenders might be treated before actually committing offences is that the traditional system of punishment affords the citizen the maximum freedom. So long as he confines his activities within the rules laid down—and these he knows or can find out—he is free from interference. This freedom he only forfeits by breaking the rules of the society in which he lives, whereupon society may make use of him to prevent further crime. A system of social hygiene would deny the individual this choice of accepting or rejecting society's terms and would leave him quite uncertain whether he was liable to interference at any given moment.

The justification of punishment

Sir James Stephen claimed that 'the criminal law stands to the passion of revenge in much the same relation as marriage to the sexual appetite'.[1] Now, important as may be the part played by the desire for revenge in the establishment of a system of criminal law, the picture conjured up in most people's minds by the term 'punishment' would surely be neither that of taking revenge nor of some substitute for this. The underlying picture we have is more likely to be based on punishment as most people first encounter it, namely parental chastisement. Akin to this is the idea—too often overlooked yet worth remembering because of the way it has dominated our thoughts about punishment—the idea of divine punishment.

The importance of stressing that parental and divine punishment is central to the ordinary notion of punishment may be seen when we come to consider the aims of punishment. For this central position of parents and gods in the concept of punishment may lead to the aims and objects of divine and parental punishment being carried over and applied by some people to the problem of state punishment.

We are not concerned here with the justification of divine and

[1] Stephen, *General View of the Criminal Law of England*, p. 99.

parental punishment; we are concerned merely with the purposes with which they are associated. The aim of parental punishment, most people would agree, is to prevent children from behaving in certain undesired ways. But this is, it would equally be agreed, only one of the purposes which most parents have for punishing their children. Most parents also wish to instil into their children a sense of right and wrong, together with an inclination to prefer the former for its own sake, and this they do by various means including the infliction of punishment. Accordingly, a parent whose child only learned to behave in such a manner as to avoid being punished would feel that he had not fully achieved his aim.

So far as divine punishment is concerned, in traditional Christian thinking it appears to be regarded less as a means to an end than as an end in itself. Temporal punishment can indeed be looked on as a means whereby the victim achieves the end of expiating for his sin and becoming reconciled with the Deity. Eternal punishment, however, would seem to be thought of as an end in itself. The eternal damnation of Lucifer, for example, though it might serve as a deterrent, is primarily something complete in itself; it is as complete as is the eternal reward of Michael the Archangel, however much an inducement and encouragement this in its turn might prove to others. Divine punishment as the reward for sin, then, as retribution, appears as an end in itself.

Now an attempt to justify state punishment for crime is sometimes made on the same ground, that it is a retribution for wrongdoing. Here, however, we must first distinguish the purpose societies have for punishing and the purposes which might justify this activity. For punishment consists in the infliction of suffering, and this is an evil which needs to be justified. We must separate from the aims societies have, the aims which might justify the infliction on the victims of the misery which punishment entails.

The aims fall into two categories, according to whether they are connected with the protection of society or not. One category comprises such aims as the exaction of retribution, the expiation by the criminal of his crime, and the satisfaction of the demand of the members of society for justice. The other category comprises the aim of protecting society and its individual members by preventing certain kinds of conduct. The infliction of punishment secures this aim by deterring potential offenders, by reforming actual offenders, and sometimes by preventing an actual offender from further criminal activity.

The first category of aims presents a difficult problem. The problem roughly is whether there can be any justification for punishment except in so far as it is aimed at the protection of society by preventing crime. It is sometimes urged that the state should punish in order to exact retribution, to preserve the balance of justice. The difficulty with this suggestion is that of discovering the justification for this. If one man does some wrong or immoral act, it is not easy to see what right another man has to exact retribution for this. Edgar Wallace's 'four just men' and other fictitious private agencies of justice might be said to be justified in punishing wrongdoers in order to prevent them committing further harm, but for one man to play at being god and to ensure that wrong should reap its reward involves an assumption of rights over others which surely needs positive justification. Such justification is hard to find and indeed few would seek to support such activities. But if individuals have no moral right to exact retribution it is hard to see how a society, a group of individuals, can acquire such a moral right either.

What holds good of retribution likewise holds good of expiation and atonement. The idea of expiation and atonement is that the wrongdoer by suffering pays the debt demanded by justice and owed to the authority inflicting the suffering, and so becomes reconciled once more with that authority. We see this idea at work in the conception of non-eternal divine punishments. It is sometimes said that punishment for crime enables the criminals to 'pay their due in the hard coinage of punishment'.[1] The difficulty of justifying state measures aimed at making an offender pay such a debt is the difficulty of showing that this debt is owed to society. Just as it is hard to show that society any more than an individual is entitled to exact retribution, so it is difficult to show that society any more than an individual has a right that the offender should make expiation and atonement to it for his wrongdoing. With Blackstone[2] we may urge that atonement and expiation should be left to the Supreme Being

---

[1] Mr. Winston Churchill in the House of Commons, 1910, cited by Sir Lionel Fox, *The English Prison and Borstal Systems*, p. 64.   [2] Blackstone, *Comm.* iv. 11.

There is, however, a valuable claim concealed in the notion of expiation, namely the idea that the wrongdoer who has been punished has by paying his debt wiped the slate clean for a fresh start; and this claim is worth pressing in the face of practical considerations which operate to prevent the criminal making a fresh start. The known fact that a man has been convicted, the stigma of a prison sentence, together with various other factors make it impossible for his start to be entirely fresh, but in so far as the notion of expiation involves the demand for a possibility for such a start it goes hand in hand with the demand for reformation and rehabilitation.

Yet another aim put forward to justify state punishment is the denunciation of the offence.[1] It is true that to prohibit an act without fixing a penalty for contravention would be an empty threat, and to fail to execute the punishment fixed would likewise reduce the law to an empty threat. But is is again hard to see what justification there can be for such denunciation unless the acts are denounced for the further purposes of preventing their performance. The aim is in fact part of the overall aim of protecting society.

We are left with the reason sometimes advanced as an important factor to be taken into account by any government: the need to satisfy the demand for justice.[2] The suggestion here is not that society, any more than its individual members, has a right to exact retribution for wrongdoing, but that if such retribution is not exacted, the public conscience will be so outraged as to take the law into its own hands, to riot, revolt, and so forth. If negroes, it has been urged in some countries, are not executed for raping white women, the white population will resort to lynching. While, as a matter of practical politics, no government can remain oblivious to the feelings of the governed, the mere existence of a desire to see justice done—in these cases to see those who commit certain acts suffer certain punishments—does not automatically justify its gratification. Although the members of a society may be entitled to be ensured that they are being

---

[1] e.g. by Lord Denning and Archbishop Fisher, quoted in Royal Commission on Capital Punishment, Cmnd. 8932, at p. 18. The Lord Chancellor agreed with this view in the House of Lords Debate in 1956, 198 H.L. Deb. (5 July) 576, 577, 696 (1956).

[2] Bentham went so far as to accept this as a justifiable incidental effect of punishment.

protected against crime, there are many desires whose satisfaction at the cost of harming other people no one would seriously seek to justify, such as a lust for war, a greed for wealth, and so on; and the passion for justice carries with it no unique qualification for such satisfaction. Where an actual offender is punished and the aim of preventing crime is pursued, the demand for justice may be incidentally satisfied. But to punish merely in order to satisfy this demand, to sacrifice an offender to this passion for justice, is no more justified than to ill treat one person in order to gratify the sadistic desires of another. Moreover, the popular passion for justice may, like many other popular feelings, be based on error and prejudice. Further, it can lead to disproportionate penalties and the punishment of the innocent. Here the rulers should lead, not be swayed by, popular opinion.

One further possible justification might be advanced, the aim of making the citizens behave morally.[1] This is akin to what we have seen to be one of the aims of parental punishments. Now though this is not often suggested as the purpose of punishing criminals, it must surely be one of the purposes underlying the retention in the criminal calendar of conduct which may be immoral but which occasions no harm to the community. The punishment, for example, of homosexual acts committed in private by consenting male adults, when there is no question of corruption or outrage to public decency, cannot serve to protect society against harm, unless it be supposed harmful even to know that such events privately take place. The only plausible reason for punishing such acts is to secure conformity with a moral code. The objections to such a purpose are, first, that external conformity with a moral code is not the same as behaving morally; and that in any case to treat adult citizens as parents treat their children and force them to conform to the current notions of morality is an encroachment on their liberty and involves the infliction of pain without any corresponding lessening of misery. It is easy to justify on grounds of self-defence society's forcing the individual to obey rules prohibiting killing and similar acts; it is difficult to see what entitles a society, any more than an individual, to seek to make a person obey moral canons whose contravention causes no harm.

[1] See pp. 79 ff.

The second category of aims is easier to support as a justification of punishment. If individuals are justified in defending themselves against violence, attacks on their property, and similar harm, it is not difficult to argue that a group of such individuals, a society, is similarly entitled to protect itself and its members against such attacks. The problem which then arises is against what kinds of conduct societies and individuals are justified in protecting themselves. The misery entailed by punishment of certain conduct must be balanced against the misery involved in leaving the conduct unpunished. The misery resulting from punishing murderers would be agreed generally to be outweighed by the misery which would ensue if murder could be committed with impunity. The unhappiness caused by the punishment of prostitution and homosexuality on the other hand may well outweigh the unhappiness resulting from tolerating such conduct.

At this level the retributive aspect of punishment plays an important role by limiting the pursuit of the aim of self-protection of society in two different ways. First, punishment may only be inflicted for an offence, as we have seen; and further it may be argued that it should only be inflicted on the offender, since he alone should be taken to have forfeited his right not to be interfered with. To penalize one person for another's offence is to make use of an innocent person for the greater good of the community, and human beings ought not to be used as mere means to an end in this way. Secondly, the retributive aspect prohibits the infliction of punishment totally out of proportion to the offence. Death for speeding might end this sort of anti-social conduct, but the price paid would be too great. But given the justification of the use of punishment to prevent crime, and given the requirement that it should be restricted to actual offenders and proportional to the offence, the major problem here is the practical one of deciding what type of punishment will best achieve this aim, whether deterrence, reclamation, or prevention offers the best prospect.

2. PUNISHMENT AS A MEANS TO AN END

In 1764 the Italian writer Beccaria[1] put forward the view that

---

[1] Beccaria, *On Crimes and Punishment*, published 1764. For an interesting account of the history of this essay see Margery Fry, *Arms of the Law*.

the only justifiable purpose of punishing offenders is the protection of society by the prevention of crime. Though this view does not command universal acceptance—as can be seen from the support given to the object of retribution by such writers as Sir James Stephen[1] and Professor Kenny[2] and by some of the advocates of capital punishment[3]—yet this much could be said, that crime prevention is accepted as the prime purpose of punishment. The practical problem is to discover how punishment can best achieve this end.

Punishing an offender may serve to lessen the incidence of crime in three different ways. The most obvious result is the effect on the rest of the community produced by the example made of the offender. Indeed the mere assignment by law of a penalty to an offence operates as a threat to deter people from committing the offence. If the offence is in fact committed, then the threat has failed so far as that particular offender is concerned, but at this stage the infliction of the penalty prescribed or allowed by law constitutes proof that the threat is no mere empty one. The suffering of the offender in such a case serves to deter others from emulating him. Among possible future offenders stands also the accused himself, and he too may be deterred by a taste of punishment from repeating his crime.

This use of punishment as a deterrent has by many been accepted as its major function. Amongst others, Blackstone[4] in the eighteenth century urged that the end of punishment is to deter from crime, and was led by this view to the conclusion that the death penalty should only be inflicted when no other penalty would be effective, and this at a time when in England more than a hundred and sixty offences were capital. The example afforded by the suffering of the offender played the largest part too in Bentham's scheme of punishment.[5] Starting from the premiss that the overall end was to control human action, he pointed out that punishment achieved this partly by reforming or disabling the offender himself and partly by providing an example to others. But example, he claimed, was the more important function.

---

[1] See Howard Jones, *Crime and the Penal System*, p. 126.
[2] *Outlines of Criminal Law* (1902), p. 33.
[3] See Royal Commission on Capital Punishment, p. 17.
[4] Blackstone, ibid.   [5] *Principles of Penal Law*, part ii, chap. 3.

It was Bentham who made the important and interesting distinction between what he termed the 'real' and the 'apparent' value of punishment. The real value is the effect which it has in fact on the victim, and constitutes the cost of the penalty in terms of suffering. The apparent value is the effect which it has on the minds of the community in general, which for the most part consists of the uninformed; and it is this that gives us the profit gained by the infliction of the penalty. Arguing on utilitarian grounds for a minimizing of suffering, Bentham claimed that the real value should be as small and the apparent value as large as possible; for the delinquent too is a member of society and his suffering is part of the total misery. One might imagine a situation in which the administrators could obtain all the profit of the apparent value without the cost of the real value, by perpetrating a fraud on the community; e.g. they could announce that the criminal had been executed, whereas in fact he had been released. To maintain such a deception would be in practice extremely difficult, and as Bentham pointed out, real punishment must be given to preserve the appearance of it.

The eighteenth and nineteenth centuries formed an era in which deterrence was firmly established in the centre of the penal system. Sir Lionel Fox[1] quotes the example of an eighteenth-century judge who passed sentence of death, saying, 'You are to be hanged not because you have stolen a sheep but in order that others may not steal sheep'. At a time when there was little in the way of an organized police force and crime could flourish undetected and unpunished, it was only to be expected that the lack of certainty of detection should be compensated by the severity of the punishments meted out to those who were convicted. By about the year 1800 over two hundred offences, it has been estimated, were punishable by death.[2] In some cases the carrying out of the sentence was accompanied by savage tortures, the victim being dragged to the scaffold, mutilated, and disembowelled. Even young children were not exempt from barbarous penalties of this nature.

However, it must be remembered that in the majority of cases a sentence of transportation was substituted for the death

---

[1] Cited by Fox, op. cit., p. 11.
[2] Radzinowicz, *A History of English Criminal Law from 1750*, vol. i, p. 3.

penalty, and this served the twofold purpose of acting as a deterrent and ridding the community of its criminals. When transportation became impossible in the mid-nineteenth century, its place as the primary punishment was taken by imprisonment. Here too, though this development was to have considerable repercussions on penal practice and our attitude to punishment, for the rest of the century the emphasis still remained on deterrence. The House of Lords Committee on Prison Discipline in 1863 stated firmly that the object of imprisonment was deterrence and that the régime should consist of 'hard labour, hard fare, and a hard bed'. The judges of that time were convinced that reform and imprisonment were a contradiction in terms. Indeed for the next generation deterrence by severity of prison conditions remained the rule. As Fox observes, 'for death itself the system had substituted a living death'.[1]

Although today we have moved far from the views of the nineteenth century on this matter, nevertheless there are still many who would give pride of place to the deterrent aspect of punishment. Of those who are opposed to the abolition of the death penalty a great number base their objections on the ground that death provides the only effective deterrent to murder. The campaign for the reintroduction of birching and flogging is founded largely on the feeling that such treatment would afford the best deterrents for offences of violence. Within the field of actual sentencing practice we are familiar with the 'exemplary sentence', where the increasing frequency of a particular crime leads the court to pass a heavier sentence than that usually awarded for that offence in order to deter others. The inordinately long sentence of forty-two years' imprisonment passed on *Blake*[2] in 1961 for contravention of the Official Secrets Act can only be regarded as a living death sentence imposed for deterrent reasons.

Since the end of the nineteenth century, however, there has been a change in attitude in penal practice which has resulted in more emphasis being placed on the reformative aspect of punishment. Before considering this, it is worth noting another way in which punishment can be used as a means to the end of crime prevention.

The punishment inflicted on the offender may not only act as

---

[1] Fox, op. cit., p. 51.   [2] [1961] 3 W.L.R. 744.

a deterrent to others but can operate to render the offender himself incapable of committing further crimes. The offender's own
behaviour is controllable, in Bentham's language, by reform
and by disablement. The prevalence of capital punishment in
England in the eighteenth century is evidence of the importance
attached to the idea of using the penalty to prevent the actual
offender from further wrongdoing, for whatever the success of
the death penalty as a deterrent, it is a uniquely successful preventive measure. At the present time much of the opposition
to the abolition of capital punishment stems from a feeling that
a man who has committed one murder must be prevented from
doing so again in the future and from a dissatisfaction with the
substitution of a term of life imprisonment which in fact results
in the release of the prisoner after, on the average, a period of
nine or ten years.

Despite the demise of the once-common alternative measure
of transportation, which performed a preventive function by
ridding the community of the offender, there remain today
several types of punishment with a partial or total preventive
effect. Imprisonment itself results in temporary prevention,
while the lengthy periods of preventive detention provided for
persistent offenders by the Criminal Justice Act, 1948, are based
on the need of removing such an offender from society in order
to protect the community. Another example of a penalty partly
aimed at the incapacitation of the offender himself is disqualification. People unfit to have charge of motor-cars may be disqualified temporarily or even permanently from holding a
driving licence; or the court may order that such a person be
disqualified until he passes a special driving test. Similar orders
can be made disqualifying people from keeping dogs. The use of
punishment to prevent the actual offender as well as to deter
others is also manifest in the punishment by the law of attempts
and conspiracies to commit crimes, of the offences akin to burglary and housebreaking, and of certain offences under the
Vagrancy Act, in all of which cases the law steps in to penalize
the accused before the object or purpose of the attempt or conspiracy is achieved.

The use of punishment solely to deter or prevent presents certain difficulties. On moral grounds the objection has been put
that this involves the complete subordination of the interests of

the individual to those of the community, whereas morally each person should be treated as an end in himself. To this Bentham seems to have given a convincing answer in asserting that if we are to prevent crime and attain security, then the punishment of offenders is an indispensable sacrifice.

The real force of this objection lies in the moral objections to inflicting punishments without regard to any other considerations than those of deterrence and prevention. Even though it is granted that society is justified in trying to prevent crime and even though it is admitted that punishment is a successful method of achieving this, at the same time there are other factors which may limit the degree of punishment which it is thought morally right to make use of. Most people would argue that punishment producing needless suffering should not be used and that the minimum penalty which would effectively achieve the object of crime prevention is the one to be selected. We can, however, go further than this and object to certain kinds of punishment, even though they might be highly effective, on the ground of their barbarity. Maiming, blinding, mutilating, and other forms of torture once prevalent in England could be objected to on this ground. Within the range of punishments which we are prepared to employ, moral considerations are a further brake on the amount of punishment which should be imposed, in that the penalty must not be wholly disproportionate to the offence. The much-criticized *lex talionis*, 'an eye for an eye and a tooth for a tooth', was in origin an advance in that it served to limit the punishment: no more than an eye for an eye, and no more than a tooth for a tooth was to be the rule. If the harm to be prevented is outweighed by the suffering inflicted, this results in an abuse of the criminal law. Moral considerations further limit the distribution of punishment to those who actually commit the offence charged and to those actual offenders who could have chosen not to have offended, so providing an objection to vicarious and to strict liability, and affording the moral basis for the excuses and justifications accepted in most systems of criminal law.[1]

Closely connected with such moral considerations are certain practical drawbacks to a system relying entirely on deterrence[2]

[1] See Hart, op. cit., pp. 10 ff.
[2] The inadequacy of deterrence is clearly examined in Margery Fry, op. cit., part ii.

and prevention. As societies become more civilized, the public conscience refuses to tolerate harsh and barbarous penalties, and the weapons in the armoury of the criminal law decrease in number. The great variety of punishments once in use in England involving physical torture or public humiliation have been abolished and we are left for the most part today only with loss of property, loss of liberty, and, in rare cases, death. A system wedded to the idea of deterrence, however, tends to rely on the severity of the punishment, and the more prevalent the offence or the more persistent the offender, the heavier becomes the penalty imposed. The result of this is to transfer public sympathy to the offender and to render the law ineffective by virtue of the refusal of judges and above all juries to see the accused convicted. In the nineteenth century many an accused was found guilty of stealing property valued at less than a shilling when the whole weight of the evidence showed that the value was higher, simply because larceny of property to the value of a shilling or more carried the death penalty. In 1830 a petition signed by over 700 bankers was presented to Parliament 'praying that Parliament would not withhold from them that protection to their property which they would derive from a more lenient law'.[1] In our own day the refusal of juries in the face of clear evidence to convict motorists of manslaughter, which carries a maximum penalty of life imprisonment, led Parliament to create the new offence of causing death by driving, the maximum penalty for which is imprisonment for five years.

The main practical objection, however, to founding a penal system on deterrence alone came to light after the end of the system of transportation. While this system remained, England was in the happy position of being able to export its criminals overseas. After the independence of the American colonies was established, new centres for transportation were found in the recently discovered colonies of Australia. By the middle of the nineteenth century, however, Australia had closed its doors to the import of convicts, and from this time forward England found that it would have to live with its ex-convicts after they had served their terms. This brought to light two factors not hitherto sufficiently realized. In the first place there was discovered the existence of a category of persistent offenders who

[1] Sir Leo Page, *Crime and the Community*, p. 54.

are not deterred by penalties adequate to deter the ordinary citizen from crime and to check the ordinary offender's criminal career. A further discovery was that a form of punishment, the threat of which might have excellent deterrent value on such members of the community as were never subjected to it, might have an entirely detrimental effect on those upon whom it is imposed. Indeed some of the aspects of imprisonment which may serve to make most individuals behave in such a way as to avoid being sent to prison, were found to be the very factors which combined to confirm the actual prisoner in his criminal ways. The contamination to which a prison sentence exposed the offender, the new contacts which it gave him with other criminals, the stigma which it imposed on him in the eyes of law-abiding citizens, and the respect which he derived from it among other criminals all combined to render a prison sentence a passport to the underworld. This practical difficulty arising from the fact that a certain type of punishment may have a dele-terious effect on the criminal has also been encountered in the field of corporal punishment. The evidence available shows that a higher percentage of young offenders sentenced to birching committed further offences than of similar offenders subjected to any other form of penalty.

The need to provide some form of punishment which would act as a deterrent without producing harmful effects on those subjected to it led to the setting up of the Gladstone Committee to examine the problem. Their report in 1895 emphasized the need for reclamation of the offender. The subsequent develop-ment of our penal system displays an acceptance of the impor-tance of reformation as an element of punishment. The prison régime has been adapted to allow for the execution of this pur-pose. Side by side with this there has been a gradual move away from imprisonment, so that today the courts could be said to strive to keep the offender out of prison rather than to send him there. The Children Acts and the Criminal Justice Acts ensure that young offenders should not be confined in the same institu-tions as adult criminals. The establishment of probation officers provided an alternative method of treatment of offenders, and enabled the court to avoid sending first offenders in many cases to prison. Another important development was that time for the payment of fines was allowed by the Criminal Justice Act, 1914, and the Money Payments Act, 1935, required magistrates to inquire into the means of an offender before committing him to prison for non-payment of fines. At the same time the practice of sentencing an offender to a short term of imprisonment as a sharp lesson has fallen into comparative disuse. Since 1945 the average annual number of offenders sent to prison for less than five weeks amounts only to 8,000-odd, as compared with a figure of 100,000 for the year 1913.

Alternatives to imprisonment have been found in various types of punishment which cater more for the reform of the offender. The obvious example is that of probation, to be dealt with later. Special reformatory institutions have been devised for young offenders. For certain classes of adult criminals there has been created a system of corrective training. Indeed today it could fairly be said that the practice of the courts is to avoid committing an offender to prison unless there is no practical alternative.

The emphasis on reform and reclamation, however, is not without its difficulties. One danger is that of concentrating so much attention on the actual offender as to lose sight of the need for the penalty to act as a deterrent to the potential offender. Yet another is that the old 'tariff' system, according to which the punishment was made to fit the crime, is being replaced by a system whereby the punishment is made to fit the offender. In so far as justice would seem to demand that like cases are treated alike, and that the same crime should receive the same punishment, the new system runs counter to this demand. It is not wholly satisfactory to see one person put on probation and another sent for a long period of corrective training for the same sort of offence. A further difficulty is that some of the measures of treatment for juvenile offenders involve the use of indeterminate sentences. The reason for this is that only those in charge of the offender are able to judge when he is sufficiently reformed to be released. On the other hand some uneasiness is naturally felt at the prospect of a person's length of sentence being decided behind closed doors instead of by judges in open court where the accused has a right to be heard.

It is clear, therefore, that even if it is accepted that the only purpose for which punishment ought to be inflicted is that of preventing crime, practical disputes can arise as to what constitutes the most effective means of achieving this purpose. Today it is not uncommon to find a conflict between lawyers on the one hand, who pin their hopes on deterrence, and psychiatrists, probation officers, and social workers on the other, who place reliance rather on the reformation of the offender. The choice of the appropriate penalty, however, is a matter for the courts. As we have seen, with rare exceptions, Parliament is content to prescribe only the maximum penalty, leaving the courts free to impose any lighter sentence. The practice of laying down a minimum sentence is rare, applying chiefly in the field of driving offences, for some of which disqualification or imprisonment are automatic and compulsory. The legislature's reluctance to provide minimum penalties is to be supported, partly because cases not infrequently arise where technically an offence has been committed but where no harm has been done and the offender was not really at fault. In such cases the power of imposing a nominal penalty or of discharging the accused absolutely is extremely valuable. Secondly, as social conditions and moral attitutes change, the law tends to lag behind and certain obsolete offences remain on the statute book. Examples of such offences are to be found in the Sunday Observance Act, some of whose provisions are no longer in accord with present views. Here again the imposition of nominal penalties allows the courts to do justice in such cases. Of course in an ideal legal system offences would be abolished as soon as they become obsolete and mere technical offences devoid of harm or wrongful intention would not exist. But the courts must operate within the framework of existing law, which falls short of this ideal and which takes time to alter and bring up to date.

The selection of the appropriate penalty is no easy matter, for the courts must bear in mind the effect of the penalty both on the offender and on the community. To forecast what this effect will be requires detailed knowledge both of the general deterrent effects of different kinds of sentence and of the reformative results of such sentences on different kinds of offender. Such knowledge can only be acquired by detailed consideration of evidence gained by sociological investigations and by familiarity with the particular problem presented by the offender in question. Obviously the courts have not the time to undertake such investigations themselves, and must rely on the reports of probation officers, medical experts, the prison commissioners, and others. The sentencing textbook envisaged by the Streatfeild Committee, by placing before the courts information derived from researches in this field, would go far to assisting the courts to substitute a more scientific approach to the problem.[1] In this connexion use might be made of prediction tables,[2] which are in essence actuarial tables based on experience and showing the probability of different kinds of offenders responding to varying types of treatment. Based on the manner in which individuals with certain characteristics have tended to respond to treatment, such tables, when applied by criminologists to predict the response to Borstal treatment, have proved significantly more reliable than the prognostications of Borstal staff members who had lived with and got to know the offenders. Tables have also been designed to predict the response to probation and other forms of treatment.

3. CAPITAL PUNISHMENT

The history of capital punishment in England for the last 200 years presents a continuous decrease in its incidence. At the end of the eighteenth century, a time of great ferocity, due partly to the lack of adequate police forces to detect and prevent crimes, as many as 200 offences carried the death penalty, which was often carried out with extreme cruelty, the victim being dragged to the scaffold, strangled, and disembowelled. The severity of the law was mitigated, however, by two different factors.

In the first place the incidence of the death penalty was limited by the curious right known as 'benefit of clergy'. This was the anomalous privilege of clerks in holy orders to be tried not by the ordinary courts, but by the Ecclesiastical Courts, which had no power to sentence the offender to death. This valuable right was later extended to all those eligible for holy orders, i.e. all males who were able to read, this latter ability being usually proved by the prisoner's reciting a verse of the Psalms, normally the first verse of Psalm li, which consisted of the three words

---

[1] See p. 195.
[2] For a discussion of the use of such prediction tables see Baroness Wootton, *Social Science and Social Pathology*, pp. 193–9.

'Miserere mei, Deus' and which became known as the 'neck verse'. Later even the requirement of the ability to read was dropped, and benefit of clergy was also extended to women. Meanwhile the range of offences to which it applied was gradually reduced until benefit of clergy was finally abolished in 1827.

The second mitigating factor was the practice of transportation. After the colonization of North America the practice arose of pardoning condemned felons provided that they agreed to be transported to the colonies, and in 1767 the courts were empowered to pass sentence of transportation. For clergyable felonies transportation for seven years was prescribed; for non-clergyable felonies the term was fourteen years. In this way the execution of the death penalty was to a great extent avoided. In the last half of the eighteenth century for instance, according to Radzinowicz, out of 3,680 persons convicted in London and Middlesex on a capital charge, only 1,696 were executed. In 1827 death as a general punishment for felony was abolished, and, accordingly, when the transportation system came to an end, it was replaced in 1853 by the new punishment of penal servitude. Transportation had therefore one beneficial result in that it lessened the severity of the penal system and brought about a reduction in the use of capital punishment.

Today only four offences are punishable by death, and in the case of two of these, viz. piracy and arson of a royal ship or dockyard, sentence of death may be recorded, whereupon the accused is automatically reprieved and imprisoned. There remain treason and murder. Though both World Wars reaped a small crop of treason trials, for which the offenders were executed, treason is today, at any rate in peacetime, a rare offence. In fact since 1861 sentence of death has only been executed in three cases of treason, and fifteen cases of offences under the Treachery Act, 1940, committed during the Second World War. In practice the only crime punished capitally is murder. Even with regard to murder there are considerable limits to the use of the death penalty, the Homicide Act of 1957 having added further restrictions.

First of all there are certain categories of person who may not be executed. It had long been the practice not to execute anyone below the age of eighteen; indeed no one below this age has been executed since 1887; and since 1948 no one who was below

the age of 18 at the time the offence was committed may by law
be executed.[1] The Royal Commission on Capital Punishment[2]
recommended in 1953 by a majority of six to five that the age
be raised to twenty-one, but this recommendation has not so far
been implemented. Expectant mothers also are exempt from
capital punishment, and accordingly if a woman convicted of
a capital offence is found by the trial jury to be pregnant, she
must instead be sentenced to life imprisonment. A third category of persons exempt from capital punishment, a category
already provided for before the 1957 Act, was that of the insane.
This exemption applies not only to those who are found to have
been insane at the time of the offence (see pp. 131 ff.) but also
to those who are insane when the time comes for execution. To
these the 1957 Act added a further category by providing for the
defence of diminished responsibility, which serves to reduce a
murder charge to manslaughter. Both these categories have been
already considered.

Secondly, the 1957 Act has narrowed the definition of murder
by abolishing constructive malice, it has further singled out
certain kinds of murder which are alone to constitute capital
murder, and it has provided that even in the case of capital
murder only an offender who has actually used force himself
upon the victim may be sentenced to death. These provisions
have been discussed earlier.

The position today is that in spite of the retention of the death
penalty executions are rare. In the first fifty years of this century 39 per cent. of men and 91 per cent. of women sentenced
to death were reprieved.[3] During the years 1900–49 the number
of men arrested for murder was 2,834. Of these, 2,176 were sent
for trial, 1,080 sentenced to death, and only 621 actually executed. The corresponding figures for women during the same
period were: arrested 1,339, sent for trial 954, sentenced to
death 130, and executed 11. Since 1957 many of the cases for
which a reprieve was granted are no longer capital and the percentage of those sentenced but not executed might be expected
to fall. Yet in 1959 of the six persons sentenced to death for
capital murder only four were executed.

---

[1] Criminal Justice Act, 1948, s. 16.   [2] Cmnd. 8932, p. 275.
[3] These figures are taken from Report of the Royal Commission on Capital
Punishment, Appendix 3.

Capital punishment then appears to be on the way out. The question remains whether it should be allowed to go altogether. One of the great difficulties surrounding this problem is the amount of emotionalism generated by the argument, which at times begins to seem like a slanging match between 'blimpish' reactionaries and woolly-minded idealists, and there is little doubt that the most vociferous champions of each side do their cause more harm than good simply by arousing antipathies in the minds of many of the uncommitted who might otherwise agree with them. It might well be that the abolition of capital punishment might come all the sooner if the campaign for it relaxed and allowed the opposition to relax likewise. This, however, is a matter of practical politics. Here we are only concerned with the reasons for and against capital punishment, and its possible justification.

Since it is the abolitionists who are advocating a change in the law, it is often said that it lies with them to justify such a change. In other words the onus is on them to show that capital punishment is not defensible. The abolitionists, on the other hand, have been quick to point out that there are certain features regarding the death penalty which are such that it should only be tolerated if there is no practical alternative. Accordingly, they claim, it is for retentionists to prove that there is no such alternative and to justify the *status quo*. Now though the abolitionists may be right here, it is one thing to decide whether in a new penal system the death penalty should have a place and another to determine whether from the system which now obtains this penalty should be removed. We must begin by inquiring what are the reasons for the dissatisfaction with capital punishment, and what are the considerations that suggest that this particular form of punishment needs special justification.

The main objection to the law of murder in the view of the Royal Commission was its rigidity. 'The outstanding defect in the law of murder is that it provides a single penalty for a crime widely varying in culpability.' The mitigation of this rigidity by the use of the Royal Prerogative for Mercy they regarded as open to criticism first on the ground that the executive should only intervene with the due process of the law in those exceptional cases which the law cannot foresee and so provide for; and, secondly, on the ground that it is undesirable for the death sentence to be pronounced in many cases in which it is not carried out. Since the Homicide Act of 1957 many of these cases of the latter category are no longer capital, and to some extent the defect of undue ridigity has been remedied.

There would seem to be four broad objections to the use of the death penalty for the remaining types of capital murder. In the first place it is argued that to put a prisoner to death is a barbarous survival from a crueller age. The same considerations which led to the abolition of the more savage accompaniments of executions and to the restriction of the number of capital offences should operate to move us to abolish the death penalty altogether. The argument is partly that the amount of suffering caused by it is excessive, being more than is necessary for the protection of the community. Here of course the abolitionists have to fight their major battle to show that society could be protected without the death penalty. But the argument also involves the view that this kind of punishment is objectionable not only on the basis of the excessive amount of suffering caused, but on account of the type of treatment entailed. To kill a prisoner in cold blood according to an inexorable ritual, it is urged, is to do something which should not be done to any person, whatever his crime, and this is because it falls below the standard of conduct which our respect for human beings in general requires. It was partly such complete disregard of human personality by those in charge of the concentration camps in Germany that so disgusted the Western world, as well as the excessive suffering caused by the atrocities committed. Indeed the Royal Commission, when asked to consider possible alternatives to hanging as a method of execution, paid attention to what they termed the quality of 'decency', by which they meant that judicial executions in a civilized country should, so far as possible, be conducted with decorum and without brutality. It is only a slight step to go further and claim that all executions necessarily involve such a degree of brutality as to fall below the standard which decency dictates.

To these contentions, that capital punishment involves an excessive amount and an inhuman type of punishment, it is often objected that sentiment has led the abolitionists to pity the murderer who is still alive and to forget the unfortunate victim of the crime. This is partly to miss the point of the argument. The argument is not merely that hanging will be too harsh a punishment for the criminal; it is that our own self-respect for our own personality is offended by capital punishment. No one is trying to condone the murder or save the murderer from severe punishment. But in a civilized society there are certain things which we should not do. For example, no one would seek to subject those who committed atrocities in Germany to the same sort of treatment as they meted out to their captives. Admittedly they treated their prisoners as no human beings should treat another, but we, in punishing them for that, should not fall into the same error. Now the argument of the abolitionists is that putting to death is yet another example of the sort of thing one man should not do to another, and that because a murderer kills his victim, this does not mean that the community, to punish him, should treat him as he treated his victim. For judicial execution reduces men to the level of dogs and horses, to be put down when they become dangerous.

These considerations have led in other spheres of our penal practice to a lessening of the severities of punishment and to a more constructive approach based on the idea of reformation. This provides a second attack on capital punishment, namely that it is the one punishment in which reformation has no place. As such it is now out of line with the rest of our penal system. When a person is executed for capital murder, society either despairs of turning him into a law-abiding citizen or else sacrifices such an objective to the aim of deterrence or prevention. Yet such evidence as there is suggests that the prospects of reformation with murderers are as favourable as with lesser offenders.[1] In this context it is sometimes contended that reformation does play its part in capital punishment in that it is a unique stimulus to repentance. This may well be so, but it is quite a different matter from that of the prisoner's re-establishment in normal life. Moreover, it is not a convincing argument for capital punishment, since it would involve the use of the criminal law other purposes than the protection of society. We have already considered the objections to using the law to enforce morality and observance of religious codes.

A third objection to capital punishment is its finality. Once it has been carried out, there is no room for correcting an error.

[1] Cmnd. 8932, p. 228.

Occasionally utterances are heard by members of the judiciary to the effect that it is impossible in England today for an innocent man to be executed, but it would surely be extraordinary if of all human activities the English murder trial alone was free from fallibility. There have been occasions when people convicted of crimes other than murder have later been proved to be innocent, have been released and compensated, the most celebrated case being that of *Oscar Slater*,[1] who was wrongly convicted and served several years before his innocence was established. Slater was duly released and received compensation, but had his crime been a capital one it would have been too late to put the matter right. In more recent times a case did arise where the defendant was convicted and hanged, though many people are, to say the least, alarmed by the possibility that he may have been wrongly convicted. *Timothy Evans*[2] was convicted of murder partly on the evidence of a witness, Christie, who at that time appeared to have an irreproachable character but who was later convicted and hanged for murder. Had the jury in Evans's trial known what is now known about Christie, their verdict might well have been different. A public inquiry which concluded that there was sufficient other evidence to support the jury's verdict has not entirely succeeded in allaying public anxiety. Admittedly such cases would be rare, but this very possibility is a reason for substituting some less irrevocable penalty.

Besides these arguments against capital punishment there are certain objections on account of some of the undesirable incidental effects of such punishment. One harmful result is that popular sympathy may be diverted from the victim of the murder to the murderer himself awaiting execution. Another is the obnoxious sensationalism which surrounds the murder trial. Yet another is the morbid interest aroused by executions in the public, which flocks in crowds to the prison where a murderer is due to be hanged. Indeed according to one of the Prison Commissioners no less than five applications a week are received on an average for the post of hangman.[3]

---

[1] *Notable British Trial Series* (4th. ed., 1950, ed. J. Hodge).
[2] See pp. 187 n. 2, 190 n. 1.
[3] Margery Fry in *Arms of the Law* paints an alarming picture of the effect of capital punishment on those whose function it is to carry it out.

All these are serious, though not necessarily conclusive, arguments against capital punishment. If we accept these arguments, as many people today do, then we must admit that the death penalty should be abolished if, but only if, there is some other penalty that could serve as a practical alternative while not involving its undesirable effects. At this point those who favour the retention of capital punishment claim that there is no practical alternative. The main bone of contention in this whole dispute is really this, whether any other penalty could achieve what the death penalty achieves.

This brings us back to the problem we have already considered, viz. the purpose of punishment. We saw earlier that the aims men and societies have in punishing could be divided into two groups, depending on whether they were concerned with protecting society or not. It was then argued that the punishment of criminals is justified only by the aim of protecting the community by preventing crime.

Some of the upholders of capital punishment, however, support their view by advancing as justifications for punishment aims other than the protection of society. According to Lord Denning in his evidence to the Royal Commission, 'the ultimate justification of any punishment is . . . that it is the emphatic denunciation by the community of a crime; and from this point of view there are some murders which, in the present state of public opinion, demand the most emphatic denunciation of all, namely the death penalty'.[1] Archbishop Fisher[2] in his evidence agreed that this is the ultimate justification of any punishment. In the House of Lords debate in July 1956 the Lord Chancellor, too, agreed with this view.[3] One criticism that has been made of this argument is that emphatic denunciation does not imply the deliberate imposition of suffering and that it is this feature of punishment which needs justification. This is not altogether a fair criticism, since advocates of the 'emphatic denunciation' theory could argue that although denunciation does not necessarily imply such imposition of suffering, it is only by translating the denunciation into action by such imposition that it is made emphatic. The main criticism which may be made of this view of the justification of punishment is that in a curious way it puts the cart before the horse. The further question is never asked:

[1] Cf. p. 204 n. 1.   [2] Ibid.   [3] Ibid.

why we should denounce any crimes, emphatically or otherwise. The denunciation by one community of crimes committed in another is rarely made, nor would it often be advocated; whereas it seems perfectly reasonable for the community to denounce crimes committed within its own sphere. What makes this seem reasonable is, of course, that such denunciation serves, partly by fostering an abhorrence of the crimes, to lessen the incidence of such crimes and so to protect the community. Consequently what is advanced as the ultimate justification of punishment is itself only a means to an end, i.e. the prevention of crime.

As for other attempts to justify capital punishment on some ground other than that of protecting society, the same objections could be made as were made earlier to such attempts to justify punishment in general and nothing further will be said here. This leaves us with the argument that the justification of the death penalty is that it serves to prevent crime by deterring and by preventing the murderer from committing further crimes. There is no doubt that the death penalty is a deterrent, like most other penalties, and clearly it is uniquely successful as a preventive measure. In view of the special objections, however, which can be made to capital punishment, it could only be justified if it was more effective as a deterrent than any other penalty, or if it was particularly necessary for murderers to be prevented from committing further crimes. Most people who wish to retain it do so on these grounds, while most people who favour its abandonment do so on the ground that these two claims cannot be substantiated.

It is difficult to establish with any degree of certainty how far the death penalty acts as a more powerful deterrent than such punishments as imprisonment. When a murder is committed, obviously the deterrent has failed, but as the Royal Commission wisely observed, 'We can number its failures. But we cannot number its successes.'[1] The arguments here fall into two different categories, the first of which consists of *a priori* arguments from common sense and a knowledge of human nature, while the second consists of conclusions drawn from statistical evidence. The common-sense argument is that since death is a harsher punishment than imprisonment, the former would surely be a greater deterrent than the latter. It would seem obvious that there might be circumstances, therefore, where

---

[1] Cmnd. 8932, p. 20.

imprisonment might fail to deter and where the death penalty would succeed. This common-sense view is backed up by evidence of individuals who have admitted that on occasions it was only the fear of capital punishment that deterred them from murder. In the House of Commons debate in 1956 Mr. Knox Cunningham asserted that he on one occasion was only deterred from murder by the death penalty.[1] Moreover, criminals have stated that they have refrained from committing murder only because they might have to 'swing for it'. With such isolated statements the Royal Commission was unimpressed, pointing out that what an offender says later is not necessarily a valid indication of what was in his mind at the time he committed the offence. Much more importance was attached by the Commission to the views of experienced representatives of the police and prison service, who were virtually unanimously agreed that the death penalty has a uniquely deterrent effect. In addition to this, certain distinguished members of the judiciary with wide experience of criminal cases, notably Lord Goddard and Mr. Justice Humphreys, felt that they were right. On *a priori* grounds, therefore, supported by the experience of those who have had to deal with criminals and fight against crime, it would seem obvious that the death penalty has a unique deterrent effect.

At this point, however, it should be remembered that murders fall into many different types. Sex-murders and murders committed by the mentally abnormal are unlikely to be deterred by any threats. Impulsive murders, including *crimes passionelles*, are likewise unlikely to be deterred by any sanction. On the other hand, the ordinary person, who may assert that the death penalty would deter him more than imprisonment, is unlikely in any event to commit murder, because to do so would be contrary to his moral beliefs, while in any case the threat of imprisonment will assist him to act according to those beliefs. Murderers like Crippen, who are not professional criminals, are not likely to be deterred by any threat because they calculate on escaping detection. This leaves us with the professional criminal. The police and prison officers were at one in arguing that these are deterred by the death penalty. For the professional criminal imprisonment is an occupational hazard, while death comes into a quite different category. Criminals, it is

[1] H.C. Deb. 16 Feb. 1956, vol. 548, col. 2600.

argued, prefer to work unarmed so as to avoid the temptation of using a weapon in a tight corner. Moreover, instances are cited of criminal activity subsiding after executions. This would seem to justify the death penalty for professional criminals, and indeed this was partly, it seems, the aim of the Homicide Act, 1957.

This being so, we might expect statistical evidence to confirm the deterrent value of capital punishment. Curiously, however, such evidence seems to warrant no such conclusion. There are two different methods of compiling such evidence. In the first place the incidence in countries without capital punishment can be compared with the incidence in countries with capital punishment. Such comparisons are not altogether satisfactory because of the different social conditions, the differences in the practice of prosecutors, the differences in the categorizing of crimes, and the differences in compiling statistics. There are, however, certain states which are very similar and which can be usefully compared, notably certain groups of states of the United States of America. The conclusion drawn by the Royal Commission from the comparison of such states was that there was no clear evidence that the death penalty influenced the homicide rate.

The other method of compiling evidence is by comparing the incidence of murder in a state during a period when the death penalty was exacted with its incidence in the same state while the death penalty was in abeyance. Here, again, caution is needed, because often the formal abolition of capital punishment has followed a period when in practice it was not enforced. But here, again, the Commission concluded that there was no clear evidence that the abolition of capital punishment led to an increase in the murder rate. A most interesting piece of evidence is furnished by the position of Denmark, where during Nazi occupation in 1944 the police were deported and there ensued a marked rise in the number of crimes of dishonesty but no increase in murder or other crimes of violence.[1] We are left then with a conflict between the argument from common sense and that from statistics, the former suggesting that the death penalty is a unique deterrent and the latter showing that no conclusion can be drawn either way.

[1] S. Hurwitz, *Criminology*, 1952, p. 303; Howard Jones, *Crime and the Penal System*, p. 123.

Before reaching any decision we must first consider the other effect of capital punishment, that of preventing the murderer from committing further murders. Considerable opposition to the abolition of the death penalty would seem to be based on the fear of letting convicted murderers loose on the public. If a genuine sentence of life imprisonment were the alternative, many perhaps would no longer object to its abolition. Yet a careful study of the behaviour of released murderers has shown that such persons rarely commit any other crimes of violence.[1] Of 112 such prisoners released in England between April 1928 and May 1948 only five had by 1948 been convicted of serious offences and only one of murder. It must be remembered, however, that those released during this period would not of course include those guilty of the more serious types of murder, since these would have been executed. But the evidence of those countries which have abolished capital punishment suggests that the detention of sane murderers in prison for the rest of their days is not necessary for the protection of society.

The decision, therefore, whether capital punishment should be abolished is clearly a difficult one. The question is whether the repulsive features and the undesirable effects of such a penalty are outweighed by its unique force as a deterrent. The fact that the evidence on this unique deterrent force is far from conclusive would seem to tilt the scales in favour of abolition. Nevertheless, those who campaign ardently for an amendment to the law should remember that they themselves are not the persons in the front line in the war against crime. The effect that abolition would have on the police and on the prison service must be taken into account. The result of abolishing the death penalty for the murder of a police officer might well be that the police would have to be armed. Looking across the Atlantic, the retentionist can conjure up a frightening picture. If he looks across the Channel, however, to Belgium, where the police are armed, the prospect is far less ominous. While it is to be hoped that in the not-too-far-distant future we may be able to abolish the death penalty altogether, this is a matter in which we should proceed with caution. Nothing could be more unsatisfactory than the precipitate manner in which the death penalty was suspended in England on 16 April 1948 only to be reintroduced

[1] See Cmnd. 8932, p. 228.

on 10 June of the same year. When the death penalty goes, it should go for good. Its abolition, therefore, should be the result of careful thought and consideration, not of emotionalism and snap decisions.

4. CORPORAL PUNISHMENT

The same tendency to reform which has limited the use of the death penalty has also brought about the virtual abolition in England of corporal punishment. With one exception, no offence today is corporally punishable. Yet, if this type of punishment itself is a dead letter, the issue whether or not to reintroduce it is very much a living one, and as recently as 1960 the Advisory Council on the Treatment of Offenders was asked to consider the desirability of such a course.

In this connexion the history of corporal punishment in England is not without relevance, since many are under the mistaken impression that its abolition was not effected until just after the Second World War, whereas in fact it had been practically done away with considerably before this. In early times whipping was a common form of punishment, being administered in public either at the cart's tail or at the public whipping-post. While death was the general penalty for felonies, whipping was the general penalty for misdemeanours. The beginning of the nineteenth century, however, saw the gradual curtailment of corporal punishment. In 1820 whipping for female offenders was prohibited, and has never since been allowed in England, though some of those who gave evidence before the Advisory Committee urged that corporal punishment should be allowed for both sexes. In 1824 the Vagrancy Act deprived the justices in petty sessions of the power to sentence offenders to corporal punishment and provided that such power should be restricted to Quarter Sessions, which were authorized to order whipping only for second offences. Death as the general penalty for felonies was abolished in 1827 and there followed then various attempts to reform and codify the criminal law, which resulted in the passing of the Acts of 1861 relating to offences against the person and offences against property. In the legislation of 1861 no provision was made for the corporal punishment of anyone over sixteen, so that for all practical purposes whipping for adults was abolished. To this there were four relatively unimportant exceptions. The offence of instituting proceedings against foreign ambassadors contrary to the Diplomatic Privileges Act, 1708, the irregular slaughter of horses and cattle contrary to the Knackers Act, 1786, and certain offences against the Vagrancy Act, 1824, remained punishable by whipping. In addition the Treason Act, 1842, had provided that such punishment was to be inflicted on anyone discharging a fire-arm against the sovereign.

By 1861, then, corporal punishment for adults was virtually abolished. It was still allowed for juveniles, however, for certain offences against the person and against property. At that time it is to be remembered that for a juvenile the only alternative punishment would have been imprisonment, which might well have had more harmful consequences.

The position achieved by the 1861 legislation was not, however, maintained. In the following year an outbreak of robbery with violence by garrotting the victim led Parliament to enact what the Home Secretary of the day (against whose advice the statute was passed) stigmatized as a panic measure after the panic was over. The Garrotters Act, 1863, reintroduced corporal punishment for garrotting and for robbery with violence. The Criminal Law Amendment Act of 1885 introduced it for males under sixteen found guilty of unlawful carnal knowledge of a girl under thirteen. In 1898 the Vagrancy Act was extended to include the crimes of soliciting and living on the immoral earnings of prostitutes, both of which offences accordingly rendered the offenders liable to corporal punishment. Fears of the growth of 'white slavery' activities resulted in the extension of whipping to procuration by the Criminal Law Amendment Act, 1912. By 1937, however, the position in practice was that corporal punishment for adults was used for the most part only for robbery with violence, while the corporal punishment of juveniles had almost died out.

In that year the Cadogan Committee was set up to examine this question and their report was presented in 1938 (Cmnd. 5684). The report contains a careful discussion of the available evidence on this matter. So far as adult offenders are concerned, the committee were of the opinion that there was no evidence that corporal punishment produced a decrease in the offences for which it was administered. Several incidents advanced as examples of the beneficial results of its use were examined but the evidence did not support, in the eyes of the committee, the conclusions drawn. Apart from the fact that there was no evidence for the proposition that corporal punishment was a deterrent to potential offenders, there was some evidence that it had a detrimental effect on the actual offender, in whom it was found to produce resentment and bitterness. As a form of punishment it was considered to be unconstructive and out of tune with the growing emphasis on the aim of reclamation. In those circumstances the Cadogan Committee recommended the abolition of flogging for adults, except for those guilty of certain prison offences, for which flogging was the only ultimate sanction, the offender having already lost his liberty, and with regard to which there was evidence that other prisoners were deterred by such penalties.

With regard to juveniles the Committee were impressed by the fact that many Juvenile Courts had long abandoned sentencing offenders to the birch, not on *a priori* grounds but simply because they had found it less effective in practice. Here the Committee stressed that the more important consideration was not the effect of corporal punishment on potential offenders but its effect on the offender himself. Many of the advocates of birching are inclined to argue from their own experience at school or at home and to conclude that what benefited them would obviously benefit the young delinquent. But, as the report is at pains to point out, judicial corporal punishment is very different from that administered by parents and teachers. In the first place corporal punishment is used to its best advantage when administered summarily, as is the case at school or at home where it follows soon after the offence. Judicial punishment, however, cannot be inflicted with this immediacy because of the legal requirements that the offender must be tried and his guilt proved before he can be punished. Thereafter he has a right of appeal. The result is that a delay sometimes of weeks intervenes between the offence and the punishment, which, when finally administered, no longer in the juvenile's mind bears that obvious relation to the offence that is desirable. Secondly, when a boy is punished by his parent or teacher, there is a relationship between the two which is of great importance in this context. The person who decides that the punishment should be inflicted and the person who inflicts it are either one and the same or else closely connected. The boy has feelings of affection or at least respect for the person who punishes him, and realizes that the punishment is administered for his own good. After he has been punished, he continues in close relationship with his father or teacher, as the case may be, who is in a position to observe the effect on him of that punishment. If we look now at judicial corporal punishment, we find the position is entirely different. There was no relationship between the offender and the policeman whose function it was to administer the birching. The latter was someone unknown and remote to the boy, someone of whom he knew nothing and for whom he had no feeling whatsoever, and moreover someone quite distinct from the magistrate ordering the punishment. After he had been birched, neither the court nor the policeman was in a position to observe the results of the punishment on the offender. It was not surprising, therefore, that there should have been evidence that the tendency of corporal punishment administered in this cold-blooded and impersonal way was to produce undesirable effects. Some offenders were made resentful by this impersonal infliction of pain, the more so in view of the sympathy bestowed on them by friends and relations, while others became local heroes to be emulated by their contemporaries. In those circumstances the Committee had no hesitation in recommending the abolition of corporal punishment for young offenders.

The recommendations of the Cadogan Committee were not implemented until 1948 when the Criminal Justice Act of that year did away with corporal punishment for juveniles and for adults, with one exception. It has been retained for certain offences committed by inmates of prisons, notably mutiny and offering gross personal violence to prison officers.

Since 1948, however, the increase in certain crimes of violence has led to widespread and persistent demands for the reintroduction of corporal punishment. One public poll conducted by a newspaper in March 1960 showed that 74 per cent. of those canvassed were in favour of some measure of flogging or birching. Accordingly, in 1960 the Advisory Council on the Treatment of Offenders was asked to consider the question and they presented their report in November of that year (Cmnd. 1213).

The Council entirely agreed with the conclusions of the Cadogan Committee, holding that judicial corporal punishment had no special or unique influence as a deterrent and was unlikely to affect the incidence of crime. The reason behind the demand for its reintroduction was the increase in violence since 1948; yet before that year corporal punishment in practice had only been inflicted for one particular type of violent crime, namely robbery with violence, so that the prevalence of many other forms of violence today can hardly be due to the abolition of flogging and birching.

The Council sounded the views of various interested and experienced bodies and associations. The police were divided on this matter and declined to give evidence. The judiciary, chairmen of Quarter Sessions, and magistrates were likewise divided, a majority of judges of the Queen's Bench Division (the division chiefly concerned with crime) being in favour of corporal punishment. Among prison governors also there seems to have been considerable divergence of opinion. Borstal governors and probation officers were almost unanimously against corporal punishment.

After considering all the evidence the Council concluded that to reintroduce such penalties would be a retrograde step, out of line with modern penal methods and militating against the establishment of the relationship necessary to the task of reclamation. There were, moreover, certain serious practical difficulties regarding the question by whom such punishments should be administered. The police were unanimously opposed to this function being allotted to them since it might worsen their relations with the public. For similar reasons members of the prison service were likewise against being burdened with this duty, since it would adversely affect their relationship with the prisoners and hinder the work of reform. Probation officers naturally are utterly opposed to having anything to do with its administration. Nor did the Council consider it a practical possibility to order parents to chastise their children and to visit the parents' failure with some legal sanction.

Although the recent prevalence of violence is admittedly a cause for serious concern, it should be borne in mind, as the Council pointed out, that some of the methods of treatment for young offenders envisaged by the 1948 legislation have not yet been able to be put into practice to any great extent. It is to be hoped that the availability of more attendance and detention centres may provide the answer to this problem.

Meanwhile the reintroduction of corporal punishment was not recommended and it would appear that its abolition has come to stay.

5. IMPRISONMENT

The decline in the use of capital and corporal punishment has established imprisonment as the major sanction of the English criminal law. Today the criminal pays for his wrongdoing with his purse or his liberty, loss of the latter being the chief penalty in the criminal law. Despite the move which there has been since the Gladstone Report of 1895 away from imprisonment, it is clear that some such form of punishment must remain as the ultimate penalty. Fines and other monetary penalties are not always practical alternatives, because the offender may not have the means to pay. Moreover, prison must be retained in reserve for the offender who refuses to pay the fine inflicted or to suffer the penalty imposed; there must be some final sanction for contumacy. Indeed this requirement exists equally in the civil law, which the courts must have power to enforce in the last resort by physical coercion.

The punitive function of imprisonment however is in fact by no means its only function, and furthermore the use of prison as a form of punishment is comparatively recent.[1] Traditionally it was held that imprisonment should be used only for the custody of offenders until such time as they could conveniently be dealt with, and this view prevailed in Europe from the time of the Roman Emperor Justinian for the next thousand years or so. In medieval England prisons were places where suspects were detained until the royal judges came round on circuit with a commission of 'jail delivery', to empty the jails and inquire into the alleged crimes. The punishments inflicted were generally of a physical form, death, torture, flogging, and so forth. Indeed it was not until the nineteenth century that imprisonment began to constitute an important sanction and not really until the eighteen-fifties that, with the abolition of transportation, it moved into first place.

[1] Fox, op. cit., p. 16,

Meanwhile imprisonment has never lost its other important functions, viz. its custodial and coercive functions. It is often overlooked that by no means all the inmates of our prisons are undergoing punishment. According to the figures produced by the Prison Commissioners in 1959, 37,844 males were sent to prison as a punishment, 28,063 were detained in prison while awaiting trial, 9,132 were either committed there for inquiries about them to be made or to await sentence, and 7,707 were received as civil prisoners. These latter were committed for contempt of court, i.e. disobeying a court order, usually an order to pay a sum of money, e.g. civil debts, rates and taxes, or wife-maintenance or affiliation. At one time imprisonment was a regular consequence of non-payment of debts, as any reader of Dickens will know, but this policy has been abandoned and today only 'fraudulent' debtors are committed. Before sending him to prison the court must be satisfied that the debtor has the means to pay and has refused or neglected to do so. Civil prisoners and untried prisoners are to some extent differently treated from the other inmates. They are separately confined, can wear their own clothes, and are not forced to work. Imprisoned debtors are of course released on payment of the sum ordered.

One further category of prisoners deserves mention. Persons convicted of certain political offences such as sedition should, the Criminal Justice Act, 1948, provided, receive special treatment. Prior to this statute certain offenders who had not been convicted of dishonesty or serious violence and who had not broken the law for 'criminal' motives were given preferential treatment, notable examples being the suffragettes. In some ways this type of detention, known as 'First Division' treatment, was similar to the *custodia honesta* occasionally imposed for political offences in Norway and Denmark. Though the 1948 Act abolished the distinction between the divisions, it has prescribed that rules should be made to deal specially with such prisoners. To the student of penology the incarceration of such persons is not without advantage, since they tend to be drawn from the more educated ranks of society and to be therefore more articulate than the general run of inmate. Consequently they are able to portray for the outside what life inside is really like for the prisoner and what imprisonment means to him.

Indeed we are indebted to such writers as Wilde and Wildeblood (neither in fact convicted of political offences, but of sexual offences) for accounts of prison life from the inmate's viewpoint. The form which imprisonment takes will depend partly on the administration of the prison system and partly on the aims and objects of imprisonment. Before the nineteenth century while prisons were used largely for custodial purposes, it was common practice for those who owned the jails, whether public or private authorities, to farm them out to private jailers who made what profit they could from them. This they did by charging each prisoner an admission and a release fee, and by providing him during his imprisonment with food, drink, and other amenities at a price. A fee was even charged for putting on and off the irons which the prisoners wore, and the better the fit, the higher the price. For the most part the inmates lived in indescribable squalor and debauchery in overcrowded buildings with no separation of the sexes or of young and old. Jail fever was rife, as many as a quarter of the prisoners dying as a result every year.

The movement to reform this vicious state of affairs began with John Howard, who in the eighteenth century inspected many of the prisons on his own account. Appalled by his findings, he urged the abolition of the system of farming out to private contractors and campaigned for better treatment for prisoners, pleading for separation of the sexes, better sanitation, proper supervision of prison-keepers, the prevention of corruption by the provision of separate cells, the provision of work for prisoners, and the appointment of chaplains. Although some of these improvements were being made by the time of Howard's death in 1790, most of the reforms for which he had hoped were still to come. The movement which he started, however, was continued, led by various Quaker families, the most notable worker in this field being Elizabeth Fry, who instituted a committee of women to visit and comfort women prisoners. Her main object was that prisoners should be treated as human beings with human feelings and that their co-operation should be sought. To this end she campaigned for separate prisons for women supervised by women, for separate cells, for work, training, and religious instruction in prisons. In the course of the nineteenth century many of the abuses of the system were swept away. The practice of letting jails to private contractors was abolished, the prison system was centralized, and a measure of uniformity was introduced into the conditions in all the different prisons.

Today the administration of the prison system is the function of the Home Secretary and the Home Office. The Home Secretary makes the rules regarding the administration of prisons, is responsible for the appointment of prison governors and other 'superior' prison officers, and appoints Boards of Visitors to each prison. These powers are vested in him by the Prisons Acts, 1865–98, and the Criminal Justice Act, 1948. Subject to his overriding control, the superintendence of the prisons is vested in the Board of Prison Commissioners, full-time civil servants who are responsible for the control and inspection of these institutions. The Board is obliged by statute to present to the Home Secretary an annual report, which is then laid before Parliament. The local administration of each individual prison is the responsibility of the governor and his officers, under the supervision of the visiting committees. An unofficial and independent body, consisting of members appointed either by the Home Secretary or by local magistrates, the Board of Visitors meets regularly, visits the prison periodically, and deals with the more serious offences against prison discipline, in particular with offences meriting corporal punishment. A prison visitor has the right to see any prisoner at any time, while any prisoner may apply to see a visitor and make a complaint to him. In this way the Board of Visitors forms a useful independent local check on the running of the prison.[1] The person primarily and immediately responsible for the administration of the prison is of course the governor, assisted by his chaplain and medical officer (both often local men appointed to work part-time) and by his other officers. There is therefore under the aegis of the Home Secretary a three-tier system of administration and supervision, with functions divided amongst the commissioners, the visitors, and the prison officers.

---

[1] One of the difficulties confronting the independent inquirer here is the conflict in testimony of officials and ex-prisoners. The latter claim that realities of prison life are very different from what outsiders read and even see. According to Wildeblood in *Against the Law*, the prison visitors never saw those parts of the prison where the inmates spent most of their time. Cf. also Hignett, *Portrait in Grey*. The former, on the other hand, discount this by stressing that the prisoner has a chip on his shoulder, is prone to exaggerate and magnify each minor irritation, and is out to exploit the market for sensationalism.

While improvements in the organization and administration of the prison system are naturally reflected in the form and conditions of the prison régime, these conditions are bound ultimately to be determined by what society considers to be the purposes of imprisonment. In other words the kind of life the inmate leads will be dictated by the use to which the jails are put. When prisons were used chiefly as places of custody and farmed out into private hands, the position was that conditions were made as pleasant as possible for those willing to pay and as unpleasant as possible for those who either could not or would not pay for amenities. Later, when imprisonment began to be used more for punitive purposes, the accent was on deterrence. The prisoner's life, it was thought, should be severe enough to ensure that he would have no desire to return. As the House of Lords Committee in 1863 put it, 'hard labour, hard fare, and a hard bed' were the proper foundations of the régime. Prisoners were separately confined and given monotonous forms of work such as the crank and the treadmill rather than useful industry. The legacy of this period has been handed down in the form of our present prisons, those grim edifices designed by Victorian architects to carry out the purposes of their time, which remain as perhaps the chief obstacle to progress in penal reform.

Underlying the enforcement of this soulless type of régime was what has been termed the principle of 'less eligibility'[1] or 'non-superiority'. Basically the notion is that convicted prisoners should not be pampered. Here what was one of the principles of the Poor Law, namely, that the condition of the pauper should be less eligible than that of the lowest grade of independent labourer, was translated into the penal system. According to Bentham the condition of a convict ought not to be made more eligible than that of the poorest class of subjects in a state of innocence and liberty. At first sight this might seem good common sense. To give a convicted person a better life than some persons not convicted of offences would be unjust to the latter and would set a premium on crime. So, for example, in times of unemployment prisoners must take their place at the end of the queue for work; in times of hunger they cannot expect to be well fed.

Closer inspection, however, reveals serious practical as well

---

[1] Mannheim, *The Dilemma of Penal Reform*, pp. 56 ff.

as moral objections to the implementation of the principle of less eligibility. From the practical standpoint it is essential in any institution, penal or otherwise, to maintain certain standards of diet and hygiene in order to avoid disease. No one would seriously suggest that prisoners should be so poorly housed, clothed, and fed as to endanger their health, even though there might be some people outside the confines of the prison whose condition of life was of this low order. Secondly, any hope of reforming offenders and preparing them to take their place once more in society would be vain if the first step was to ensure their inhuman treatment, merely in order to put them at a disadvantage compared with the least fortunate members of the community.

On moral grounds the rigid application of the principle is open to objection in that in many cases it would involve excessive hardships resulting in injustice. Bentham's idea was based on the assumption that none but the poorest members of the community were liable to suffer imprisonment. This is certainly not the case today, when inmates of prisons may be found drawn from many different classes and many different walks of life. Consequently the rigid enforcement of such a principle would expose prisoners who in ordinary life enjoyed quite high standards of living to very considerable suffering indeed and result in penalizing them excessively. As it is, the burden of imprisonment is bound to fall on different prisoners unequally so long as prison life is institutionalized and while there exists but one general standard of living in the institution. But the fundamental punishment involved in a prison sentence is loss of liberty, and in this one vital respect the offender has an inferior position to that of those outside the prison. Today it is generally accepted that in the words of Alexander Paterson, appointed as a Prison Commissioner in 1922, 'offenders are sent to prison as a punishment, not for a punishment'.[1] The punishment which they suffer by being deprived of their freedom should not be increased by rendering their living conditions as irksome as possible.

This new and enlightened attitude to imprisonment is part of the general approach to punishment which was first adopted by the Gladstone Committee, which in 1895 urged that the

[1] Paterson on Prisons, p. 23.

emphasis should be placed on reclamation so that the offender might be re-established as a member of the community and enabled once more to take his place in society. To this end they argued for more elasticity in the prison system so that it might be more adaptable to the individual offender and better able to turn him out a better man than when he came in. Recent years have seen these ideas brought to fruition. Today there is greater classification of different prisoners together with more specialized treatment for the different categories. Much has been done, too, to alleviate the hardships of prison life. The old separate system of solitary confinement was abandoned. Prisoners now take their meals together and the notorious rule prescribing silence has been abolished. Recreational and educational activities are provided in the evenings. Brutalization of prisoners is prohibited. No mechanical restraint may be placed on any prisoner unless it is ordered by the medical officer or unless the prisoner is liable, if unrestrained, to do damage to himself or others. The only penalties which the governor has authority to impose are forfeiture of remission and privileges, cellular confinement, stoppage of earnings, and special diet. Corporal punishment can only be ordered by the Visitors' Committee and must be confirmed by the Home Secretary. Meanwhile during his term an attempt is made to enlist the prisoner's co-operation. By good conduct he may earn a remission of part of his sentence, the rate of remission today being one-third of any sentence more than a month.[1] It would be more true, however, today to describe the position as one in which remission, like other privileges such as that of receiving letters and visits and of having tobacco, is not so much earned by good behaviour as forfeited by bad.

While prison conditions were being improved, a new attack on the problem of recidivism was launched by the Criminal Justice Act, 1948. This statute provides special methods of treatment for the persistent offender. An offender over twenty-one, whose previous convictions show that he is liable if unchecked to turn into a confirmed criminal, may be sentenced to a period of corrective training, which in practice usually lasts for three

---

[1] The Prison Act, 1952, s. 27 (i), empowers the Home Secretary to release on licence at any time anyone undergoing a sentence of life imprisonment. Home Office practice has been to release such prisoners after ten years.

years. Such offenders are meant to be confined in special prisons
or in parts of ordinary prisons specially set aside for this purpose.
During their training particular attention is to be paid to education and to teaching the prisoner a trade so that he may be
able to support himself after release. An offender over thirty,
whose previous convictions and record show that he is a confirmed criminal, may be sentenced to a term of preventive
detention, not so much as a punishment as for the protection of
the community, the maximum period being fourteen years and
the usual term being not less than eight years. There is some
evidence that these new forms of treatment, designed to fit the
offender rather than the offence, have come as a shock to the
criminal world, but the view of the Home Office in 1959 set out
in the report *Penal Practice in a Changing Society*[1] was that it was
too soon yet to say whether preventive detention was achieving
the objects for which it was devised.

In spite of this new approach to the problem of imprisonment
many practical difficulties remain. Perhaps the chief obstacle to
progress has been the buildings available for use as prisons.
Relics of earlier eras, when the system of separate confinement
was in force, they provide little accommodation for community
work and recreation, and in some cases even community meals
are not altogether possible. As a result the prisoners are in many
cases locked up too often and too long. Moreover, there are not
enough buildings for the number of prisoners, so that cells are
often overcrowded and there is much unnecessary discomfort.
The lack of accommodation has also resulted in different categories of prisoner being housed in the same institution, so that
in some of the local prisons are to be found not only offenders
undergoing punishment but prisoners awaiting trial or sentence,
civil prisoners, and offenders sentenced to corrective training or
preventive detention who are waiting for transfer to the appropriate institutions. This unsatisfactory state of affairs can only
be overcome by a building programme to provide a sufficiency
of institutions. Such a programme has been put forward by the
Home Office but its execution will cost a great deal of money
and take considerable time.

One of the most serious problems connected with the reformative approach to imprisonment is the question of work in

[1] (1959) Cmnd. 645.

prison. Originally when the function of imprisonment was purely custodial, there was no right to make the inmates work. This rule still applies today with regard to untried prisoners detained in custody and to persons convicted of certain political offences. Yet it has been wisely observed that there is only one thing which a man can do for eight hours a day every day and be contented, and that is work. While the Houses of Correction, or Brideswells, established in the sixteenth century, recognized the truth of this and tried, not without success, to reform vagrants by setting them to work, ordinary prisons had no place for work. Howard, and after him Bentham, Elizabeth Fry, and other reformers, emphasized the importance of work for prisoners, but it was not until 1865 that it became a regular feature of prison life.

Its introduction in this year, however, was made not for any reformative value it might have so much as for its punitive effect. Dull, monotonous hard labour from now on was to be part of the punishment of the prisoner, who was not to be remunerated for it. The Gladstone Committee, despite its inauguration of the modern approach to the treatment of offenders, failed to tackle the question of prison work adequately, and it was not until the report of the Departmental Committee on Employment of Prisoners (Cmd. 4462, 1933) that suitable employment was stressed as 'the most important factor in the physical and moral regeneration of the prisoner'. Not only has the cruelty of enforced idleness been recognized as a gratuitous addition to the loss of liberty entailed by imprisonment, but it has been accepted that one of the objectives of modern penal treatment is to render the offender willing to lead a good and useful life, while fitting him to do so. Such useful labour aims to enlist the prisoner's interest and give him a sense of purpose, to afford him an opportunity to exercise his skill and gain confidence in his ability to work, and to instil into him good working habits. As Dr. Grünhut says, the object of prison labour is 'training for work and training by work'.[1]

Notwithstanding the acceptance of prison labour as the most important factor in a reformative programme, the translation of theory into practice has encountered serious difficulties. The existing prison buildings are badly short of adequate workshops, not having been built for this purpose. Shortage of staff too

[1] Grünhut, *Penal Reform*, p. 209.

renders it difficult to allow as much communal work under supervision as is desirable. For obvious security reasons it is not altogether possible to permit prisoners to engage in employment outside the prison, on farms, for example, though the success which has attended the development of open prisons suggests that this might be tried. Indeed arrangements have been made whereby selected prisoners are allowed to work in civilian jobs outside during the last months of their sentence. The prisoners themselves constitute another obstacle, in that they form a continually fluctuating labour force over whose composition the prison authorities have no control. Some are completely without skills of any sort, and the shortness of their sentences makes it in many cases impossible to teach them a trade. Consequently the only available and suitable work tends to be low both in quantity and quality, the repairing of mailbags forming the major standby. In addition to these considerations there must be taken into account the attitude of the outside world to prison labour. Demand tends to be low, the main source of work being contracts for government departments. Moreover there is a natural hostility on the part of trade unions to what they consider unfair competition and sweated labour, while at the least sign of unemployment the principle of less eligibility begins to militate against the prisoner in this context above all. This problem, as the Home Office Report[1] stresses, can only be solved when society as a whole accepts that prisoners do not work in an economic vacuum and that though temporarily safeguarded, they are not economic outcasts.

Closely connected with this is the question of prisoners' earnings. In theory it is agreed that payment for work would produce advantageous effects. The prisoner would have more incentive to work. The fact of having something to spend would increase his self-respect and give him something to think about. In practice, however, prisoners' earnings amount on the average to only about 2s. 8d. a week, which is not even enough to buy a packet of twenty cigarettes. Although suggestions have been made that they should be paid an economic rate for the job, there are serious difficulties inherent in any such practice. Not only would it be difficult to calculate what the economic rate was, but presumably the cost of the prisoner's keep should

[1] *Penal Practice in a Changing Society* (1959), Cmnd. 645, p. 17.

be deducted from his pay packet by the authorities, so that payment at an economic rate would strike him as arbitrary and unrealistic. Further, the cost to the taxpayer might prove excessive. Moreover, such a policy would have to be combined in fairness with some practice whereby the prisoner was forced to make restitution to his victim.

Once prison came to be regarded as a place of training to fit the offender for a useful life in the community after his sentence, it began to be realized that there were certain features inherent in the concept of imprisonment which tended to defeat the whole object of the sentence. As Alexander Paterson, a leading reformer in this field, observed, 'you cannot train men for freedom in a condition of captivity'. Though much had been done to ameliorate the prisoner's lot by allowing him to receive visitors, by improving the prison garb, and removing some of the more unpleasant material conditions, the fact remained that to become a model prisoner was not a step to becoming a model citizen. Self-respect, confidence, and self-reliance are not developed by merely learning to obey the rules inside an institution. One result of the realization of this has been the establishment of open prisons and camps, of which there are now several. The prisoners are carefully selected before being transferred to these open camps and so far there have been surprisingly few absconders. The relation between prisoners and staff is improved and something like a normal free community is produced.

Another serious drawback to a punishment such as imprisonment is the contamination to which the convict is exposed. The inexperienced offender falls under the influence of more hardened criminals. His contacts with the criminal world are widened, and his sentence becomes a passport to the underworld. To avoid such undesirable effects a practice is made of separating the different categories of offenders. Those under twenty-one are separated from older criminals, and confirmed criminals are sent to special institutions. Moreover, today the aim of the courts is to avoid sending anyone to prison if any practical alternative exists. As we have seen, the use of the short sentence to teach the offender a sharp lesson has fallen out of favour.

Yet another special difficulty involved by a term of imprisonment is the deprivation of normal sexual life. For the homosexual offender of course, it has been aptly remarked, imprisonment as a cure is as futile as giving a chronic alcoholic occupational therapy in a brewery.[1] But for the ordinary criminal, too, the abnormality of prison life in this respect causes considerable problems. In certain prison systems in Europe and South America arrangements are made for 'connubial visits' between husband and wife. Indeed the suggestion has been made that prisoners should be allowed to continue their family life within the prison, but it is questionable how far this is a practical proposition.[2]

Perhaps the worst effect of imprisonment so far as the offender is concerned is the stigma incurred by a prison sentence. Indeed it is this factor which makes this punishment such a powerful deterrent to the ordinary citizen. Though it is often said that it is the conviction rather than the penalty which creates the disgrace, convicted offenders who are sentenced to imprisonment seem to incur a higher share of it than those let off more lightly. Admittedly a prison sentence does not involve forfeiture of civil rights. The prisoner retains his right to vote and can, with the permission of the prison authorities, pursue his legal remedies in the courts. Certain public offices, however, must be vacated if the holder is imprisoned and certain pensions are forfeited. Moreover, professional associations may strike off one of their members who has been sent to prison. Indeed for the business or professional man, imprisonment, with the social ostracism which ensues, can spell ruin. As Oscar Wilde complained, society 'is really ashamed of its own actions, and shuns those whom it has punished, as people shun a creditor whose debt they cannot pay'.[3] The offender from the labouring classes, too, may find such a sentence ruinous. Prospective employers not unnaturally distrust the ex-prisoner and he emerges from prison facing economic as well as emotional difficulties. Indeed prisoners often complain that their real punishment begins when they leave prison.

To overcome such difficulties much is done in the way of 'after-care', and Wilde's reproach is no longer true, that society abandons the prisoner at the very moment when its highest duty towards him begins. Before release, prisoners are prepared by

[1] St. John-Stevas, op. cit., p. 225.
[2] Fox, op. cit., p. 223.   [3] Oscar Wilde, *De Profundis*.

special pre-release courses and in some cases by being allowed to work outside, and hostels are being established where such workers can live like free men. Another important aspect of pre-release training is home leave to allow the individual to make family adjustments and see prospective employers. On release the authorities see that the prisoner is properly clothed and given his fare back home. Sometimes he is provided with the necessary tools or stock-in-trade for his new job. There is, in addition, a system of 'after-care' for discharged prisoners. All prisoners discharged from Borstal, corrective training, and preventive detention are compelled to undergo compulsory after-care, as are those sentenced to life terms and certain other categories of prisoners, for whom provision has been made by the Criminal Justice Act, 1961. These comprise prisoners serving terms of four years or more, prisoners serving terms of at least six months who have previously undergone a sentence of Borstal training, imprisonment, or corrective training, and prisoners serving terms of at least six months who were under twenty-six years of age at the commencement of the sentence. Such prisoners become the responsibility of the Central After-Care Association, which consists partly of representatives of voluntary organizations and partly of representatives of government departments, while the actual supervision of the discharged prisoner is performed by probation officers. For prisoners other than those mentioned above there is a voluntary system of after-care carried out by local Discharged Prisoners' Aid Societies. The Advisory Council on the Treatment of Offenders has recommended, however, that the compulsory system should be extended to all classes of prisoner.

Now since the idea prevailing today is that prison should be used chiefly as a training to reform and rehabilitate the offender, it is a curious commentary on the type of training employed that so much time and energy have to be devoted to assisting the ex-prisoner to get over the effects of his training. Much of this might perhaps be avoided, as might also such undesirable features of imprisonment as the danger of contamination, by the adoption of some form of non-institutionalized punishment to replace imprisonment. At present the only alternatives for adults are fines, conditional discharges, and probation, none of which would be adequate for many of the cases in which a prison sentence is imposed. By no means every offender is suitable for probation nor is every offender in a position to pay a monetary penalty. For juveniles, however, the Criminal Justice Act, 1948, provided for the establishment of attendance centres which involve loss of leisure without loss of liberty, the offender being compelled to attend at such hours as will not interfere with his school or working hours. Some parallel to this might perhaps be established for adult offenders. Dr. Mannheim[1] has suggested that compulsory labour without loss of liberty might provide a suitable penalty while avoiding the harmful effects of a term of imprisonment. Another alternative which might usefully be employed is to impose a suspended sentence, as is done in some countries, the offender being sentenced to a term of imprisonment but the sentence not being carried out if the offender behaves himself over a period fixed by the court. Meanwhile if the success of imprisonment is to be measured by the subsequent records of those sentenced to it, statistics show that about 20 per cent. of those who serve such sentences return to prison. These constitute the recidivist element, for whom no final solution has been found. The remaining 80 per cent. appear to have benefited either by training or punishment and not to trouble the courts further.[2]

One final comment on imprisonment is that it is a form of punishment which makes little distinction between the different offences which result in the offenders' being sent to prison. The violent, the dishonest, the sexually abnormal, the doctor who performs an illegal abortion, and the offending motorist are all sent to the same sort of establishment. In the eyes of the ordinary citizen, however, there is a vast difference between the last of these offenders and the others. It is no wonder, therefore, that juries are reluctant to convict defendants of traffic offences so long as such offences are likely to be visited with the same penalties as are offences which are generally regarded as real crimes.

6. ALTERNATIVES TO IMPRISONMENT: DISCHARGE AND PROBATION

Where a court is of opinion, having regard to the circumstances of the offence and the character of the offender, that it is

[1] Mannheim, op. cit., p. 134.   [2] Howard Jones, op. cit., p. 191.

inexpedient to impose a punishment, it may order that he be discharged. If there has been a mere technical breach of the law, it may be content to discharge him absolutely, and his conviction is disregarded except for certain purposes. These are the defendant's right of appeal against conviction, his right to rely on a plea of *autrefois convict* if subsequently charged with the offence for which he is discharged, and certain special rules relating to restitution of stolen property and compensation. Instead of discharging him absolutely, however, the court may discharge him subject to a condition that for a period not exceeding twelve months he commits no further offence. Should no further offence be committed before the period expires, then the conviction, as in the case of an absolute discharge, is disregarded. If, however, the defendant breaks the condition by committing another offence, he is liable to be sentenced both for that and for the original offence for which he was discharged.

Besides these powers the courts may in certain cases bind an offender over to keep the peace and be of good behaviour.[1] Here the defendant is required to enter into a recognizance to be of good behaviour for a time specified in the order, in default of which he forfeits his recognizance. The court may also when binding a defendant over require him to find sureties, who will enter into recognizance and guarantee his good behaviour.

It was this practice of binding offenders over which contained the germs of what later became the probation system. When sureties were required, those who entered into recognizances guaranteeing the defendant's good behaviour could be relied on to keep an eye on him and see that he fulfilled his promise. Early in the nineteenth century certain magistrates, notably Matthew Hill, Recorder of Birmingham, followed the practice of releasing offenders on condition that they returned to the care and supervision of their parents or masters. So far, however, there were only isolated and spasmodic attempts to employ this new approach to crime, and it was not until 1876, when the Church of England Temperance Society began to establish its Police Court Missions to reclaim drunkards convicted by the courts, that anything like a regular system appeared. The success of these missions led them to apply the same treatment to

---

[1] Magistrates have in certain cases the right to bind a person over to keep the peace even though no offence has been committed.

other offenders, and the co-operation of the magistrates who were prepared to release the offenders on bail to the missioners resulted in this practice gaining recognition from the legislature by the Summary Jurisdiction Act, 1879, and the Probation of First Offenders Act, 1877, which gave magistrates the power to suspend sentence in certain cases. The value of probation was soon recognized and in 1907 the Probation of Offenders Act authorized the courts to appoint probation officers and to make orders committing offenders to the care and supervision of such officers. It was not, however, till 1925 that the legislature positively required the courts to appoint probation officers, but since the Criminal Justice Act of that year every court has been bound to have such an officer.

The appointment of probation officers is in the hands of local Probation Committees set up by the magistrates in each area. This local feature of the Probation Service assists in bringing about collaboration between the courts and the probation officers and to some extent makes up for the fact that those who pass sentence know little about the defendant or about the effect on him of the sentence they impose. A measure of centralization and uniformity is introduced by the fact that the Probation Branch of the Home Office supervises and inspects the administration of the local Probation Services throughout the country. Moreover, the Probation Branch provides courses of training for those who wish to enter the service, and so seeks to maintain a high general standard throughout the different services.

A probation order can be made for a period of not less than one and not more than three years. To such an order the court can add certain conditions. It may for instance make it a condition of the order that the offender lives in a certain hostel, or that he undergoes certain treatment. A condition frequently attached to a probation order is that he should abstain from alcohol. Except where the defendant is under fourteen years of age, a probation order cannot be made without the offender's consent. This harks back of course to the former practice of binding offenders over in their own recognizances, but it preserves the essential characteristic feature which links it with the present system and which underlies the whole notion of this approach to crime. Probation rests on the willing co-operation of the offender, who from the start is required to show himself ready to make a positive effort to make good.

Although putting a defendant on probation may seem like letting him off altogether, it would be a mistake to imagine that being on probation was no burden to an offender. Whereas a fine can be paid then and there, a probation order may last for as long as three years, during the whole of which time the probationer is under the care of the probation officer, to whom he will have to report and whom he will have to satisfy that he is making progress. The basic idea of probation, which is a sort of domiciliary treatment not involving complete loss of liberty, is that the offender either redeems himself and is purged of his offence, or, failing this, is punished for it. For, meanwhile, the probation officer supervising him has the twofold duty of helping the offender and keeping the court informed of his progress. Failure to make progress may result in his being brought back before the court for breach of the order, whereupon he may be liable not only to punishment for such breach but also for the original offence in respect of which the probation order was made.

This feature, which provides the punitive element in probation, is also responsible in a number of cases for some degree of resistance on the part of the offender. The threat of further punishment if he fails to make good is continually present in the mind of the probationer, who may not unnaturally tend to regard the probation officer, whose duty it is to report any such failure, as a sort of police court spy. This may well prevent the establishment of that confidence and trust which are essential to enable the officer to assist the probationer. This kind of difficulty would seem unavoidable in any system which gives an offender a chance to make good but insists on observing what use he makes of the opportunity, and can only be overcome by skill and tact on the part of the individual officer.

There are other difficulties which are not inherent in the probation system itself but which arise from external factors. Most important is that there are insufficient probation officers to cope with the work to be done. Their duties are many and various. After-care of discharged prisoners, as we have seen, is one of their functions. Another is that of making general preliminary inquiries about a defendant if the court so requires before

sentence is passed. Trying to effect matrimonial reconciliations
is yet another of their duties, which consumes a large amount of
their time. Finally there is the primary function of supervising
those put on probation. With the present numbers of probation
officers the burden of case-work is heavy, one officer on the average handling as many as sixty cases, a considerable load when
it is remembered that much of such work has to be done not
only with the offender himself but with his family also. Certain
countries have attempted to surmount this difficulty by making
use of voluntary helpers, who can relieve the officers of part of
their burden. Holland and Sweden both utilize volunteers in
this way to a considerable extent. The drawback, however, is
the lack of skill and training on the part of such helpers, who
cannot be expected to be competent to deal with individual
cases of any difficulty or complexity. The only satisfactory solution would be to appoint more probation officers, and this, of
course, is open to objections on economic grounds.

As it is, the courts today make extensive use of probation as
a method of dealing with offenders. Before the war Magistrates'
Courts put on probation an average of 20 per cent. of the
offenders with whom they dealt, and this is without taking into
account the Juvenile Courts, where the percentage figure was
even higher. The superior courts in 1938 put over 10 per cent.
of offenders on probation. Since the war there has been some
decrease in the percentage in the Magistrates' Courts, but the
higher courts have shown a significant increase in the percentage of cases in which they have adopted this method of treatment. The figures for those over twenty-one years of age put on
probation in 1959 were 15·5 per cent. by Assizes and Quarter
Sessions and 10·3 per cent. by Magistrates' Courts for indictable
offences, 0·5 per cent. for non-indictable offences.

If the question is posed as to the effectiveness of probation,
the answer is that the surveys carried out by the Home Office
and by individual criminologists have shown that roughly
70 per cent. of those put on probation have made good. This
shows a slightly lower success rate than does imprisonment,
which seems to result in 80 per cent. of ex-prisoners keeping out
of prison subsequently. In measuring the success of the system
we must also not overlook the fact that those put on probation
are usually those guilty of less serious crimes, who are in any

event not so likely to commit further offences as are more confirmed criminals, and that the results must to some extent be
attributed to this as well as to the system. It would be a mistake
to think that an equal measure of success could be necessarily
achieved with more hardened and more serious cases. Indeed
for this very reason the Departmental Committee on Social
Services in the Courts of Summary Jurisdiction (Cmnd. 5122)
recommended that no one should be put on probation without
a full preliminary inquiry into the circumstances of his offence,
so that only suitable cases should be chosen for this type of
treatment. Nevertheless the fact remains that the subsequent
records of those selected as suitable cases by the courts amply
prove the value and usefulness of the probation system.

7. FINES

For all offences other than those carrying a fixed penalty the
courts have power to impose a fine. In the case of misdemeanours
this is a power which existed at common law. With regard to
felonies, since originally the general penalty was death, and
since conviction entailed automatic forfeiture of the felon's property, the power to impose a fine does not seem to have existed.
In 1861 criminal legislation authorized the courts to inflict a
monetary penalty for certain felonies and later enactments contained similar provisions in respect of specific offences, but it was
not until 1948 that the courts were given a general power of
fining persons found guilty of felonies. No general limit has been
set by law to the amount of the fine which may be imposed for
either felonies or misdemeanours, though both Magna Charta
and the Bill of Rights contain provisions prohibiting excessive
and unreasonable fines and assessments. For summary offences
the Magistrates' Courts have had a general power to impose
fines since the Summary Jurisdiction Act, 1879, which fixed
a limit of £25. The maximum fine which the Magistrates'
Courts can impose for indictable offences tried summarily
is £100.

With certain exceptions money recovered in the form of fines
must be handed over to the Secretary of State and transmitted
to the Exchequer. The exceptions relate to cases where the proceeds of fines are by special enactment made payable to the
Customs and Excise, to the party aggrieved or injured by the

offence, or must be used towards repairing damage done by the offender.

When an offender is ordered to pay a fine, there must be some method of enforcing the penalty. One method exists by virtue of the fact that when the fine is recorded it becomes a judgment debt due to the Crown, which can accordingly sue the offender in the Civil Courts. In 1957 the case of *The Treasury* v. *Harris*[1] raised the problem whether such a debt was a personal one to the debtor and died with him. Harris, who had been convicted in 1952 of certain offences for which he was sentenced to imprisonment and a fine, died in 1953 before the completion of his term and without paying the fine. It was held that the debt was not extinguished by his death and was accordingly recoverable from his estate at the suit of the Crown.

The other method of enforcing the penalty is by imprisoning the offender. Formerly the courts had power to order that the offender should remain in custody till the fine was paid. Today, however, we have accepted the view that none save fraudulent debtors, i.e. those with means who refuse to pay, should be imprisoned, and the severity of the criminal law has been mitigated to bring it into line with this attitude. The Criminal Justice Act, 1948, has provided what may be termed a code relating to imprisonment in default of payment of fines. By this enactment Assizes and Quarter Sessions are empowered to allow time for payment and to order payment by instalments if necessary. The term of imprisonment in default of payment must not exceed twelve months. The Court of Criminal Appeal has also decided[2] that the courts no longer have the right to order the accused to be detained until the fine is paid.

Similar rules governing the powers of Magistrates' Courts are contained in the Magistrates' Courts Act, 1952. In imposing a fine the magistrates must take account of the offender's means. It is also laid down that he is to be given at least seven days' time to pay in all cases unless he appears to the court to have adequate means or informs the court that he does not want time to pay or the court is satisfied that he has no fixed abode or there is some other specific reason why he should not be given time to pay. In addition to this provision the courts are authorized to

---

[1] *H.M. Treasury* v. *Harris*, [1957] 2 All E.R. 455.
[2] *R.* v. *Brook*, [1949] 2 K.B. 138.

allow further time to pay and if such time is allowed, no term of imprisonment in default may be fixed except in the presence of the offender and for some special reason such as the gravity of the offence or the character of the offender. When time to pay is allowed, the offender may not be imprisoned in default without a subsequent inquiry into his means. The magistrates must hold such an inquiry in his presence and satisfy themselves that he has the means to pay the fine. If the offender is without the means to pay, he cannot be committed to prison in default.

The use of the fine as a form of punishment has become increasingly common in the courts. In 1959, 44 per cent. of male persons over twenty-one found guilty of indictable offences were fined as compared with a figure of 26·6 per cent. for 1938. It is with regard to non-indictable offences, however, that the fine is seen to be the chief weapon of the courts. Of those convicted of all non-indictable offences, 94·5 per cent. were fined by the magistrates in 1959. The percentage of fines for traffic offences is considerably higher than for other non-indictable offences, being 97·5 per cent. as against 86·9 per cent.

The reasons for the popularity of this type of penalty with the courts are obvious. For trivial offences it is a quick summary punishment. So far from costing society anything it provides a credit balance for the Exchequer. Moreover it is clearly of deterrent value. One difficulty, however, is to adjust the penalty to the offender's means so as to make him feel the punishment. Payment of a £2 fine for a parking offence would mean little to the very wealthy. Some countries have a system whereby the fine is made proportionate to the defendant's earnings so that instead of being fined a certain sum he is fined a certain proportion of his wages. Whether such a system would prove acceptable in England, however, is doubtful.

8. COMPENSATION AND RESTITUTION

One feature notably lacking in the different types of punishment so far considered is the element of reparation. While it would seem an elementary demand of justice that the wrongdoer should be made to compensate the victim of his crime, the various sentences available to the Criminal Courts take little account of this. Capital punishment, imprisonment, fines, and probation orders serve to reduce crime either by deterrence or reformation or by a combination of the two. The death penalty and imprisonment have the additional effect of incapacitating the offender, the former permanently and the latter temporarily, from further crime. Reparation, however, is entirely absent.

The Criminal Courts do, however, possess limited powers with regard to compensation and restitution. For example, if a person is convicted of a felony, the court may by virtue of the Forfeiture Act of 1870 order him to pay compensation not exceeding £100 to anyone who has suffered a loss of property by reason of the offence. Another provision is contained in section 11 of the Criminal Justice Act, 1948, which authorizes a court which places an offender on probation or discharges him absolutely or conditionally, to order him to make reasonable compensation for injury or loss.

The powers of the Criminal Courts to order restitution concern stealing and other offences of dishonesty. When an offender is prosecuted by or on behalf of the owner of the dishonestly acquired property, the Larceny Act, 1916, provides that on his conviction the court can order him to restore the property to the owner. The obvious limitation on the usefulness of this power is that in most cases the wrongdoer will have disposed of the property before the trial. To remedy this defect the Act provides that he may also be made to restore any property for which he has exchanged or into which he has converted the property dishonestly acquired. Even this provision will not entirely protect the owner, since the offender may have disposed of the property and spent the proceeds. What the owner needs is the power to recover his goods from the person into whose hands they have fallen, and to a limited extent the Criminal Courts are able to assist him by ordering that the person in possession of the property restore it to the owner.

In this context we must return to the distinction which English law makes between stealing and swindling. As we saw earlier, a thief does not acquire ownership of the stolen property, while a swindler who obtains it by false pretence does obtain ownership. The position of the latter is that he obtains a voidable title to the property; he acquires the ownership subject to the true owner's right to recover the goods from him. If the owner does not act quickly he may lose this right; for if the swindler sells the goods to a third person who buys them in good faith knowing nothing of the fraud perpetrated on the owner, the law holds that the new owner's right to the goods prevails over that of the former owner. This is undoubtedly hard on the latter, who may not have discovered the fraud till after the new owner acquired the goods, but in deciding which of two innocent parties should bear the loss the judges were activated partly by the consideration that commercial dealings would become impossible unless purchases in good faith were protected, and partly by the fact that though both parties were innocent, the former owner was careless in consenting to the fraud. In other words the law expects a man to exercise care not to be swindled into parting with his property, but does not require purchasers of goods (as opposed to land) to take time and trouble investigating the vendor's title to sell the goods.

So far as false pretences are concerned, therefore, the scales are weighted by commercial convenience against the former owner. The same considerations, one might expect, would have led the courts to adopt the same approach with regard to property obtained by stealing. We have seen, however, that while a thief gets possession of the property which he steals, he never gets the ownership; and since he has no title, he can give no title to a third party, for the law takes the view here that a man cannot give what he has not got, expressed in the often-quoted maxim *nemo dat quod non habet*. Consequently the owner has the right to recover the property from any third party to whom it is sold or otherwise disposed of, regardless of the latter's good faith. In such cases the ultimate sufferer is the innocent third party who subsequently acquires the property, and the law provides that in such cases the court may order compensation to be paid to him by the offender.

Inroads on this rule too have been made, however, in the interests of commercial convenience. The most important exception to the revesting rule concerns money and negotiable instruments, e.g. cheques. The function of coins, bank-notes, cheques, and other such items of property is to serve as articles of exchange. Their usefulness would clearly be severely limited if people who subsequently acquired them were liable to restore them to the former owner. Such items remain, therefore, outside the scope of the rule that stolen property revests in the owner on the thief's conviction. Another exception is provided

by the venerable rule of law that a thief can give a good title if
he sells the goods in market overt, e.g. certain fairs, shops in the
City of London. Later and more important exceptions are provided by the Factors Act, 1889, and Sale of Goods Act, 1893,
concerning disposition of goods for consideration by mercantile
agents and others in a similar position. These matters are outside the scope of this inquiry and belong rather to the field of
contract and commercial law. Here we may only note that on
conviction of the thief, the property revests in the original owner
and the court has power to order its restitution even though
a good title may have been acquired in market overt, but that
this does not apply if the goods have been disposed of by a mercantile agent or a person in a similar position.

It is sometimes urged that the Criminal Courts should have
the power to order offenders in all cases to make compensation
to the victims of their crimes. This is not in fact necessary, since
the victim has in any case his remedies in the Civil Courts. If
A assaults B, the latter can sue A for damages. If A steals C's
watch, C can bring an action for conversion. In theory, therefore, there is no need to reduplicate the remedies which the injured party already possesses.

In practice, however, these remedies are often rendered
nugatory by the offender's inability to pay compensation. To
order such an offender to make reparation over a period of
years would hardly be feasible in view of the supervision which
would be required. So far as motor accidents are concerned the
Road Traffic Act has wisely required that drivers should be
insured against accidents to other persons, so that injured parties
shall not go without compensation, regardless of the financial
position of the driver himself. This could hardly be extended
to crimes in general. It would hardly be practicable to demand
that every individual insure himself against all harm which his
conduct might inflict on others.

Nevertheless if the victim of a crime has to shoulder the whole
burden of the injury, justice seems to be lacking. One remedy
would be to allow compensation from public funds. This at
least would spread the load of suffering and thereby reduce
unhappiness. The courts have long had a discretion to award
compensation to the relatives of persons killed in attempting
to effect lawful arrests and a power to order rewards to those

who have been active in apprehending offenders in certain cases. In both cases the money is paid from public funds. Miss Margery Fry advocated a system whereby public compensation should be paid from public funds to the victims of crime. According to the Home Office, any such scheme raises a multiplicity of practical problems.[1]

9. COSTS

In addition to the loss and injury which the aggrieved party may have suffered by virtue of the offence committed against him, the actual trial of the offender may have put him out of pocket and caused him to lose time which he might more profitably have spent otherwise. This is particularly the case where the injured party is the prosecutor, but is also true to an extent where the prosecution is conducted by the police or some other authority, because even here he may have to lose time in appearing as witness at the proceedings. The provisions of the law relating to this matter are now contained in the Costs in Criminal Cases Act, 1952, which lays down one rule for indictable offences and a different rule for summary offences.

Since indictable offences are more serious than summary offences, prosecutions for these will consume considerably more time and involve more expense than summary prosecutions. Accordingly, where the offender is convicted, the courts may either order him to pay all or part of the costs of the prosecution, or it may order that the costs be paid out of local funds. The second of these rules, which holds not only for trials on indictment, but also for summary trial by Magistrates' Courts of indictable offences, provides for the case where a private prosecution is brought but the defendant has no money to reimburse the prosecutor. In addition the courts are empowered to order that witnesses be compensated for loss of time and expenses by payment out of local funds. Special regulations have been made prescribing the maximum allowances payable to expert and other witnesses from such funds.

In trials of summary offences the Magistrates' Courts have no power to order payment out of local funds. Since the procedure is informal and speedy and the prosecutor is not obliged to be legally represented, he is unlikely to be greatly out of

[1] 30 June 1961, Cmnd. 1406.

pocket and the defendant could probably reimburse him. The court can, therefore, where the defendant is convicted, order him to bear the costs of the prosecution.

Where the prosecution fails, the question arises whether the defendant should be compensated. Here again the law differentiates between summary and indictable offences. As regards the former, the magistrates may order the prosecutor, if they think fit, to pay the costs of the defence, but have no power to order payment out of local funds. In the case of indictable offences the courts have only a limited power of ordering the prosecutor to foot the bill but have a general discretion to order payment of the defence costs out of local funds.

How this discretion should be exercised is a matter which has caused some controversy. In the Civil Courts the judges have a discretion as to costs, but the general practice is that costs 'follow the event'. In other words the successful plaintiff's costs are paid by the defendant, while the unsuccessful plaintiff pays the defendant's costs. This practice has two valuable effects, since it serves to discourage plaintiffs from bringing frivolous claims and defendants from putting forward worthless defences, and at the same time it tends to put the successful party in the position in which he would have been had no trial taken place. The successful plaintiff is restored to his original position by being awarded damages or other relief together with the cost of recovering that relief, while the successful defendant by being awarded costs is put back in the position which he would have enjoyed if no action had been brought against him.

Now the general practice of the Criminal Courts appears to be not to exercise their discretion in favour of a defendant who is acquitted unless they consider that the prosecution should not have been brought. To order costs to be given in all cases out of local funds might hamper the police and other prosecuting authorities in carrying out their duties, for the public interest may often demand that a prosecution be brought even though its outcome is by no means a certainty. A local authority which found that unsuccessful prosecutions constituted a drain on its funds might wish to restrict the activities of the police within its jurisdiction. On the other hand it seems unjust that a person who is acquitted should be nevertheless prejudiced by being made to pay for defending himself; he surely could claim that he is entitled to be restored to the position he would have had if he had never been prosecuted. This would appear all the more true in the light of the fact that impecunious defendants can be granted legal aid to defend themselves. Why then should the defendant with means have to bear the loss even when he is acquitted? If the public interest demands that prosecutions be brought, then it is only right that the whole cost should be borne by the public purse when an acquittal results. Perhaps a satisfactory solution would be to allow successful defendants to recover their costs in all cases from a central fund, but to order payment from local funds in the case of prosecutions which should not have been brought.

10. THE YOUNG OFFENDER

The most notable difference between our modern penal system and that obtaining in the nineteenth century is the special provisions which now exist with regard to young offenders. Admittedly most societies can be found to display some measure of lenience towards the young, of whom the same standards are not demanded as of their elders who have had time and experience to learn the requirements of their society. In England the courts had long adopted rules whereby a child under seven (raised by statute subsequently to eight) cannot be convicted of a crime, while a child between the ages of seven and fourteen can only be convicted if he is shown to have realized that his conduct was morally wrong. These rules apart, children were dealt with on exactly the same footing as adults. Young boys and girls were prosecuted in the ordinary courts for the most trivial offences such as throwing stones, bathing in canals, and so forth; they were sentenced to the same penalties as adults, death, transportation, and imprisonment; and they served their sentences in the same institutions as grown and hardened criminals.

When the new emphasis on the importance of reclamation was accepted, it was only natural that this should have repercussions in the treatment of juvenile crime. Perhaps the most obvious criticism of the nineteenth-century system or lack of system is the contamination to which thousands of youngsters were annually exposed by being incarcerated with confirmed criminals. While the threat of imprisonment might just possibly stop other miscreants from bathing in canals, one certain effect would be to ensure that the actual offender would be given ample opportunity, scope, and encouragement to develop into a thorough-going criminal. If on the other hand the protection of society is best served by measures which not only deter but also reform the actual offender, then it is clear that children will require special treatment. An adult offender needs to be diverted from the path he has followed back to the normal course of behaviour. A child has barely had time to follow a path at all and must be helped on to the right lines. What a child requires is not so much reformation as formation.

But if the young offender is to be helped and encouraged to grow up into a reasonable member of society, it is essential to discover the causes preventing him from doing so. One child's offence may be the result of excess of high spirits. Another may be slow in developing a sense of what is required by membership of a community. Yet another may be turning to crime as the result of bad home influence and environment. To sort out the reasons for his misbehaviour requires careful inquiry into his case by courts experienced in dealing with young people, together with investigation into his background and circumstances. Once this has been done the courts must find the treatment best suited to train him to become a respectable law-abiding member of society.

To deal with this problem special courts have been created to try cases of juvenile crime and special methods have been devised for treating young offenders.

(a) Juvenile Courts

Juvenile Courts were first established in England by the Children Act, 1908. Today they are governed by the Children and Young Persons Act, 1933, and by rules made by the Lord Chancellor under its provisions. These courts consist of magistrates who are members of a special Juvenile Court panel, to which the rules provide that only those specially qualified for dealing with juvenile cases may be appointed. Not more than three magistrates may sit together to form such a court. A larger number, besides being unwieldy, would only serve to intimidate the child. If possible one of the magistrates should be a woman, an important requirement for obvious reasons but one not always fulfilled.

A Juvenile Court differs from an ordinary court in that it is less public, less formal, and so less formidable. The court sits if possible in a different building from the ordinary court-house, or else in a separate part of the court building. The general public is excluded, the only persons allowed inside being the police, probation officers, officers of the court, and of course the parties and witnesses. Newspaper reporters are permitted to be present but there are restrictions in the reports which may be given of such proceedings. The name, address, and school of the accused or of any juvenile witness may not be revealed; neither photographs nor anything else which might lead to the identification of any such young person may be published in a newspaper unless the court or the Home Secretary so directs. The child's parents may attend the court, and indeed must do so unless the court considers that it would be unreasonable to require their attendance.

According to the Departmental Committee on the Treatment of Young Offenders (Cmd. 2831) (1927) the principle of guardianship should be at the root of all Juvenile Court procedure. While our Juvenile Courts have not gone so far in this direction as their American counterparts, whose primary function from the beginning has been the guardianship of the child, nevertheless the 1933 Act laid down as a guiding principle that—

Every court in dealing with a child or young person who is brought before it, either as being in need of care and protection or as an offender or otherwise, shall have regard to the welfare of the child or young person and shall in a proper case take steps for removing him from undesirable surroundings, and for securing that proper provision is made for his education and training.

As can be observed from this section, a Juvenile Court has not only a criminal jurisdiction but also in certain matters important civil powers. The law provides that any child, that is a person under fourteen, and any young person, that is a person between the ages of fourteen and seventeen, who is summarily tried must be tried by a Juvenile Court. To this rule there are certain exceptions, the most important concerning the case where there is an adult co-defendant. With regard to indictable offences the law lays down that children must be tried summarily except in the case of homicide or where there is a co-defendant not a child; and that young persons may, if they consent, be summarily tried in all cases except homicide. The result of these provisions is that the vast majority of offences committed by juveniles are dealt with by those courts most fitted to deal with them.

The civil jurisdiction of the Juvenile Court covers three types of case. First there are 'beyond control cases'. Children and young persons brought before the court by their parents or guardians as beyond their control may be removed, with the parents' consent, from their homes and sent to some appropriate establishment. Secondly, there are the 'care and protection cases'. The local authority, the police, or an authorized person may bring such a case if there are reasonable grounds for believing that the child or young person is in need of care and protection. Such a child or young person is one who, having either no parent or guardian or one who is unfit to exercise care and guardianship or one who is not exercising proper care and guardianship, is either falling into bad associations, or exposed to moral danger, or beyond control. 'Care and protection cases' also extend to children against whom certain specified offences, e.g. offences of cruelty or sexual offences, have been committed. In such cases the court may order the appropriate treatment even against the wishes of the parent or guardian. Thirdly, a child who persistently plays truant from school may be ordered to be brought before the Juvenile Court.

A consideration of these three types of case is outside the scope of this book. It should be noted, however, that while a child under eight cannot be found guilty of an offence, his conduct may render him liable to be brought before the court as beyond control or in need of care and protection, in either of which cases he may be accordingly dealt with. Secondly, the difference between the civil and the criminal cases is not so wide as might be thought. The commission of an offence is frequently a symptom of the delinquent's need for care and protection, and the moral danger of those brought before the courts as beyond control or as in need of care and protection is often greater than that of those accused of some minor offence. While truancy might at first sight seem unconnected with juvenile crime, experienced magistrates have stressed the close relationship between it and delinquency. Truancy at the least gives the young child time to get into mischief; at the worst it is a sign that something is wrong, either with the child himself or with his home, and is a warning that something must be put right. It is only reasonable, therefore, that such cases should fall within the jurisdiction of the Juvenile Courts.

An important stage in the trial and treatment of juveniles is the making of inquiries into the delinquent's background in order to discover the causes of his misconduct. Except in trivial cases it is impossible for a court to perform its duty of having regard to the child's welfare without making such inquiries. John Watson, the chairman of a London Juvenile Court, in his book *The Child and the Magistrate* illustrates all too clearly the need for this vital stage.[1] The duty of conducting such inquiries falls primarily on the local authorities, but the court may direct instead that they be made by its probation officers. The latter is the preferable course, since if probation is later decided on as the appropriate treatment, this means that the probation officer has made his entry at the earliest possible moment, at a time when the parents' co-operation is more easily obtained than after an order is made. Some difficulty arises in connexion with the right time for making inquiries. The presumption of innocence and considerations of freedom militate against their being made until after there has been a finding of guilt. Such post-trial inquiries, however, involve a remand, and this is often impracticable where the Juvenile Courts meet only at long intervals. As one experienced magistrate has said, 'the choice is not between pre-trial and post-trial inquiries, but between pre-trial inquiries and no inquiries at all'.[2] While post-trial inquiries or remand are preferable, therefore, circumstances often preclude these and necessitate the use of pre-trial inquiries.

(b) Treatment of Young Offenders

The treatment of offenders may conveniently be divided into those forms of treatment involving removal from home and those not involving such removal.

The latter category consists of such measures as discharges,

[1] Watson, op. cit., pp. 71–84.
[2] Sir Leo Page, cited Watson, op. cit., p. 81.

fines, probation orders, and attendance at attendance centres.
The use of the first three of these punishments has already been
considered, but there are some special provisions and considerations relating to their application to young offenders. Except in
the case of very trivial offences, it is doubtful whether absolute
and conditional discharges or fines are suitable for such offenders, since many of the offences committed are probably due to
the delinquent's inability to come to terms with the problems of
life without help.

Fines present further problems. In the case of a child it must,
and in the case of a young person it may, be imposed not on the
child but on the parents, unless the court is satisfied that they
have not conduced to the offence by failing to exercise due care
of the child. While this is a reasonable provision, it is doubtful
how far the imposition of a fine on parents who are responsible for the child's offence by virtue of their neglect, will result
in remedying the position. If the parents are themselves unable
to cope with the problems of a family, a fine will not help them.
The most likely effect is to make the parents take revenge on the
child and so kill what affection there is between them. Where
the fine is imposed on the offender himself, it is obvious that it
should be proportionate to his pocket money or earnings. Moreover it is important to ensure if possible that it is paid not by the
parent but by the child himself, so that he may appreciate that
he is being punished. One method of achieving this is to order
payment by instalments.

The disadvantage of the fine is that it is merely a punishment
and provides no remedy for the young offender's difficulty. It is
all the more disturbing, therefore, that in recent years the use
of the fine has increased in such cases at the expense of probation, that form of treatment above all so appropriate to the
needs of the juvenile delinquent.[1] The reasons for the suitability
of probation for the young offender are twofold. In the first
place supervision may give him that help and guidance the lack
of which is preventing him from coping with life's difficulties.
In the second place much delinquency results from unsatisfactory home circumstances. Here, by careful case-work with the
whole family, the probation officer may be able to eliminate
these background difficulties and establish normal, happy

---

[1] See Winifred A. Elkin, *The English Penal System*, pp. 72-73.

relationships without which the child cannot be prevented from embarking on a life of anti-social behaviour. It has been suggested that in such cases the courts should be empowered to put the parents themselves on probation, though how far this would be possible in view of the need for the probationer's consent (unless he is under fourteen) is doubtful.

The attendance centre is the creation of the Criminal Justice Act, 1948. The idea of such institutions is to deprive the offender of his leisure without depriving him of his liberty. Any person between the ages of ten and twenty-one who is guilty of a breach of probation or of an offence for which an adult could be imprisoned, may be ordered to attend for twelve hours at a centre, the maximum attendance on any one day being three hours. The times are so arranged as not to interfere with his work or schooling. What this means in fact is that the offender will lose a succession of free Saturday afternoons.

Over thirty centres for those under seventeen are now in existence and one for those over seventeen was started in 1958. The centres are under the control of the police, and this seems to work well and to promote better understanding between police and probation officers. The time is spent partly in tedious work and partly in education, in order to educate the offenders in the proper use of the leisure of which the court has deprived them. It is early yet to say how satisfactory such centres are as a form of treatment. Some have questioned whether twelve hours is a high enough maximum to achieve any results. The Criminal Justice Act, 1961, has provided that the normal total of twelve hours' attendance may in certain circumstances be increased to a maximum of twenty-four hours if the court considers that in the circumstances twelve hours would be inadequate. On the other hand, an offender under fourteen years of age may be ordered to attend for a lesser aggregate of hours if the court considers that in the circumstances twelve hours would be excessive.

Domiciliary treatment will not always fit the case, however. The child's environment may be so bad as to preclude all hope of any remedy being successful while he remains there. Or he may be so unruly that nothing short of some kind of institutional training will be adequate. Or again there may exist some temporary difficulty or crisis within the home which renders it essential for the child to be removed from it for a short while until things return to normal. In all these cases the offender must be taken from home and detained elsewhere.

For adults this would, of course, mean prison. This form of punishment, however, has been increasingly restricted so far as juveniles are concerned, until we have now reached the position laid down by the Criminal Justice Act, 1948, as amended by the Criminal Justice Act, 1961. Under these statutes no court may sentence an offender under seventeen years of age to imprisonment and the later Act eliminates intermediate and short prison sentences for those under twenty-one. The number of young offenders sent to prison on conviction in 1959 was 31 boys and 1 girl under seventeen, and 1,057 young adults between the ages of seventeen and twenty-one.

(i) *Short-term treatment away from home*

To take the place of imprisonment various different schemes and institutions have been devised. First we may consider the methods available for juveniles needing only a short period of removal from home. Where home conditions are difficult and removal is desirable, the court may make it a condition of a probation order that the offender resides elsewhere. There are three different courses available. He can be boarded out in a family; he can be ordered to reside in a probation hostel; or he can be directed to live in a probation home. The first of these depends on the number of families willing to accept the addition of a problem child, and these are naturally limited. The hostels and homes are run by voluntary organizations, but grants are made by the local authorities and the Home Office is to some extent responsible for financing them. Residence in a hostel means that the probationer is free to go out to work each day and returns at the end of the day; in a home the probationers work on the premises, remaining in the home the whole time. The hostel would seem preferable to the home, since it is more in tune with the idea of probation. We have seen that probation aims to treat the offender and help him overcome his difficulties without removing him from his environment and depriving him of his liberty. Where circumstances are such as to warrant his removal, it would seem logical, if he is on probation, to leave him nevertheless in the community rather than to withdraw him from it altogether. Probation and any form of detention appear incompatible.

Boarding out, probation hostels, and probation homes are short-term measures for those whose own homes are unsatisfactory. There is also a need, however, for means of dealing with offenders who need a short sharp shock to bring them to their senses. For such people probation is not the solution and fines are inadequate; yet at the same time we have set our faces against both imprisonment and birching. Some type of short-term detention is required to take their place. The Children and Young Persons Act, 1933, allows the courts to punish young offenders for crimes for which adults can be imprisoned by ordering them to be detained in a remand home. The maximum period of detention is one month. This, however, is an unsuitable solution to the problem, since the remand home is already used for the custody of children and young persons about whom inquiries are being made, or who are waiting for trial or for removal to an approved school or Borstal. The undesirability of using the same place for custody and for punishment has led the courts to make comparatively little use of this power.

An alternative type of treatment was provided by the 1948 Act in the form of the detention centres. These were intended to afford a sharp lesson for those offenders for whom fines and probation are inadequate but for whom long-term residential training is unnecessary. From the outset the emphasis has been on strict discipline rather than constructive training. The day of the inmate is long and is spent in exercise and hard work. Experience has shown, however, that it is possible even in the short period of detention which the offender serves to include some positive form of training.[1]

The law provides that a person between the ages of fourteen and twenty-one found guilty of an offence punishable in the case of an adult with imprisonment may be committed to a detention centre. No such person, however, may be committed there if he has already served a term of imprisonment of six months or more, or undergone a period of Borstal training. For such persons it was estimated that this form of treatment would not be beneficial. The normal period of detention is three months, though in exceptional cases this may be increased to six months.

[1] Cmnd. 645, p. 9.

Certain criticisms have been made of this scheme. In the first place it was perhaps a mistake not to have provided compulsory after-care for those released from the centre. Moreover, a system of recall to act as a sanction might well have proved beneficial. Both these measures have been shown to be valuable elements in approved school and Borstal training. Accordingly, the Criminal Justice Act, 1961, provides for compulsory supervision for a period of twelve months after the date of release, during which time failure to comply with the requirements of supervision will render the offender liable to recall. One fact that has emerged from the evidence as to the effects of the treatment is that it is not wholly successful for offenders who have been committed to approved schools. These are perhaps too institutionalized to respond to the detention centre as intended. It might have been better had the Act added this category to the other categories of offender for whom the detention centre is not permitted.

It is too early yet to judge fully of the efficacy of this treatment. As yet there are few centres, two for those under seventeen and two for those above that age, while two more are being planned. The increase in juvenile crime has subjected the system to severe strain and it is clear that the existing centres are not enough. As it is, the courts are frequently unable to commit an offender to a centre because of the lack of a vacancy and have had to fall back on the short-term imprisonment, the very thing that the detention centre was designed to avoid. The Home Office estimates that at present there is need for a further six centres if this object is to be achieved. In so far as one can judge at this early stage from the effects of the treatment on those sent to the centres it seems that a certain measure of success is being achieved. Dr. Grünhut, who has made a study of over 400 boys before, during, and after treatment at a detention centre, has concluded that the results are encouraging in terms both of reappearance in court and of character improvement, and that the detention centre 'has a legitimate place in a variegated system of treatment for young offenders'.[1]

(ii) *Long-term treatment away from home: approved schools; Borstal training*

Where it is necessary to remove an offender from his home

[1] Cmnd. 645, p. 9.

for a period of some length, there are three possible courses available to the courts. They may make a 'fit person order', committing him to the care of a fit person. They may send him to an approved school. Or they may direct that he undergo a period of Borstal training.

A 'fit person order' is usually made where it is considered desirable to remove the child permanently from his home. The main ground for making such an order is that the child or young person is in need of care and protection, although a considerable proportion of orders are also made in the case of offenders. The order lasts until the child reaches the age of eighteen. In the meantime it is open to the parents to apply at any time to the court, which may revoke the order, if it thinks it expedient to do so. The fit person to whom the child is committed may be either an individual or the local authority. A relative may be willing to take the child under his roof and bring him up with his own family, but naturally such cases are not frequent. More commonly the child has to be committed to the care of the local authority, which by virtue of the Children Act, 1948, must comply with such an order. Having committed the child to the local authority, however, the court has no further control over his upbringing. The authority may board him out with foster parents, put him into a children's home, or send him to a boarding-school. The one restriction on the autonomy of the local authority is that it may not send him to an approved school without an order from the court.

The approved schools are the descendants of the earlier reformatory and industrial schools set up in the nineteenth century for homeless, destitute, and delinquent children. Largely as the result of the pioneer work of Mary Carpenter, legislation was enacted to permit the courts to commit children to these institutions and the state began to assist towards their finance. Finally in 1908 the Children's Act placed the schools under the supervision of a special department of the Home Office. Today there are over a hundred different approved or Home Office schools, as they are sometimes called, run by voluntary organizations or by local authorities, catering for children of different age, sex, and religion. The financial burden falls almost entirely on the local authorities and the state, which are bound to pay the cost of maintenance of each child at the schools, though where the parents can afford it they may not unreasonably be ordered to contribute. State control exists by reason of the fact that the schools are subject to the approval and inspection of the Home Secretary, who is empowered to give directions to the managers of the schools and to make provisions for regulating the constitution and proceedings of the school.

The purpose of the approved school is to provide training where other treatment such as probation has failed or is unlikely to succeed or where the home background is unsatisfactory. Consequently the cases where the courts have power to commit a child or young person to an approved school fall into various categories. Such power exists on finding of guilt for an offence punishable in the case of an adult with imprisonment; in the case of a child or young person found to be in need of care and protection, beyond control, or failing to attend regularly at school; and where, having been committed under a fit person to a local authority, he proves too unruly to remain in the family or institution in which he has been placed. Children under ten, however, may not be sent to an approved school save in exceptional circumstances.

In this form of treatment the emphasis is on training the child to live a normal social life. The schools are open institutions where the children are trained and educated rather than prisons where they are kept under lock and key. Despite the problem of absconding, which is frequent and often accompanied by stealing in the neighbourhood, the authorities prefer to retain an open institution. For persistent absconders closed blocks within the school may be established. The education provided is much the same as in ordinary schools, with considerable opportunity in boys' schools for technical training. Since only the managers of the school can judge whether a child's training has fitted him to re-enter society, the logical step has been taken of transferring from the courts to the school managers the right of deciding on the length of time each individual must spend in the institution. There is no set period, each person being released when those in charge consider that he has had sufficient training to warrant allowing him to return to the outside world, although no person may be released within the first six months without the consent of the Home Secretary. This kind of indeterminate sentence, however, runs counter to the traditional notion that a person should only be deprived of his liberty by a court and that the court in sentencing the offender should fix the period of loss of liberty. To safeguard the freedom of the individual and prevent abuse by the school authorities of their powers, the law sets a maximum term to detention in such a school. In most cases, there being some special exceptions, this maximum period is three years. In fact the majority of inmates are released considerably earlier. At any time after the first six months a child may be released, but the managers of the school retain supervision over him for the next two years and may, if they think fit, make use of the valuable sanction of recalling him to the school. After the expiry of the period of supervision the managers may, at his request, give him further assistance, so providing a further measure of after-care after his release from the school. Supervision is carried out by the school staff, by special welfare officers, or by probation officers, depending on the circumstances of the case. If the child has no satisfactory home to return to, the managers must arrange for him to enter a hostel or must find lodgings for him. They must also, if he is over school-leaving age, try to find employment for him.

The approved school system is open to several criticisms. We have seen that children may be detained in the schools for a variety of reasons. The child in need of care and protection may find himself side by side with the delinquent, and while it may seem enlightened to send the latter to a place of training rather than of punishment, it is questionable how far it is fair to the former to send him to the same place as actual offenders. Apart from this, there is the problem of coping with the varying types of children committed to the schools, the backward, the unruly, the persistent truants, and so on. Their variety makes it difficult to provide education suitable to their different needs. To some extent this is being remedied by setting up classifying schools to sort out the various types of children and determine what school is appropriate in each case.

It has been suggested that the period of detention is too long and that in many cases an equal measure of success could be achieved by a shorter period. There are now certain short-term schools where release normally takes place after nine months. If on the other hand the child appears not to be responding to the training provided, he can be transferred to an ordinary approved school.

The system has also been criticized for pampering the children, giving them a standard of material comfort far above that to which they are used. Occasionally one hears of a young defendant asserting that he committed the offence in order to get into an approved school, and certainly the conditions compare favourably with those in certain public schools. But it is to be remembered, as Watson points out, that while the public schoolboy from a luxurious home needs hardening, the approved schoolboy from the slum needs to be taught the decencies of life. Moreover, it must not be forgotten that the loss of liberty for what may be quite a long time constitutes in itself in most cases a heavy punishment. Perhaps the most serious objection to the system is that its products become too institutionalized to be able to find their place in the outside world. The training which they receive in the school teaches them to conform to the rules and regulations of a self-contained institution instead of curing their inability to stand on their own two feet. To some extent this may be unavoidable; to some extent it can be remedied by post-release supervision and after-care.

Nevertheless such evidence as is available shows that roughly two-thirds of those released from approved schools do not trouble the courts further.

The third type of long-term treatment away from home, and perhaps the most admired institution in our penal system, is Borstal training. The name derives from the village of Borstal, where in 1902 Rochester Prison was turned into an institution for boys. Borstal training did not, however, become a separate feature of the penal system until 1908, since when it has continued without serious alterations. It is here that so much is due to the influence of Alexander Paterson, who regarded it as the task of Borstal training not to 'break or knead the offender into shape, but to stimulate some power within to regulate conduct aright, to a preference for the good and the chance to make him want to use his life well, so that he himself and not others will save him from waste'.[1] It was as a result of this sort of attitude that in 1930 one Borstal governor led a group from Middlesex to Nottingham to camp at Lowdham and build

[1] Alexander Paterson, *The Principles of the Borstal System* (1932).

their own institution. Since then other open settlements have followed.

Borstal training is reserved for the young adult rather than the child. Only those between the ages of fifteen and twenty-one may be committed to Borstal. Secondly, only offenders found guilty of offences punishable with imprisonment may be sent for a period of such training. One important difference, however, between committal to Borstal and committal to an approved school is that only Assizes and Quarter Sessions may pass such a sentence; if a court of summary jurisdiction thinks that this would be the appropriate sentence for an offender, it must commit him to Quarter Sessions for sentence with a recommendation for Borstal training. Before sending him to Borstal the court must be satisfied that having regard to his character and previous conduct and to the circumstances of his offence, it is expedient that he should be detained for training for not less than six months. The court must also obtain a report from the Prison Commissioners regarding his physical and mental condition and his suitability for Borstal.

One respect in which Borstal training resembles the Approved School system is in the indeterminate length of sentence. The maximum has now been set at two years and release is possible at any time after six months. After release the offender remains subject to supervision and recall until two years from the date of his release. Although the essence of the system is training rather than punishment, the burden of loss of liberty for anything up to three years followed by restrictions on the released boy's activities for a further four years ensures that a Borstal sentence provides an effective deterrent to the potential offender.

A Borstal, however, is not a prison. The inmates of a prison are confined under lock and key and kept separate from the rest of the community. Borstals are basically open institutions. There are, it is true, two different types of Borstal, closed and open Borstals. The latter, of which there are now several, are without walls and bars. Some are converted country houses, others camps of huts. The closed Borstals are housed in the premises of former prisons and are reserved for tougher and more difficult offenders. Even in these institutions, however, the gates remain open and the inmates perform many activities outside the Borstal. The system of training is one of progression from grade to grade, in each successive grade further freedom and responsibility being given to the inmate. In the final grade he is allowed to go out alone and to work without supervision. He is also allowed five days' home leave to prepare himself and his family for his return. Contacts with the outside world are encouraged. Football and cricket matches are arranged with local teams. The institutions have clubs which are affiliated to national organizations. In the summer camps are held where the 'lads', as the inmates are termed, mix with other young people.

The training in a Borstal is vigorous. The day is a full one, devoted to productive work such as maintaining the buildings or agricultural work. Education is provided, emphasis being laid on vocational instruction. Particularly important too is the place of religion within the institutions. One interesting feature, which no doubt contributes to their success, is that they are modelled on the house system of the public schools. This means that the staff are better able to get to know the inmates and to develop a feeling of belonging to a community.

As in all institutions, disciplinary measures are necessary. Such measures consist of loss of privileges, transfer to a closed Borstal or to a closed block within a Borstal. The chief sanction, however, is the indeterminate length of the period of detention, since release is unlikely unless the offender is seen to make progress.

Despite foreign admiration the Borstal system as it works in practice is far from perfect. The use of former prison buildings for closed Borstals is unsatisfactory since it preserves the taint and stigma of the very punishment which Borstal is meant to replace. More disturbing is the lack of sufficient institutions. The Home Office[1] reported that this was resulting in offenders spending as long as twelve weeks in local prisons before a vacancy occurred in a Borstal, while far too many young adults are being sent to prison for short periods. In 1957 as many as 1,000 boys and 100 girls received sentences of six months or less. So far as the already existing Borstals are concerned, their work of training and education is seriously hampered by the high proportion of inmates of low mentality. The institutions have also been criticized for their lack of adequate facilities for

[1] Cmnd. 645, p. 10.

psychiatric treatment. One serious defect of the system is that persistent absconders from approved schools may be sent to Borstal. As a result young boys and girls committed to approved schools in the first place as being in need of care and protection may end up in Borstal, although never guilty of any criminal offence. A particularly formidable problem is that of absconding. The average proportion of escapes in recent years has been over one in six.

To estimate the results of Borstal training one may look at the figures for subsequent convictions after release. Before the war, it was estimated, on the basis that more than one conviction in the seven-year period following release was a failure, that the success rate for boys was 75 per cent. and for girls 70 per cent. Since the war, however, the figures have been slightly lower. The Prison Commissioners have proposed the integration into a single system of Borstal and imprisonment for young adults. Borstal training may well be modified therefore in the near future and will have to be reassessed accordingly.

SELECT BIBLIOGRAPHY

Criminal Law

CROSS and JONES, *Introduction to Criminal Law* (4th ed.).
KENNY, *Outlines of Criminal Law* (17th ed.).
GLANVILLE WILLIAMS, *The Criminal Law* (2nd ed.).
—— *The Sanctity of Human Life.*
C. K. ALLEN, *The Queen's Peace.*
N. ST. JOHN-STEVAS, *Life, Death and the Law.*

Trial

P. ARCHER, *The Queen's Courts.*
LORD DEVLIN, *The Criminal Prosecution in England.*
—— *Trial by Jury.*
GLANVILLE WILLIAMS, *The Proof of Guilt.*

Punishment

LIONEL FOX, *The English Prison and Borstal System.*
HOWARD JONES, *Crime and the Penal System.*
WINIFRED A. ELKIN, *The English Penal System.*
MARGERY FRY, *Arms of the Law.*
J. A. WATSON, *The Child and the Magistrate.*

INDEX

INDEX OF CASES

PRINTED IN GREAT BRITAIN
AT THE UNIVERSITY PRESS, OXFORD
BY VIVIAN RIDLER
PRINTER TO THE UNIVERSITY

10 11 12 1 2 3 4 5 6 7
1 2 3 4 5 6 7 8